# A Journalist's Guide to Sources

Titles in the series

Series editor: F.W. Hodgson

# A Journalist's Guide to Sources

David Spark

Focal Press
An imprint of Butterworth-Heinemann
Linacre House, Jordan Hill, Oxford OX2 8DP
A division of Reed Educational and Professional Publishing Ltd

ℛ  A member of the Reed Elsevier plc group

OXFORD   BOSTON   JOHANNESBURG
MELBOURNE   NEW DELHI   SINGAPORE

First published 1996
Reprinted 1997

**British Library Cataloguing in Publication Data**
Spark, David
    A journalist's guide to sources
    1. Investigations 2. Information services – Directories
    I. Title
    070.4'3

ISBN 0 240 51470 X

Composition by Scribe Design, Gillingham, Kent
Printed and bound in Great Britain by
Hartnolls Limited, Bodmin, Cornwall

# CONTENTS

# FOREWORD

What do journalists use to find out about planning decisions, the protection of badgers, the rules of hockey or the background of a local hero? Their contacts book of course. Names, addresses, telephone numbers, people, organizations...there, carefully jotted down and carried about, are the contacts the prudent reporter hopes will help provide the answers a story needs.

Picture the ultimate in contacts books and you have David Spark's *A Journalist's Guide to Sources*.

No one book could contain every source that every story by every journalist needs, but here is one that covers a huge area of inquiry by distilling the very essence of information-providing, both printed and electronic.

Here can be found the telephone number of the National Ankylosing Spondylitis Society, of a professor willing to talk to the press about the origins of hymns, another about acid rain and yet another about crocodiles.

There is an organization that advises on the problem of bedwetting and a magazine that has an expert on stolen art. And did you know that Britain has a Hedgehog Preservation Society, a Domesticated Ostrich Association and a Reedgrowers Association? That Christmas tree growers have their own federation and that Hull University can offer the press the services of an expert on pollution from fish farms?

Carefully listed, alphabeticized and indexed, with information on Internet providers and on-line services, *A Journalist's Guide to Sources* is set to be the ideal one-volume companion for reporters and feature writers and those planning a career in journalism.

*F. W. Hodgson*
*Editor, Media Series*

# 1 WHERE TO LOOK

## AT HOME

When I was looking for information about the sinking of the Titanic, I found what I needed in a book in my own house. It was more informative than all the volumes in our local library. Never overlook sources of information and ideas within your house and family circle.

The experiences and tip-offs from family and friends have led me to stories on students-and-landlords, poor compensation for compulsory purchase, university staff pensions, crossing roses with brambles, making dummies for shop windows and legs for beached yachts, and a six-hour session with two double-glazing salesmen.

The snag is knowing what material you have in the house. Things you set aside as possibly useful in future are easily forgotten if not properly filed.

Keeping well-organized cuttings is probably a counsel of perfection, unless your interests as a journalist are limited to specific fields. Some of the names and phone numbers in a contacts book can prove to be long out of date when next you try them. But a contacts book is worth keeping because sometimes you find yourself looking for the same name and telephone number over and over again.

Here are some other places to look for information which you as a journalist should keep in mind.

## AT THE OFFICE

A newspaper office, local or national, is a rich source of information. It will have files of the newspaper and also of its competitors and of all the national press. National stories may draw attention to a local newspaper situation or have a local impact or suggest a story on a related theme. An account of a trek through the Pakistan mountains organized by a company at Keswick, in Cumbria, raised for me the questions how the company came to be doing this and why from Keswick.

The office probably buys periodicals (such as *The Economist* which surveys and comments on British and foreign news) and will have sent to it other publications from books to parish newsletters which their editors or publishers would like written about.

It will also have reference works such as:

*A–Z Street Directory.*

*The Writers' and Artists' Yearbook*, which lists publishers, newspapers and magazines, and literary agents.

*Crockford's Clerical Directory*, a who's who of Church of England clergy which also lists parishes and their priests.

*Dod's Parliamentary Companion*, which gives election details and short biographies of MPs.

Encyclopaedias.

French, German, Spanish dictionaries. If you are not a linguist, do look up foreign words. Many papers get them wrong as often as right.

A gazetteer – vital if you want to locate or spell a place you never heard of.

*Halliwell's Film Guide*, or *Ephraim Katz's International Encyclopaedia of Film* (Macmillan: £30). These have synopses of films and also assess their quality.

*IPO Directory* (Information and Press Officers in Government Departments). It also covers press officers in a wide range of public agencies from the electricity and gas regulators to the Metropolitan Police (and their areas), the National Rivers Authority (and its regional offices) and the Serious Fraud Office. It is issued twice yearly, on subscription, from IPO Directory, PO Box 30, Wetherby LS23 7YA. Tel: 01937-541010).

*Keesing's Record of World Events*, a monthly digest of world news, with index.

*Oxford Dictionary of Quotations*, or *Stevenson's Book of Quotations*.

Railway timetable.

*Roget's Thesaurus*. If you are fed up using the same word, it will give you alternatives.

*The Times Atlas.*

*Vacher's Parliamentary Companion*. This guide to Parliament is revised and republished four times a year.

*Whitaker's Almanack* (published annually) lists Members of Parliament and British Members of the European Parliament; Government departments and officials; local councils; employers associations and trade unions; publishers; bishops; international organizations. It gives basic facts about the countries of the world.

*Who's Who* – easily overlooked as a source about someone you need to know about. It even lists some addresses.

*Wisden.* Everything about last year's cricket.

A press directory *(*Hollis, Benn, Willings*).*

Get from major publishers their brochures about forthcoming books, if your office doesn't get them already. Authors, including well-known ones, are usually available for interview. Book subjects could also be important nationally or locally. Some brochures (e.g. Headline and Hamish Hamilton) say where authors live.

Many senior journalists are sent *The Journalist's Handbook* (distributed free four times a year by Carrick Media, 2–7 Galt House, 31 Bank Street, Irvine KA12 0LL. Fax: 01294-311322). It lists news contacts at many organizations.

A companion volume, *The Media Yearbook*, lists anniversaries, birthdays of well-known people, major forthcoming events, and has 80 pages of contacts at organizations and PR consultancies.

*The UK Press Gazette* lists some contacts including police forces and regional offices of the post and railways. It also offers a computer disk of contacts called ContactPro (£29.95 plus VAT). Users can add their own.

## NEWS DESKS

The news desk diary remains the bible of news editors. They also monitor TV news headlines. The **Press Association** provides news schedules for the day and week.

Offices may buy other services. **Future Events News Service** (8 Wiseton Road, London SW17 7EE. Tel: 0181–672–3191; fax: 0181–672–2282) gives a diary of each day's events including celebrity stories and offers a twice weekly service on world events distributed by UPI. **Celebrity Press Service** issues its *Celebrity Bulletin* on Mondays and Thursdays. Many London news desks use *London at Large*, a weekly guide to who will be where.

A news desk usually has detailed maps of the area it covers.

Often a story behind a diary engagement is more interesting than the event itself. For freelances this is specially important because staff writers will be quickly in print with obvious news.

A press briefing on schizophrenia offered pointers to two intriguing stories in other fields: a genetic explanation of why more people are right-handed than left-handed, and a claim that Britain is the world leader in brain imaging.

## PUBLIC LIBRARIES

A small local library might have most of the publications you need to consult: national papers, *The New Scientist*, *The Times Educational Supplement*, UK phone books, *Willing's Press Guide*, and *Kelly's Directory* (its pink pages list many but unfortunately not all of the smaller companies which elude other directories).

A major town reference library offers a huge array of books and material useful to journalists. Here are some:

### Arts, music

> *New Grove's Dictionary of Music and Musicians* (twelve volumes, and also a concise one-volume version).
> *Oxford Dictionary of Music* (one volume).

### Books

> *Directory of Book Publishers.*
> *Encyclopaedia of World Literature in the 20th Century.*
> *The Writers' Directory 1994–6* (published in America).

### Commerce

> *Bankers' Almanac* (covers the world).
> *Business Monitors.*
> Company annual reports.
> *Dun and Bradstreet's Key British Enterprises.*
> *Dun and Bradstreet's Who owns Whom* – lists companies and their subsidiaries.
> *FT Smaller Companies Handbook* – gives a page to each.
> *Insurance Directory.*
> *Macmillan's Unquoted Companies* – 20,000 not quoted on the stock exchange; what they do, who runs them.
> *Stock Exchange Year Book* – financial and some other details on companies listed on the stock exchange.

### Education

> *Directory of Technical and Further Education.*
> Education magazines.

*International Handbook of Universities.*
*Times Higher Education Supplement.*

### Entertainment

*Kemp's Film, TV and Radio Handbook* – a lot of information but aimed
  at people in the trade.
*Spotlight* – lists actors with their pictures and their agents.

### Environment

*Who's Who in the Environment.*

### Europe

*Encyclopaedia of European Community Law* – a whole shelf of it, as
  you would expect.
*FT European Handbook* – companies of Europe.

### Government publications

Acts of Parliament.
Business monitors – giving production statistics.
*Civil Service Year Book* – who holds important jobs.
Command papers – reports published by the Government.
*CSO Annual Abstract of Statistics* (and *Monthly Digest of Statistics*).
*CSO's Blue Book* – UK national accounts.
Digest of UK Energy Statistics.
*Economic Trends* (periodical).
Hansard reports of Parliament.
Labour Force Survey – quarterly survey of 60,000 households.

### Health, local government

*Directory of Independent Hospitals and Health Services.*
*Housing Year Book* – includes aid and advice groups, housing associations,
building societies, builders.
*IHSM Health Services Year Book.*
*Key Indicators of Local Authority Social Services* (covers counties,
metropolitan districts, London boroughs).
*Medical Directory* – a doctors' who's who.
*Medical Register* – of doctors authorized to practise.
*Municipal Year Book* – includes health authorities, hospital trusts, development corporations and central government, as well as councils.

## International

Bookcases full of world history, including the *Cambridge History of Islam.*
*Encyclopaedia of Terrorism.*
*Monthly Bulletin of Statistics* (United Nations' periodical).
*Motor Industry of Great Britain* – world automotive statistics.
*Who's Who in Classical Mythology.*
*World Bibliographical Series* – lists books written about all the countries in the world.

## Jobs

*New Earnings Survey.*

## Law

*Halsbury's Statutes.*
Law Reports.

## London

*London Hostels Directory.*
*London Housing Statistics.*
*Names of Streets in London.*
*Survey of London* (detailed account of history and buildings).

## Museums

*British Museum Guide.*
*Museums Yearbook.*

## Phone books

For overseas as well as the UK (American books in microfilm).

## Pictures

*Picture Sources in the UK.*

## Religion

*Crockford's Clerical Directory* (of the Church of England) and directories for other churches.

### Science

*Handbook of the Birds of Europe, the Middle East and North Africa.*
*Van Nostrand's Scientific Encyclopedia.*

### Sea

*Jane's Fighting Ships.*

### Society

*British Social Attitudes.*
*Disability Rights Handbook.*
*Encyclopaedia of Feminism.*
*Social Security Statistics* – not divided by area.

### Sport

*Guinness International Who's Who of Sport.*

Many libraries, including the British Library Newspaper Library, have indices to newspaper articles. *The Times*, *Financial Times* and *Herald (Glasgow)* publish indices. The Library Association publishes quarterly the *British Humanities Index*.

Clover Publications publishes the *Clover Newspaper Index* covering the national broadsheets: its bulletins can be kept together in a loose-leaf binder.

## THE LOCAL COUNCIL

Most councils now employ press officers who will help you find informants and information in their council's domain. Council staff are usually well informed about the area they administer (see pages 216–18).

## UNIVERSITIES

Your nearest university might well have experts on subjects you want to know about who can make your story more thorough, even on such out-of-the-way subjects as Frisbees (Warwick), and dry rot (Strathclyde). If you want independent information on the countries of Europe, for example, you have little alternative to trying the universities.

University men and women through their research come across important points not obvious in day-to-day news reports and appear often in television news bulletins. Some are acknowledged national experts on certain news subjects. Keele (tel: 01782–583371) and Kent (tel: 01227–451805) have radio links to studios.

Many universities publish lists of their experts willing to talk to the media, and the subjects on which they are willing to talk. Some give direct phone numbers and even e-mail addresses. Others insist on an approach via the university press office or department.

In format, these university who's whos vary from A4 size (University College London, London School of Economics, Durham) down to pocket size (Strathclyde, Warwick). In style, Keele's is the least inhibited. It presents its dons' pictures at jaunty angles, with detailed but succinct accounts of their expertise, as if they are seeking auditions for TV (which perhaps they are). Cambridge, at the other extreme, goes for small print. A problem with the Cambridge guide is that it fails to draw attention to centres of excellence.

## MAGAZINES

Many editors of specialist magazines are prepared to talk to journalists about their speciality, or to contribute newspaper articles. Magazines can be specially helpful concerning minor sports and pastimes which lack easily contacted national officials.

For freelances seeking a subject no-one else is working on, a specialist magazine is a good source of ideas. An article about a man who makes lightweight water drilling rigs for Oxfam stemmed from *Farm Equipment International*. One on low-cost trams started life in a magazine advertisement.

## GOVERNMENT OFFICES

Apart from their published reports, government offices will usually arrange for you an unattributable briefing on matters with which they are concerned. They may turn you down if the official you want to speak to is in a particularly newsworthy situation and therefore in big demand.

Departments commonly have regional offices and press officers. The Government also has offices for specific places such as London and Merseyside. Outside London the desire of departments to run their own show conflicts with the desire of the Government as a whole to co-ordinate its efforts. A new attempt at co-ordination is the **Business Link** network which brings together government departments, chambers of commerce and training and enterprise councils.

## PRESS AND PUBLIC RELATIONS OFFICERS

Press officers vary as much as journalists. Some joined only last week, while others know everything about the firm they have served twenty years. Some can't be too helpful, others wish you hadn't phoned. Some send more than they promised, others send nothing, others send things so late you've forgotten you asked for them. Some chase up an answer to your query straight away, others can take up to six months.

Government press officers, with packs of national news hounds chasing them, tend to be busy and to cover specific and limited fields. They also seem to switch jobs and responsibilities frequently.

Journalists, in general, take every possible advantage of PR facilities while claiming to distrust all PRs as spin doctors (except the one whose hospitality they are currently enjoying). Blatantly spin-doctored material, for example in the Come to Wonderful So-and-So mode, appears in print quite commonly. Years ago, Humbert Wolfe wrote:

> ...You cannot bribe or twist,
> Thank God, the British journalist;
> But, seeing what the man will do
> Unbribed, there's no occasion to.

Wolfe, whose main target was the press barons, might have been impressed by the skill and integrity with which British journalists have navigated the treacherous PR waters of Baghdad (in the Gulf War) and Bosnia.

The mundane truth is that in nine stories out of ten journalists and press officers form a useful partnership. Press officers provide a point of access to the complex and possibly tongue-tied bureaucracies of government, local government, companies and charities. The best are enthusiasts who can explain their organization and its aims in plain language. But journalists need to seek out what other views there may be.

One good rule is: always check the underlying arithmetic. Things won't happen unless there is the time and the money for them to happen. Labour MP Frank Dobson won his argument with water company spokesmen over the need to repair leaking pipes because he did his sums well. The company PR case foundered on the arithmetical facts.

Even the best press officers won't necessarily guess what will make the best story. On a visit to the mountainous north of Pakistan, I and other journalists listened to a series of enthusiasts explaining their work in the Aga Khan Rural Development Programme. But we missed a point hidden away in the accompanying literature which could have made the best story. It concerned the lonely lives of young women working as health visitors in remote, conservative Moslem communities.

A weakness of press officers (and even more of company managers) is a failure to see what will make their story vivid. The temptation is to reel off the company achievements and forget to mention the old man who made them happen.

Be on your guard when press officers provide information about foreign places. They may tell less than the whole story. A charity held a press conference in the 1980s to urge Britain to help Ethiopia feed its drought victims. The spokesmen omitted to mention that they were victims not just of drought but of the then Ethiopian Government's soldiers and bombers.

## THE INTERNET

The Internet uses the telephone network to link computer users all over the world. It offers free information: this is a sacred principle for university users. But it is, literally, anarchic and the information can be time-consuming and costly (in phone bills) to find.

Most British journalists using the Internet probably concentrate on e-mail, the service which enables you to send a message to any other Internet user anywhere and receive a reply. If your machine is switched off when the reply arrives, it will come when you switch on again. E-mail is good for sending fax-type messages, particularly to several people at once. It is also a good way to track down people not immediately available

**NISS Gateway** on the Internet gives a menu of services. There is no central directory of e-mail addresses. **Mailbase** offers a UK directory service, and **Paradise** one for the European Union. **MIT** and **Four 11 Directory Services** also offer address services.

E-mail brings American informants within easy reach. It is possible to receive usable photographs by e-mail, if you have the necessary decoding programme.

Organizations have their own e-mail addresses, for example foe.co.uk (which means Friends of the Earth, a registered company, in the UK). They then allocate addresses based on this to their staff.

Other simple uses of the Internet are to find experts in particular subjects and to get in touch with people interested in something you want to know about through what are called news groups. There are over 9000 news groups, and a query to members of a group will produce a handful of replies.

Some British government press releases can be picked up from the Internet.

The **World-Wide Web** (WWW), invented at the European Centre of Particle Physics in Switzerland, enables you to comb the Internet for information. For this you need a 'browser', preferably a local one. You can click on to coloured words on the screen, hopefully garnering more information as you move on from one storage computer to another. Words in one computer's memory are linked by the web to words in another. Among the companies, universities and government institutions putting pages on WWW are the Press Association, the *Financial Times* and *The Guardian*. Indexes are provided by so-called search engines.

Since the information is free, Internet is cheap to use once you have the equipment: the running costs are simply the charge levied by the agency giving you access to the net, plus the telephone charges for using that access. Even if you are in touch with the far side of the world, these charges will be at local-call rates if your service-provider is within local-call distance. So choose a provider who is as close at hand as possible. **Demon**, for example (tel: 0181–371–1234; fax: 0181–371–1150) has access points throughout Britain.

Other providers include **BBC Networking Club** (tel: 0181–576–7799), **CityScape**, Cambridge (tel: 01223–566950; fax: 01223–566951), **Direct Connection** (tel: 0181–317–0100), **EasyNet** (tel: 0171–209–0990), **EUnet**, Whitstable (tel: 01227–266466; fax: 01227–266477), **Ireland On-Line** (tel: 00–353–91–592727), **Pipex** (tel: 01223–250120) and **RedNet** (tel: 01494–513333). **EasyNet** is linked with Cyberia, Britain's first cafe for travellers on the Internet. It is at 39 Whitfield Street, London W1.

The basic equipment you need is a PC with Windows, or an Apple-Mac. You need a modem to link your computer to the telephone service. This should be Hayes compatible and operate at a minimum of 2400 bits per second: 14,400 or 28,800 bps is preferable.

Your service-provider will charge for connection and then £10 to £15 a month and send you a starter pack with software that will connect you. You will also acquire an e-mail address.

The Internet began from the US Department of Defense and has been widely used by universities. Imperial College in London stores hundreds of thousands of programmes and files available to Internet users through NISS Gateway. The **Archie** system gives you access to a million files at 800 sites.

Like other computer work, the Internet is full of jargon, for example:

**FTP** – file transfer protocol allows you to send a file to another computer or receive one. Files available to you and all-comers are called anonymous FTP.

**Hypertext** – text that contains links to other text as in the World-Wide Web.

**HTML** – hypertext mark-up language, standard language of the World-Wide Web.

## COMMERCIAL ON-LINE SERVICES

A key advantage of having a computer look something up for you, rather than ask a librarian or go through the cuttings yourself, is that the computer can report what it has found, or not found, almost immediately. For this, however, you need an organized and edited service. The anarchic Internet will not do.

**FT Profile** is one well-known 'host' offering an organized service on-line, that is, accessible over the telephone lines. Dial via your modem into FT Profile and call up a few relevant articles quickly on people in the news. Or type in a couple of words and it will summon up newspaper or other reports in which these two words jointly occur. Or, to cut down the job, you could try more words. You pay a fee per minute for the time you are linked to FT Profile plus a fee per line transmitted. So FT Profile transmits the headline of a report first before it puts you to the expense of the full text.

A report from a national newspaper would cost you only a few pence per line. Market research reports come more expensive.

FT Profile (13 Epworth Street, London EC2A 4DL. Tel: 0171–825–8000; fax: 0171–825–7999) offers compiled as well as full-text databases. It includes provincial and international newspapers as well as London ones. Hosts such as FT Profile also make available other services which do not have direct access to customers. Examples are the Hermes service of government press notices and the Department of Trade and Industry's Spearhead service on European Union measures. The European Union has its own host called **ECHO** but this has a hard time dealing with Brussels's gargantuan output of words.

Worth noting are:

MAID, which stands for **Market Analysis and Information Database**. It is a leading rival of FT Profile. Its **Profound** business information service offers news from over 4000 newspapers and agencies, reports on over 4 million companies world-wide and briefings from 113 countries. Many documents appear as in the original source, with colour charts and graphs. (MAID plc, 48 Leicester Square, London WC2H 7DB. Tel: 0171–930–6900; fax: 0171–930–6006).

**First**. This will trawl regularly for information on subjects that interest you (from Individual UK, Cedar Court, 9 Fairmile, Henley-on-Thames RG9 2JR. Tel: 01491–579600; fax: 01491–579750).

**Knight-Ridder** offers news from the world's newspapers, plus thousands of articles on industrial and medical research and even on sports medicine. You can choose which of its 800 databases (many of them American) you want access to. (Knight-Ridder Information, Haymarket House, 1 Oxendon Street, London SW1Y 4EE. Tel: 0171–930–7646; fax: 0171–930–2581)

**Lexis Nexis**, 1 St Katherine's Way, London E1 9UN (tel: 0171–369–1300), operates in a similar fashion to FT Profile. It claims to offer the world's most comprehensive, full-text, on-line libraries, with material from over 2000 newspapers and wire and broadcast services world-wide, including some British provincials and periodicals. Lexis Nexis offers three methods of payment: a fee per month, a fee per hour of use, and a pay-as-you-go scheme with payments for on-line time, searching and lineage.

**Companies House's** computer will give you details of companies, their accounts and their directors (see page 106).

**Perfect Information** provides company reports complete with their illustrations (36 Chiswell Street, London EC1Y 4SE. Tel: 0171–454–0666; fax: 0171–454–0668).

**Dun & Bradstreet International** says that Dun's Market Identifiers (Europe) is the most comprehensive on-line source of European company data. It covers over two million companies in countries from Spain and Ireland east to Austria.

Material transmitted electronically is copyright and should not be stored. In practice, a user who receives copyright material may well cut and paste it in producing a newspaper report. It is worth checking the supply contract to see what copyright stipulations the supplier makes. Re-use of other people's material needs to avoid plagiarism.

## CD-ROM

The CD-ROM system gives you information on compact discs. Once you have bought your system and your discs, you can use them without further payment. Unlike the information on on-line systems, however, the facts on a CD-ROM disc are not constantly updated.

# 2 PEOPLE

## HOW TO FIND THEM

Never overlook the **phone book**. Provided you have an approximate address, or the possible title of an organization, you can find and contact large numbers of people without stirring from your chair.

You can reach most people you need to speak to through their firm, their colleagues or an organization with which they are connected. But some people do not work for a firm and you may not know an organization they belong to. Or perhaps you have simply name and place. If so, the phone book may well help.

If necessary and the name is not too common, you can ring people of the same name and hope to find a relative.

If people are not in the phone book but you know the street or area where they live, you can look for them in the **electoral register**. Public libraries usually have a copy.

Some people may be reachable only by visit or letter.

For people outside your normal area of work, you may have only a telephone number from which you get no reply. Or the phone number may be all you have to distinguish between towns of the same name: for example, Hadleigh (Essex) and Hadleigh (Suffolk). Dialling codes are listed at the front of phone books. The list for London is particularly helpful because it lists codes in numerical order and tells you where they are in use. Codes for other areas of Britain are in alphabetical order by place, and require more patience to research if you do not have the place name.

London postal districts, often used without a local place name, are confusing. If you do not know where SE11 is, look in the index of the *London A–Z* for a street in SE11 and find its whereabouts from the map.

You may want to find people whose whereabouts or even identity are being kept secret. Ask at shops or public houses or, if you are outside your own area, a local reporter.

Other approaches:

**Your office cuttings library** – whoever you want to speak to may have been in the news before.

*Who's Who* – some of the great and good give their addresses and phone numbers in it.

**Agents and PR people** – for politicians, writers, celebrities.

**Directories and professional associations** – for lawyers, doctors and other professionals.

Beware the grey area beyond the bounds of your *A–Z*. A photographer, who had gone to Croydon on a job, was told at 5.30 p.m. to take another picture of an address in Shelton Avenue, Croydon, at 6.30. He bought a *London A–Z* which showed no such address. His news desk suggested he went to New Addington, four miles to the south-east. Still no Shelton Avenue. He took a bus to Selsdon, from where he walked two and a half miles to Shelton Avenue, which proved to be in Warlingham. He arrived at 8 p.m. His picture subject had left.

## *Finding celebrities*

Many well-known people and their associates make themselves hard to reach for obvious reasons. Yet your news desk may require you to contact them; every news desk is interested, for instance, in friends of the Princess of Wales. Here are some ideas:

1 Always check the phone book and *Who's Who*.
2 Check your own contacts book. (You should always record in it anyone who was hard to reach.)
3 Ask colleagues, especially photographers and specialists. Political correspondents are likely to have contact numbers for politicians.
4 Ask at places of work
5 Ask agents, PR representatives, friends. Actors are listed in *Spotlight*, which gives their agents' addresses.
6 Ask publishers, for whom the person you want has written a book (as many older celebrities have). Publishers won't give you a phone number but will forward a message. If you know the book, *Whitaker's* book-tracing service (tel: 0171–836–8911 up to 4 p.m.) will tell you the publisher.

7   Look for a cutting or picture showing your celebrity near or outside his home. Ask estate agents in the area where the house is. Even if they can't identify the house, they could name the street and you can walk down it with your picture.

8   Ask neighbours, if your celebrity has left his usual haunt.

## Missing persons

Some people are quite simply missing. Even their families don't know where they are. Families looking for a relative may seek the help of the **Missing Persons Bureau** (tel: 0181–392–2000; fax: 0181–878–7752) or the **Salvation Army**.

## Who to ask and where to find out

1   The office library, but watch out for inaccurate reporting. One national newspaper habitually and erroneously described Des Wilson as the founder of Shelter.

2   *Who's Who*, for the great and good.

3   Firms they work for.

4   Organizations they belong to.

5   PR representatives.

6   Friends, enemies and neighbours.

7   Books that mention them.

## Finding people for interview

You may want to find not specific people but members of a group you are interested in: for example, lorry drivers going to Bosnia.

Government agencies and some other organizations won't give names unless they seek permission from those named, a laborious task they don't often attempt. Other organizations give names because they want publicity.

For several years I was looking for people with stories to tell their local paper or radio about their work in developing countries. I searched through magazines, both commercial and from voluntary agencies, covering this work. Once names are in print, they are public.

The phone book may help you find members of groups with a recognized identity. For example, two Sikh temples and several Kurdish societies are listed in London's.

It is also worth checking entries in the business phone book beginning with the words Association or British or Society or the name of your local town. In the London phone book, this will lead you to astrologers, owners of Spanish property, Christmas tree growers, wildlife artists and glass blowers.

You can also publish a note in your own paper asking for informants; you can write letters to other papers or even advertise in a national paper. If you advertise, you will probably have to say that you are a journalist. Once you have a few informants, they can lead you to more.

## ACCIDENTS AND DISASTERS

Speak to local police, ambulance station, hospitals, county police press office, doctors, eyewitnesses (but beware of accepting allegations as fact), managers of firms or operators involved, offices of Automobile Association and RAC, railway press officers, airport managers, Defence press officers (if services are involved), river authorities (floods).

*Annual Abstract of Statistics* (in town reference libraries) gives national figures for all kinds of accident.

### *National sources*

**British Association for Accident and Emergency Medicine**, c/o Royal College of Surgeons, Lincolns Inn Fields, London.
Tel: 0171–831–9405; fax: 0171–405–0318

**British Safety Council**, 70 Chancellors Road, London W6 9RS.
Tel: 0181–741–1231

**North West Accident Unit** (Professor Rod Little), Manchester University M13 9PL.
Tel: 0161–275–2112/4, press office

**Royal Society for the Prevention of Accidents**, Cannon House, The Priory, Birmingham B4 6BS.
Tel: 0121–200–2461; fax: 0121–200–1254

### *Insurance*

**Institute of London Underwriters**, 49 Leadenhall Street, London EC3A 2BE.
Tel: 0171–240–2656; fax: 0171–836–7870

## BANKS

Reference: *Bankers' Almanac* (covers the world).

**Abbey National**, Abbey House, Baker Street, London NW1 6XL.
Tel: 0171–612–4979; fax: 0171–612–4233

**Bank of England**, Threadneedle Street, London EC2R 8AH.
Tel: 0171–601–4411/15; fax: 0171–601–5460

**Banking, Insurance and Finance Union**, 16 Amity Grove, London SW20
0LG.
Tel: 0181–946–9151; fax: 0181–879–7916

**Banking Ombudsman**, 70 Grays Inn Road, London WC1.
Tel: 0171–404–9944

**Barclays (UK Banking PR)**, 54 Lombard Street, London EC3.
Tel: 0171–699–2976

**British Bankers Association**, 10 Lombard Street, London EC3.
Tel: 0171–626–8486; fax: 0171–283–7037

**British Merchant Banking Association**, 6 Frederick's Place, Old Jewry,
London EC2R 8BT.
Tel: 0171–796–3606

**Girobank**, Bootle GIR 0AA.
Tel: 0171–396–6439; fax: 0171–396–6466

**Lloyds**, 71 Lombard Street, London EC3P 3BS.
Tel: 0171–626–1500

**Midland**, 27 Poultry, London EC2P 2BX.
Tel: 0171–260–8000; fax: 0171–260–7065

**NatWest**, 41 Lothbury, London EC2P 2BP.
Tel: 0171–726–1000

**Standard Chartered Bank**, London.
Tel: 0171–280–7500

**TSB**, PO Box 6000, Victoria House, Victoria Square, Birmingham B1
1BZ.
Tel: 0121–600–6339; fax: 0121–600–6341

## BELIEF AND RELIGIONS

Most major churches will have priests or ministers in your area. Roman
Catholic bishops have secretaries who will answer queries. Anglican
bishops have chaplains. Anglican dioceses also have full-time workers,
covering such fields as social responsibility, and possibly working from a
diocesan office. Methodist districts have chairmen (who may be women).
There are many lively ecumenical groups linking local churches, and there

may be a local council of faiths linking the churches with people of other beliefs.

*The Catholic Directory* lists Catholic priests; *Crockford's* lists Anglicans. Methodist ministers are listed in the *Minutes of the Methodist Conference*: local ministers will have copies.

See also the *Baptist Handbook, Buddhist Directory, Friends' Book of Meeting Yearbook, Jewish Yearbook, Salvation Army Yearbook.*

Other faiths have less formal structures and you will need to identify useful contacts.

## National sources:

**Centre for Advanced Religion and Theological Studies**, c/o Faculty of Divinity, Cambridge.
Tel: 01223–332590

**Comparative Religion Department**, Manchester University, M13 9PL
Tel: 0161–275–3614 or try PR 0161–275–2112/4

**Theology Department**, Durham University, Abbey House, Durham DH1 3RS.
Tel: 0191–374–2060; fax: 0191–374–4744

## BUDDHISM

**Friends of the Western Buddhist Order**, St Marks Studios, Chillingworth Road, London N7 8QJ.
Tel: 0171–700–3077; fax: 0171–700–3077

**Buddhist Society and** *The Middle Way* (journal), 58 Eccleston Square, London SW1V 1PH.
Tel: 0171–834–5858

## CHURCHES

**Churches Commission for Racial Justice**, 35 Lower Marsh, London SE1 7RL.
Tel: 0171–620–4444

**Council of Christians and Jews**, 1 Dennington Park Road, London NW6 1AX.
Tel: 0171–794–8178; fax: 0171–431–3500

**Council of Churches for Britain and Ireland**, 35 Lower Marsh, London SE1 7RL (umbrella body for all the British Isles).
Tel: 0171–620–4444; fax: 0171–928–0010

**Evangelical Alliance**, 186 Kennington Park Road, London SE11 4BT.
Tel: 0171–582–0228; fax: 0171–582–6221

Theology Department, **Leeds University**, LS2 9JT.
Tel: 0113–233–3641


## Black churches

**International Ministerial Council of Great Britain**.
Tel: 01923–239266

**Joint Council of Anglo-Caribbean Churches**.
Tel: 0171–737–6542


## Catholic

**Catholic Media Office**, 39 Eccleston Square, London SW1V 1BX.
Tel: 0171–828–8709

**International Justice and Peace**.
Tel: 0171–630–6985

**Social and Pastoral Action**, Vaughan House, 46 Francis Street, London SW1.
Tel: 0171–798–9008


## Church of England

**Bell Ringers**, Central Council, 46 Byfords Road, Huntley GL19 3EL.
Tel: 01452–831197

**Church Action on Poverty**, Central Buildings, Oldham Street, Manchester M1 1JT.
Tel: 0161–236–9321; fax: 0161–237–5359

**Church Army**, Independents Road, Blackheath, London SE3 9LG (army for evangelism).
Tel: 0181–318–1226; fax: 0181–318–5258

**Church Commissioners**, 1 Millbank, London SW1P 3JZ (they provide for the Church an income from its assets).
Tel: 0171–222–7010; fax: 0171–233–0171

**Church of England Press Department**, Church House, Great Smith Street, London SW1P 3NZ.
Tel: 0171–222–9011; fax: 0171–222–6672

**Church Urban Fund**, Millbank, London SW1P 3JZ (Anglican fund for inner cities).
Tel: 0171–620–0917

**Mothers Union**, 24 Tufton Street, London SW1P 3RB.
Tel: 0171–222–5533; fax: 0171–222–5533

## Hymns

**Hymn Society of Great Britain and Ireland**, St Nicholas Rectory, Glebe Fields, Curdworth B76 9ES.
Tel: 01675–470384

**Professor Richard Watson**, English Studies, Elvet Riverside, Durham DH1 3JT.
Tel: 0191–374–2730; fax: 0191–374–7471

## Others

**Baptist Union**, PO Box 44, 129 Broadway, Didcot OX11 8RT.
Tel: 01235–512077

**Methodist Press Office**, Central Buildings, Matthew Parker Street, London SW1H 9NH.
Tel: 0171–222–8010

**Salvation Army**, 101 Queen Victoria Street, London EC4P 4EP.
Tel: 0171–236–5222; fax: 0171–236–6272

**Society of Friends**, Euston Road, London NW1 2BJ.
Tel: 0171–387–3601; fax: 0171–388–1977

**Spiritualists National Union**, Redwoods, Stansted Hall, Stansted CM24 8UD.
Tel: 01279–816363; fax: 01279–812034

**Unitarian Churches**, General Assembly, 1 Essex Street, London WC2R 3HY.
Tel: 0171–240–2384; fax: 0171–240–3089

**United Reformed Church**, 86 Tavistock Place, London WC1H 9RR.
Tel: 0171–916–2020

## *Women and the ministry*

**Ministry of Women** (was Movement for Ordination of Women), c/o Christina Rees, Royston SG8 8JX.
Tel: 01763–848822; fax: 01763–848774

**Watch** (Women and the Church).
Tel: 0181–863–2094

**Catholic Women's Network**.
Tel: 0181–470–5977

## CHURCH OVERSEAS

**Anglican Consultative Council**, SE1 8UT.
Tel: 0171–620–1110

**Church Missionary Society**, SE1 8UU.
Tel: 0171–928–8681

**United Society for Propagation of Gospel**, SE1 8XA.
Tel: 0171–928–8681
All at 157 Waterloo Road, London SE1

**Baptist Missionary Society**, 129 Broadway Didcot OX11 8RT.
Tel: 01235–512077

**Bible Society**, Stonehill Green, Westlea, Swindon SN5 7DG
Tel: 01793–418100

**Council for World Mission** (formerly the London Missionary Society), 11 Carteret St, London SW1H 8DL.
Tel: 0171–222–4214

**Methodist Church Overseas Division**, 25 Marylebone Road, London NW1 5JR.
Tel: 0171–486–5502

**National Missionary Council** (Roman Catholic), Holcombe House, The Ridgeway, London NW7.
Tel: 0181–906–1642

**Oxford Centre for Mission Studies**, St Philip and St James, PO Box 70, OX2 6HB.
Tel: 01865–56071; fax 01865–510823

**Quaker Peace and Service**, Euston Road, London NW1 2BJ.
Tel: 0171–387–3601; fax: 0171–388–1977

**Salvation Army International Head Quarters**, 101 Queen Victoria Street, London EC4P 4EP.
Tel: 0171–236–5222; fax: 0171–236–4981

## *Persecution of Christians*

**Jubilee Campaign**, St Johns, Cranleigh Road, Wonersh, Guildford GU5 0QX.
Tel: 01483–894787; fax: 01483–894797

**Keston Research**, PO Box 226, Oxford OX2 6BF.
Tel: 01865–311022; fax: 01865–311280

## *World Church*

**John Bridge**, History, Keele University ST5 5BG (a member of World Council of Churches executive).
Tel: 01782–583197

# HINDUISM

**Anthropology Department**, **SOAS**, Thornhaugh Street, Russell Square, London WC1H 0XG.
Tel: 0171–637–2388

**Eleanor Nesbitt**, Institute of Education, Warwick University, CV4 7AL.
Tel: 01203–523523, ext. 2579; e-mail: aeran@snow.warwick.ac.uk

**Shri Swaminarayan Mandir,** 105 Brentfield Road, London NW10.
Tel: 0181–965–2651

## *In India*

**Professor Christopher J. Fuller**, Anthropology Department, London School of Economics, London WC2A 2AE.
Tel: 0171–955–7213

# HUMANISM

**British Humanist Association**, 47 Theobalds Road, London WC1X 8SP.
Tel: 0171–430–0908; fax: 0171–430–1271

## ISLAM

Most of Islam has no formal structure. Mosques are independent congregations, led by an imam who is probably the best person for local journalists to approach. Here are some sources of information on matters affecting Islam.
Reference: *Cambridge History of Islam.*

**Aga Khan Secretariat**, Aiglemont, 60270 Gouvieux, France. (The Aga Khan leads the Ismaili community of Moslems, spread throughout the world, which joins with him in contributing to a major charity, the Aga Khan Foundation.)
Tel: 00–33–44–58–40–00; fax: 00–33–44–57–20–00

**Arabic and Islamic Studies Department**, University of Exeter, Old Library, Prince of Wales Road, Exeter EX4 4JZ.
Tel: 01392–264028

**Arabic and Islamic Studies Department**, University of Glasgow G12 8QQ.
Tel: 0141–339–8855

**Centre for Middle Eastern and Islamic Studies**, Dr S.Taji-Farouki, South End House, Durham DH1 3TG.
Tel: 0191–374–2822; fax: 2830

**Centre for Study of Islam and Muslim-Christian Relations**, 996 Bristol Road, Birmingham B29 6LQ
Tel: 0121–472–4231

**Islamic and Middle East Studies**, Edinburgh University, 7 Buccleuch Place, EH8 9LW.
Tel: 0131–650–4180

**Islamic Cultural Centre**, Dr Ghamdi, 146 Park Road, London NW8 7RG. This is probably the leading UK mosque.
Tel: 0171–724–3363

**Islamic Foundation**, Conference Centre, Ratby Lane, Marfield, Leicester.
Tel: 01530–244944

**Ismaili Centre**, 1 Cromwell Gardens, London SW7 2SL.
Tel: 0171–581–2071/589–2226

**Muslim Educational Trust**, 130 Stroud Green Road, London N4 3RZ.
Tel: 0171–272–8502/9584

**Oxford Centre for Islamic Studies**, St Cross College, OX1 3TU.
Tel: 01865–278730

**Dr Peter Clarke**, Theology and Religious Studies, King's College, The Strand, London WC2R 2LS.
Tel: 0171–836–5454, ext. 3796

## JUDAISM

**Board of Deputies of British Jews**, Woburn House, Upper Woburn Place, London WC1H 0EP.
Tel: 0171–387–3952/388–7651; fax: 0171–383–5848

**Central British Fund for World Jewish Relief**, 30 Gordon Street, London WC1H 0AN.
Tel: 0171–387–3925; fax: 0171–383–4810

**Jewish Care**, 221 Golders Green Road, London NW11 9DQ.
Tel: 0181–458–3282; fax: 0181–201–8430

**Jewish Education Bureau**, 8 Westcombe Avenue, Leeds LS8 2BS.
Offers information on Jewish issues.
Tel: 0113–266–3613; fax: 0113–269–7318

**Jewish Studies**, Dr John Klier, University College London, Gower Street, London WC1E 6BT.
Tel: 0171–387–7050, ext. 3720; departmental office: 0171–380–7171

**Union of Orthodox Hebrew Congregations**, 40 Queen Elizabeth's Walk, London N16 0HH.
Tel: 0181–802–6226

## NEW RELIGIOUS MOVEMENTS/NEW AGE

**Professor Eileen Barker**, Sociology Department, London School of Economics, Houghton Street, London WC2A 2AE.
Tel: 0171–955–7289

**Dr Paul Heelas**, Religious Studies, Lancaster University LA1 4YW.
Tel: 01524–592422

**Dr Peter Clarke**, Theology and Religious Studies, King's College, The Strand, London WC2R 2LS.
Tel: 0171–836–5454, ext. 3796

## SIKHISM

**Eleanor Nesbitt** see under HINDUISM

## SUPERNATURAL

**Society for Psychical Research**, 49 Marloes Road, London W8 6LA.
Tel: 0171–937–8984

## YOGA

**British Wheel of Yoga**, 1 Hamilton Place, Boston Road, Sleaford NG34
7ES.
Tel: 01529–306851

**Dr Daniel Mariau**, Theology Department, Hull University HU6 7RX.
Tel: 01482–465646

**Iyengar Yoga Institute**, 223A Randolph Avenue, London W9 1NL
Tel: 0171–624–3080; fax: 0171–624–3080

## CHILDREN

Try education officers, directors of social services, local inspectors of the
National Society for the Prevention of Cruelty to Children. See regional
sources, in United Kingdom chapter, from page 238.

**Child Poverty Action Group**, 4th floor, 1 Bath Street, London EC1V
9PY.
Tel: 0171–253–3406

**Family and Youth Concern**, 322 Woodstock Road, Oxford OX2 7NS.
Tel: 01865–56848; fax: 01865–52774

**National Children's Bureau**, 6 Wakley Street, London EC1V 7QE.
Leading research organization.
Tel: 0171–843–6000; fax: 0171–278–9512

**National Childminding Association**, 8 Masons Hill, Bromley BR2 9EY.
Tel: 0181–464–6164

**National Foster Care Association**, 5 Marshalsea Road, London SE1
1EP.
Tel: 0171–828–6266; fax: 0171–357–6668

**Parents at Work**, 77 Holloway Road, London N7 8JZ.
Tel: 0171–700–5771; fax: 0171–700–1105

**Professional Association of Nursery Nurses**, 2 St James Court, Friar
Gate, Derby DE1 1BT.
Tel: 01332–343029; fax: 01332–290310

**Twins and Multiple Births Association**, PO Box 30, Little Sutton, South
Wirral L66 1TH.
Tel: 0151–348–0020; fax: 0151–348–0020

# ABDUCTION

**Reunite** (National Council for Abducted Children), PO Box 4, London
WC1N 2NX.
Tel: 0171–404–8356

# ADOPTION

**British Agencies for Adoption and Fostering**, London SE1 0LX.
Tel: 0171–593–2000; 0171–593–2001

**NORCAP** (counselling for adoptees and parents), 3 New High Street,
Headington, Oxford OX3 7AJ.
Tel: 01865–750554

**Parent to Parent Information on Adoption Services**, Lower Boddington
NN11 6YB.
Tel: 01327–260295; fax: 01327–260295

# BEDWETTING

**Enuresis Resource and Information Centre**, 65 St Michael's Hill, Bristol
BS2 8DZ.
Tel: 0117–926–4920; fax: 0117–925–1640

# CHILD ABUSE

**Childwatch**, 206 Hessle Road, Hull HU3 3BE.
Tel: 01482–325552

**Child Care Forum**, Barbara Kahan, Dudley DY1 1DZ.
Tel: 01384–455339; fax: 01384–254406

**Dr Bill Gillham** and **Dr David Warden**, Strathclyde University G1 1XQ.
Tel: 0141–552–4400; Dr Gillham, ext. 2589; Dr Warden, ext. 2576

## CHILDREN'S SOCIETIES

**Barnardo's**, Tanners Lane, Barkingside, Ilford IG6 1QG.
Tel: 0181–550–8822; fax: 0181–550–0429

**Catholic Child Welfare Council**, 120 West Heath Road, London NW3 7TY.
Tel: 0181–731–8028

**The Children's Society**, Edward Rudolf House, Margery Street, London WC1X 0JL.
Tel: 0171–837–4299; fax: 0171–837–0211

**National Children's Home**, 85 Highbury Park, London N5 1UD.
Tel: 0171–226–2033; fax: 0171–226–2537

**National Society for the Prevention of Cruelty to Children**, 42 Curtain Road, London EC2A 3NH.
Tel: 0171–825–2500

**Shaftesbury Society**, 16 Kingston Road, London SW19 1JZ.
Tel: 0181–542–5550; fax: 0181–545–0605

## HYPERACTIVITY

**Hyperactive Children's Support Group**, 71 Whyke Lane, Chichester PO19 2LD.
Tel: 01903–725182

## POCKET MONEY

**Wall's Ice Cream (Birds Eye/Walls)**, Walton on Thames, publishes an annual survey.
Tel: 01932–263000

## CONSUMERS

Local trading standards officers administer the Trades Description Act which ensures that people get what they think they are buying. You may also have local consumer groups.

*National sources*

**BEUC**, Brussels. European consumer's organization.
Tel: 00–322–735–3110; fax 00–322–735–1455

**GFK**, 22 Stephenson Way, London NW1 2HZ. Publishes regional consumer survey.
Tel: 0171–383–2939

**Consumers' Association**, 2 Marylebone Road, London NW1 4DX. Publishes Which magazine.
Tel: 0171–830–6061/2/4/5/6; fax: 0171–830–6063

**Consumers International**, 24 Highbury Crescent, London N5 1RX.
Tel: 0171–226–6663; fax: 0171–354–0607

**Institute of Trading Standards Administration**, 4 Hadleigh Business Centre, Essex SS7 2BT. For trading standards professionals.
Tel: 01702–559922; fax: 01702–559902

**National Consumer Council**, 20 Grosvenor Gardens, London SW1 0DH.
Tel: 0171–730–3469; fax: 0171–730–0191

**Office of Fair Trading**, Field House, Breams Buildings, London EC4A 1PR.
Tel: 0171–269–8899/901; fax: 0171–269–8961

# CREDIT

See page 46.

# DEATH

**Cremation Society**, 2nd floor, 16a Albion Place, Maidstone ME14 5DZ.
Tel: 01622–688292/3; fax: 01622–686698

**Federation of British Cremation Authorities**, 41 Salisbury Road, Carshalton SM5 3HA.
Tel: 0181–669–4521

**National Association of Funeral Directors**, 618 Warwick Road, Solihull B91 1AA.
Tel: 0121–711–1343; fax: 0121–711–1351

## EUTHANASIA

**Voluntary Euthanasia Society**, 13 Prince of Wales Terrace, London W8 5PG.
Tel: 0171–937–7770; fax: 0171–376–2648

**Andrew Williams**, Philosophy Department, York University YO1 5DD.
Tel: 01904–432029 (university PR)

## DISABLED

Many national organizations have local groups.
Reference: *Disability Rights Handbook.*

**British Council of Organizations of Disabled People**, Litchurch Plaza, Derby DE24 8AA.
Tel: 01332–295551; fax: 01332–295580

**British Limbless Ex-Service Men's Association**, 185 High Road, Chadwell Heath RM6 6NA.
Tel: 0181–590–1124; fax: 0181–599–2932

**Carers' National Association**, 20 Glasshouse Yard, London EC1A 4JN.
Tel: 0171–490–8818; fax: 0171–490–8824

**Centre for Accessible Environments**, 60 Gainsford Street, London SE1 2NY.
Tel: 0171–357–8182; fax: 0171–357–8183

**Disability Alliance**, Universal House, Wentworth Street, London E1 7SA.
Tel: 0171–247–8759; fax: 247–8765

**Disability Studies**, Professor Mike Oliver, Greenwich University, Wellington Street, London SE18 6PF.
Tel: 0181–331–9588

**Disabled Drivers Association**, Ashwellthorpe, Norwich NR16 1EX.
Tel: 01508–489449

**Lady Hoare Trust for Disabled Children**, 4th floor, 44 Fleet Street, London EC4Y 1BN. Started as thalidomide appeal.
Tel: 0171–583–1951; fax: 0171–583–1391

**Leonard Cheshire Foundation**, 26 Maunsell Street, London SW1P 2QN.
Tel: 0171–828–1822; fax: 0171–976–5704

**ME Association**, Stanhope House, High Street, Stanford-le-Hope SS17 0HA.
Tel: 01375–642466; fax: 01375–650256

**Mind** (helps mentally ill), Granta House, Broadway, London E15 4BQ.
Tel: 0181–519–2122

**Opportunities for People with Disabilities**, 1 Bank Buildings, Princes Street, London EC2R 8EU.
Tel: 0171–726–4961; fax: 0171–726–4961

**RADAR** (Royal Association for Disability and Rehabilitation), 12 City Forum, City Road, EC1V 8AF.
Tel: 0171–250–3222; fax: 0171–250–0212

**Remploy**, 415 Edgware Road, London NW2 6LR.
Tel: 0181–235–0500; fax: 0181–235–0501

**Scope** (formerly the Spastics Society), 12 Park Crescent, London W1N 4EQ.
Tel: 0171–636–5020

**AFASIC** (Association for Speech Impaired Children), 347 Central Markets, London EC1A 9NH.
Tel: 0171–236–3632; fax: 0171–236–8115

## BLIND

**Guide Dogs for the Blind**, Hillfields, Burghfield Common RG7 3YG.
Tel: 01734–835555

**National Federation of the Blind**, Unity House, Smyth Street, Westgate, Wakefield WF1 1ER.
Tel: 01924–291313; fax: 01924–200244

**National League of Blind and Disabled**, 2 Tenterden Road, London N17 8BE. Trade union for disabled workers.
Tel: 0181–808–6030; fax: 0181–885–3235

**Royal National Institute for Blind**, 224 Great Portland Street, London W1N 6AA.
Tel: 0171–636–1153; fax: 0171–388–8316

**Sense** (National Deafblind and Rubella Association), 11 Clifton Terrace, London N4 3SR.
Tel: 0171–272–7774; fax: 0171–272–6012

## CEREBRAL PALSY

**Lisa Woolfson**, Education and Psychology, Strathclyde University, Glasgow G1 1XQ.
Tel: 0141–950–3355

## DEAF

**Hearing Dogs for the Deaf**, London Road, Lewknor OX9 5RY
Tel: 01844–353898; fax: 01844–353099

**National Deaf Children's Society**, 15 Dufferin Street, London EC1Y 8PD. Has regional network.
Tel: 0171–250–0123; fax: 0171–251–5020

## LEARNING DIFFICULTIES

**Down's Syndrome Association**, 153 Mitcham Road, London SW17 9PG.
Tel: 0181–682–4001

**Learning Disabilities Department**, Floor E, South Block, University Hospital, Nottingham NG7 2UH.
Tel: 0115–924–9924

**MacIntyre Care**, 602 South Seventh Street, Milton Keynes MK9 2JA.
Tel: 01908–230100; fax: 01908–695643

**Mencap**, 123 Golden Lane, London EC1Y 0RT. Helps mentally handi-capped.
Tel: 0171–454–0454; fax: 0171–454–9193

**Rathbone CI**, 1st floor, 77 Whitworth Street, Manchester M1 6EZ.
Helps people with learning and other problems.
Tel: 0161–236–5358; fax: 0161–236–4539

**Rescare**, 23 Higher Hillgate, Stockport SK1 3ER. Helps mentally handi-capped in care.
Tel: 0161–474–7323; fax 0161–480–3668

## SPORT

**British Sports Association for the Disabled**, 13 Brunswick Place, London N1 6DX.
Tel: 0171–490–4919; fax: 0171–490–4914

# EDUCATION

Primary and secondary schools are the responsibility of local education authorities (county councils, metropolitan and London boroughs) unless they are privately-run or have opted out of local-authority control. These authorities normally have a director of education or chief education officer. Schools have boards of governors and, usually, parent-teacher associations. Other local sources: head teachers, union branch secretaries, colleges, universities, students' union officers.

Further education colleges, like higher education, are now nationally financed and not under local authority control.

## *National sources*

Reference: *Education Yearbook. Education Authorities Directory and Annual* – includes secondary schools, special schools and universities.

**Department of Education and Employment**, Sanctuary Buildings, Great Smith Street, SW1P 3BT.
Fax: 0171–925–6000
Higher education; qualifications, tel: 0171–925–6443/5109/5111
Schools, tel: 0171–925–5108/5741/5102
Further education and training, tel: 0171–925–5361/5373/5499
Curriculum and assessment, tel: 0171–925–5721/5659/5104

**CASE** (Campaign for State Education), 158 Durham Rd, London SW20 0DG.
Tel: 0181–944–8206

**Catholic Education Service**, 39 Eccleston Square, London SW1V 1BX.
Central body for Catholic schools.
Tel: 0171–828–7604

**Council of Local Education Authorities**, 66a Eaton Square, London SW1W 9BH.
Tel: 0171–235–9554

**Education Magazine**, 5 Bentinck Street, London W1M 5RN.
Tel: 0171–935–0121

**National Confederation of Parent-Teacher Associations**, 48 Hammerton Road, Gravesend DA11 9DX.
Tel: 01474–560618

**Funding Agency for Schools**, 25 Skeldergate, York YO1 2XL.
Tel: 01904–661664/1863; fax: 01904–661679

**OFSTED** (Office for Standards in Education), 33 Kingsway, London WC2B 6SF. Schools inspectorate.
Tel: 0171–421–6539/6758/6574; fax: 0171–421–6522

**Parents Opposed to Opting-Out**, 7 Queen Edith's Way, Cambridge CB1 4PH.
Tel: 01223–249646

**School Curriculum and Assessment Authority**, 45 Notting Hill Gate, London W11 3JB.
Tel: 0171–243–9419/9250; fax: 0171–243–0542

*Times Educational Supplement, Times Higher Education Supplement,* 66 East Smithfield, London E1 9XY.
Tel: 0171–782–3000

## Pupil-teacher ratios

**School of Education**, Oxford Brookes University, Wheatley Campus, Oxford OX33 1HX. Has published a national survey.
Tel: 01865–485930

## ADULT

**Adult and Continuing Education Department**, Glasgow University, 57 Oakfield Avenue, Glasgow G12 8LW.
Tel: 0141–330–4394

**Adult Education Centre**, Nottingham University.
Tel: 0115–951–6516

**Sight and Sound**, 118 Charing Cross Road, London WC2H 0JR.
Tel: 0171–379–4753

**Workers Educational Association**, 17 Victoria Park Square, London E2 9PB.
Tel: 0181–983–1515

## Distance learning

**Association of British Correspondence Colleges**, 6 Francis Grove, London SW19 4DT.
Tel: 0181–544–9559; fax: 0181–540–7657

**Distance Learning Centre**, South Bank University, London SE1 0AA.
Tel: 0171–815–7878

**Open University**, Walton Hall, Milton Keynes MK7 6AA.
Tel: 01908–274066

## DYSLEXIA

**Dr Chris Singleton**, Director of Dyslexia Research, Hull University
HU6 7RX.
Tel: 01482–465157

**Dyslexia Institute**, 133 Gresham Road, Staines TW18 2AJ.
Tel: 01784–463851; fax: 01784–460747

## ENGLISH TEACHING

**National Association for Teaching of English**, 50 Broadfield Road,
Sheffield S8 0XJ.
Tel: 0114–255–5419; fax: 0114–255–5296

*Oxford English Dictionary*, Oxford University Press, Walton Street,
Oxford OX2 6DP.
Tel: 01865–56767; fax: 01865–56646

## EQUIPMENT

**British Educational Suppliers Association**, 20 Beaufort Court, Admirals
Way, London E14 9XL.
Tel: 0171–537–4997; fax: 0171–537–4846

## EXAMINATIONS

**Joint Council for GCSE**, 6th Floor, 23 Marsh Street, Bristol BS1 4BP.
Tel: 0117–921–4379; fax: 0117–922–6700

**Institute of Education**, 20 Bedford Way, London WC1H 0AL. Useful
for comment.
Tel: 0171–580–1122

### *General National Vocational Qualifications*

**National Council for Vocational Qualifications**, 222 Euston Road,
London NW1 2BZ.
Tel: 0171–728–1957

**BTEC** (Business and Technical Education Council), Central House, Upper Woburn Place, London WC1H 0HH.
Tel: 0171–413–8400; fax: 0171–413–8437

**City & Guilds**, 46 Britannia Street, London WC1X 9RG.
Tel: 0171–294–2468

**RSA Examinations Board**, Westwood Way, Coventry CV4 8HS.
Tel: 01203–470033; fax: 01203–468080

## FURTHER EDUCATION

Reference: *Directory of Technical and Further Education.*

**Association of Principals of Colleges**, 12 Fir Close, Poynton, Stockport SK12 1PD.
Tel: 01625–859413; fax: 01625–859413

**Association of Teachers and Lecturers**, 7 Northumberland Street, London WC2N 5DA.
Tel: 0171–782–0160

**Association of University and College Lecturers**, 104 Albert Road, Southsea PO5 2SN.
Tel: 01705–818625; fax: 01705–838187

**Further Education Funding Council**, Cheylesmore House, Quinton Road, Coventry CV1 2WT.
Tel: 01203–863000; fax: 863100

**NATFHE**, 27 Britannia Street, London WC1X 9JP. Lecturers' union.
Tel: 0171–837–3636

**Sixth Form Colleges Association**, 10 Lombard Street, London EC3V 9AT.
Tel: 0171–398–4148; fax: 0171–283–9655

## HIGHER EDUCATION

See also UNIVERSITIES below.

**Standing Conference of Principals**, PO Box 190, Cheltenham GL50 3SJ.
Tel: 01242–225925; fax: 01242–263554

**Higher Education Funding Council (England)**, Northavon House, Coldharbour Lane, Bristol BS16 1QD.
Tel: 0117–931–7437/7363; fax: 0117–931–7463

## INDEPENDENT SCHOOLS

Reference: *Independent Schools Yearbook.*

**Girls Schools Association**, 130 Regent Road, Leicester LE1 7PG.
Tel: 0116–254–1619; fax: 0116–255–3792

**Headmasters Conference**, 1 Russell House, Bepton Road, Midhurst
GU29 9NB.
Tel: 01730–815635

**Independent Schools Information Service**, 56 Buckingham Gate,
London SW1E 6AE.
Tel: 0171–630–8795

## INTERNATIONAL

**International and Comparative Education Department**, Institute of
Education, 20 Bedford Way, London WC1H 0AL.
Tel: 0171–580–1122

### *School linking*

**Commonwealth Linking Trust**, 7 Lion Yard, Tremadoc Road, London
SW4 7NQ.
Tel: 0171–498–1101; fax: 0171–720–5403

**Education Partners Overseas**, 10 Barley Mow Passage, London W4
4PH.
Tel: 0171–831–4013

**Mary Stead**, UK One World Linking Association, Town Hall, Rose Hill,
Chesterfield S40 1LP.
Tel: 01246–216320; fax: 01246–221085

## MUSIC

**Choir Schools Association**, York Minster School, Deangate, YO1 2JA.
Tel: 01904–625217

**Royal Academy of Music**, Marylebone Road, London NW1 5HT.
Tel: 0171–873–7373; fax: 0171–873–7374

**Royal College of Music**, Consort Road, London SW7 2BS.
Tel: 0171–589–3643; fax: 0171–589–7740

## PASTORAL CARE AND PSYCHOLOGY

**Association of Educational Psychologists**, 3 Sunderland Road, Durham
DH1 2LH.
Tel: 0191–384–9512

**National Association for Pastoral Care**, Institute of Education, Warwick
University, CV4 7AL.
Tel: 01203–523810; fax: 01203–524110

## RESEARCH

**British Educational Research Association**, 15 St John Street, Edinburgh
EH8 8JR.
Tel: 0131–557–2944; fax: 0131–556–9454

**Centre for Educational Research**, London School of Economics,
London WC2A 2AE.
Tel: 0171–955–7809

## SCIENCE

**Association for Science Education**, College Lane, Hatfield AL10 9AA.
Tel: 0707–267411; fax: 0707–266532

**British Association for Advancement of Science**, 23 Savile Row, London
W1X 1AB.
Tel: 0171–973–3500; fax: 0171–973–3051

## SECONDARY

**City Technology Colleges Trust**, 9 Whitehall, London SW1A 2DD.
Tel: 0171–839–9339; fax: 0171–839–5898

**Secondary Heads Association**, 130 Regent Road, Leicester LE1 7PG.
Tel: 0116–247–1797; fax: 0116–247–1152

## SPECIAL EDUCATION

**National Association for Special Educational Needs**, 4 Amber Business
Park, Amber Close, Amington B77 4RP.
Tel: 01827–311500

## STUDENTS

**Association of Graduate Recruiters**, Sheraton House, Castle Park, Cambridge CB3 0AX.
Tel: 01223–356720; fax: 01223–356720

**Campaign for Bedsit Rights**, 7 Whitechapel Road, London E1 1DU.
Tel: 0171–377–0027

**NUS**, 461 Holloway Road, London N7 6LJ.
Tel: 0171–272–8900; fax: 0171–263–5713

### *Overseas students*

**UK Council for Overseas Student Affairs**, 9 St Albans Place, London N1 0NX.
Tel: 0171–226–3762; fax: 0171–226–3373

## TEACHERS

**Association of Teachers and Lecturers** (formerly the Assistant Masters and Mistresses Association), 7 Northumberland Street, London WC2N 5DA.
Tel: 0171–782–0160

**Institute of Education**, 20 Bedford Way, London WC1H 0AL.
Concerned with teachers' training.
Tel: 0171–580–1122

**NASUWT**, Hillscourt Education Centre, Rednal, Birmingham B45 8RS.
Schoolmasters and women teachers union.
Tel: 0121–453–6150; fax: 0121–453–7224

**National Association of Headteachers**, 1 Heath Square, Haywards Heath.
Tel: 01444–458133

**National Union of Teachers**, Hamilton House, Mabledon Place, London WC1H 9BD.
Tel: 0171–388–6191; fax: 0171–387–8458

**Professional Association of Teachers**, 2 St James Court, Friar Gate, Derby DE1 1BT.
Tel: 01332–372337; fax: 01332–290310

**Teacher Training Agency**, Portland House, London SW1E 5TT.
Tel: 0171–925–3758/5/3; fax: 0171–925–5957; e-mail: tta@gtnet.gov.uk

*Exchanges*

**League for Exchange of Commonwealth Teachers**, 7 Lion Yard, Tremadoc Road, London SW4 7NQ.
Tel: 0171–498–1101; fax: 0171–720–5403

# UNIVERSITIES

Reference: *International Handbook of Universities.*

**Association of University Teachers**, 1 Pembridge Road, London W11 3JY.
Tel: 0171–221–4370; fax: 0171–727–6547

**Committee of Vice-Chancellors and Principals**, 29 Tavistock Square, London WC1H 9EZ.
Tel: 0171–387–9231; fax: 0171–383–8649; e-mail: info@cvcp.ac.uk

**Universities and Colleges Admissions Service**, Cheltenham.
Tel: 01242–222444

## SOME UNIVERSITY PRESS OFFICES

**Bradford**
Tel: 01274–383088; fax: 01274–385460

**Cambridge**
Tel: 01223–332300; fax: 01223–330262

**Cardiff**
Tel: 01222–874839

**Durham**
Tel: 0191–374–2922; fax: 0191–374–7393; e-mail: P.R.Slee@durham.ac.uk

**Essex**
Tel: 01206–872400

**Glasgow**
Tel: 0141–330–4240; e-mail: MikeBrown@mis.gla.ac.uk

**Greenwich**
Tel: 0181–316–8140; fax: 0181–316–8145

**Hull**
Tel: 01482–466326; fax: 01482–466442; e-mail:
J.H.Dumsday@admin.hull.uk.ac

**Keele**
Tel: 01782–583371/74; fax: 01782–584165; e-mail:
JANETrda01@keele.ac.uk

**Kent**
Tel: 01227–451805; fax: 01227–764464; e-mail: H.G.Harrison@ukc.ac.uk

**Lancaster**
Tel: 01524–594120

**Leeds**
Tel: 0113–233–6699; fax: 0113–233–6017

**Leicester**
Tel: 0116–252–2415/2436; fax: 0116–252–2028

**LSE**
Tel: 0171–955–7060/7417; fax: 0171–405–1350

**Manchester**
Tel:  0161–275–2112/4; fax: 0161–275–2209

**Newcastle**
Tel: 0191–222–6067; fax: 5447; e-mail: tony.rylance@ncl.ac.uk

**Oxford**
Tel: 01865–278182

**Reading**
Tel: 01734–318005

**Strathclyde**
Tel: 0141–552–4400, ext. 2182; fax: 0141–552–1576

**Swansea**
Tel: 01792–295344

**UCL**, London
Tel: 0171–391–1603

**Warwick**
Tel: 01203–523708; fax: 01203–524752; e-mail:
puapjd@admin.warwick.ac.uk

**York**
Tel: 01904–432029; fax: 01904–432092

## ETHNIC MINORITIES

You need to find out what organizations and which leaders are truly repre-
sentative of local minorities. Organizations may be short-lived and may
move from one base to another. The phone book could help. So could
religious spokesmen.

There may be a local race-relations forum. Councils commonly have minority liaison officers. Voluntary bodies may also act as intermediaries, using public funds to help minority members. It is sometimes questioned whether the minorities or those helping them get the greater benefit.

The Indian caste system has produced a wealth of organizations in Britain, from temples to cricket clubs, since a caste operates as an extended family.

## National sources

**Home Office Immigration and Community Relations Press Desk**, Queen Anne's Gate, London SW1H 9AT.
Tel: 0171–273–4620; fax: 0171–273–4660

**Anti-Racist Alliance**, PO Box 150, London WC1X 9AT.
Tel: 0171–278–6869

**Asian Times**, 139 Fonthill Road, London N4 3HT.
Tel: 0171–281–1191; fax: 0171–263–9654

**Asian Who's Who.**
Tel: 0181–550–3745

**Centre for Research in Ethnic Relations**, Warwick University, Coventry CV4 7AL.
Tel: 01203–523523, ext. 2963

**Commission for Racial Equality**, 10 Allington Street, London SW1E 5EH.
Tel: 0171–932–5279/5354/5380; fax: 0171–931–0429;
e-mail: info@cre.gov.uk

**Institute of Race Relations**, 2 Leeke Street, London WC1X 9HS.
Tel: 0171–837–0041; fax: 0171–278–0623

**Professor John Benyon**, Leicester University LE1 7RH.
Tel: 0116–252–2458

**Runnymede Trust**, 11 Princelet Street, London E1 6QH. A research body.
Tel: 0171–375–1496

**Sia: National Development Agency for Black Voluntary Sector**, 49 Bedford Row, WC1V 6DJ
Tel: 0171–430–0811; fax: 831–9767

**The Voice**, 370 Coldharbour Lane, London SW9 8PL.
Tel: 0171–737–7377

## AFRO-CARIBBEAN PEOPLE

**Dr David Dabydeen**, Centre for Cultural Studies, Warwick University, Coventry CV4 7AL.
Tel: 01203–524809

## ASIAN BUSINESS

**Suhail Aziz**, 126 St Julian's Farm Road, West Norwood, London SE27 0RR. Organizes symposia sponsored by DTI and other bodies.
Tel: 0181–766–6118

## BANGLADESHIS

**Suhail Aziz**, see above

## FILIPINOS

**Commission for Filipino Workers**, St Francis's Community Centre, Pottery Lane, London W11.
Tel: 0171–221–0356

## HEALTH AND CARE

**Dr Waqar Ahmed**, Social Policy Research Unit, York University YO1 5DD.
Tel: 01904–432029, university PR

## IMMIGRATION

**Association of Visitors to Immigration Detainees**, Co-ordinator, 53 Western Road, Winchester SO22 5AH.
Tel: 01962–863317

**Joint Council for Welfare of Immigrants**, 115 Old Street, London EC1V 9JR.
Tel: 0171–251–8708/6

## PAKISTANIS

**Riaz Dooley**, 221 Westbourne Park Road, London W11 1EA.
Tel: 0171–221–6095/1729; fax: 0171–229–3595; home tel: 0181–952–2724

## REFUGEES

**British Refugee Council**, Bondway House, Bondway, London SW8 8BB.
Tel: 0171–582–6922

## TURKISH SPEAKERS (INCLUDING KURDS)

**Turkish Education Group**, 2 Newington Green Road, London N1 4RX.
Tel: 0171–226–8647

# FASHION

**Fashion Monitor** (tel: 0171–405–4455) gives a monthly listing of contacts and future events.

**London College of Fashion**.
Tel: 0171–514–7400

**London Fashion Week**, PR Lynne Franks.
Tel: 0171–724–6777

**Hairdressing Council**, 12 David House, 45 High Street, South Norwood SE25 6HJ.
Tel: 0181–771–6205; fax: 0181–771–3392

**Institute of Trichologists**, 228 Stockwell Road, London SW9 9SU. Hair specialists.
Tel: 0171–733–2056; fax: 0171–733–2056

**Pretty Polly**, Unwin Road, Sutton in Ashfield NG17 4JJ.
Tel: 01623–552500; fax: 01623–556267

**Tattoo Club of Great Britain**, 389 Cowley Road, Oxford OX4 2BS.
Tel: 01865–716877; fax: 01865–775610

# FINANCE

## *Local sources*

Banks, building societies, accountants, insurance brokers, stockbrokers, pawnbrokers, moneylenders, hire-purchase companies, big shops.

## *National sources*

**British Venture Capital Association**, 12 Essex Street, London WC2R 3AA.
Tel: 0171–240–3846

**Finance and Leasing Association**, 18 Upper Grosvenor Street, London W1X 9PB.
Tel: 0171–491–2783; fax: 0171–629–0396

**Securities and Investment Board**, 2 Bunhill Row, London EC1Y 8RA.
Sets rules for regulatory bodies in financial fields.
Tel: 0171–638–1240; fax: 0171–382–5905

## ACCOUNTANTS

**Accounting Standards Board and Financial Reporting Council**, 100 Grays Inn Road, London WC1X 8AL.
Tel: 0171–404–8818

**Coopers and Lybrand**, 1 Embankment Place, London WC2N 6NN.
Tel: 0171–583–5000; fax: 0171–213–4409

**Ernst and Young**, 1 Lambeth Palace Road, London SE1 7UE.
Tel: 0171–928–2000; fax: 0171–931–3481

**Institute of Chartered Accountants in England and Wales**, Moorgate Place, London EC2P 2BJ.
Tel: 0171–920–8100

**Institute of Chartered Accountants in Ireland**, 87 Pembroke Road, Ballsbridge, Dublin 4.
Tel: 00–353–1–680400

**Institute of Chartered Accountants of Scotland**, 27 Queen Street, Edinburgh EH2 1LA.
Tel: 0131–225–5673

**Chartered Institute of Management Accountants**, 63 Portland Place, London W1N 4AB.
Tel: 0171–637–2311

**International Accounting Standards Committee**, 167 Fleet Street, London EC4A 2ES.
Tel: 0171–353–0565

**KPMG**, 1 Puddle Dock, London EC4V 3PD.
Tel: 0171–236–8000; fax: 0171–248–6552

## ADVICE

**Independent Financial Advisers Promotion.**
Tel: 0117–971–1177

**Institute of Financial Planning**, Whitefriars Centre, Lewins Mead, Bristol BS1 2NT.
Tel: 0117–930–4434; fax: 0117–929–2214

## CREDIT

**Access Credit Cards**, Pilgrim House, High Street, Billericay CM12 9XY.
Tel: 01277–634295; fax: 01277–634303

**Barclaycard.**
Tel: 0171–699–2673, press

**CCN** (credit management and data gathering group), Talbot House, Talbot Street, Nottingham.
Tel: 0115–941–0888

**Consumer Credit Association UK**, Queens House, Queens Road, Chester CH1 3BQ.
Tel: 01244–312044

**Consumer Credit Trade Association**, 159 Great Portland Street, London W1N 5FD.
Tel: 0171–636–7564; fax: 0171–323–0096

**Credit Card Research Group,** 2 Ridgmount Street, London WC1E 7AA.
Tel: 0171–436–9937

**Equifax Europe**, 16 Harcourt Street, London W1H 2AE. Credit reference company.
Tel: 0171–724–6116; fax: 706–8740

**Institute of Credit Management**, The Water Mill, Station Road, South

Luffenham LR15 8NB.
Tel: 01780–721888; fax: 01780–721333

**Retail Credit Group** (credit-issuers), Kings Court, Goodge Street,
London W1P 1FF.
Tel: 0171–580–8715

## EUROMARKETS

These are not necessarily anything to do with Europe. They are a means
of raising money abroad, at interest rates related to LIBOR, the London
Interbank Offered Rate.

**Stock Exchange**, London EC2N 1HP.
Tel: 0171–588–2355

## FUTURES AND OPTIONS

**Futures and Options Association**, 1 Crutched Friars, London EC3N
2HT.
Tel: 0171–488–4610

**London Commodity Exchange**, 1 Commodity Quay, St Katharine's
Dock, London E1 9AX.
Tel: 0171–481–2080

**London International Financial Futures Exchange** (LIFFE), Royal
Exchange, Cornhill, London EC3V 3PJ.
Tel: 0171–623–0444

## INVESTMENT

**Association of Investment Trust Companies**, 16 Finsbury Circus,
London EC2M 7JJ.
Tel: 0171–588–5347

**Association of Private Client Investment Managers**, 112 Middlesex
Street, London E1 7HY.
Tel: 0171–247–7080; fax: 0171–337–0939

**Association of Unit Trusts and Investment Funds**, 65 Kingsway, London
WC2B 6TD.
Tel: 0171–831–0898; fax: 0171–831–9975

**Barclays de Zoete Wedd**, Ebbgate House, 2 Swan Lane, London EC4R 3TS.
Tel: 0171–956–4013; fax: 0171–956–4488

**Investment Ombudsman**, 4th Floor, 6 Fredericks Place, London.
Tel: 0171–796–3065

**Investors Compensation Scheme**, 2 Bunhill Row, London EC1Y 8RA.
Tel: 0171–628–8820; fax: 0171–382–5901

**Personal Investment Authority**, Canada Square, London E14 5AZ.
Supervises pensions, unit trusts, portfolio investment.
Tel: 0171–538–8860

**Securities and Futures Authority**, Cottons Centre, Cottons Lane, London SE1 2QB. Investment watchdog.
Tel: 0171–378–9000

**Stock Exchange**, London EC2N 1HP.
Tel: 0171–588–2355

## SWAPS

**International Swap and Derivatives Association**, 33 King William Street, London EC4R 9DU.
Tel: 0171–283–0918

## FIRE

**Chief and Assistant Chief Fire Officers Association**, 10 Pebble Close, Amington, Tamworth B77 4RD.
Tel: 01827–61516; fax: 01827–61530

**Fire Brigades Union**, 68 Coombe Road, Kingston on Thames KT2 7AE.
Tel: 0181–541–1765; fax: 0181–546–5187

**Fire Research Station**, Borehamwood WD6 2BL.
Tel: 01923–664082

**Fire Service College**, Moreton in Marsh GL56 0RH.
Tel: 01608–650831; fax: 01608–651788

## FOOD AND DRINK

Supermarket managers, any local food manufacturers and local association of food shops are obvious sources of information. Restaurateurs may help with recipes. There may be local groups interested in promoting organically-grown food, or tea and coffee imported at 'fair-trade' prices.

Hospital and academic nutritionists will talk about the nutritional value of food. Environmental health inspectors supervise the safety of shops and restaurants. The district director of public health (a health service post) will be concerned with cases of food poisoning.

On the drink side, there will be local licensed victuallers associations. There may be a branch of Alcoholics Anonymous.

Journalists' group: *The Guild of Food Writers* (48 Crabtree Lane, London SW6 6LW, tel: 0171–610–1180).

## Information sources

*Food Pocket Book (NTC Publications,* Henley RG9 1EJ).
*The Food System,* Geoff Tansey and Tony Worsley (Earthscan, 120 Pentonville Road, London N1 9JN: £15.95). An account of how the world food industry works.
*World Drink Trends* (NTC Publications, Henley RG9 1EJ).

**British Dietetic Association**, 7th Floor, 22 Suffolk Street, Birmingham B1 1LB.
Tel: 0121–643–5483; fax: 0121–643–4399

**British Refrigeration Association**, 6 Furlong Road, Bourne End SL8 5DG.
Tel: 01628–531186; fax: 01628–810423

**British Sandwich Association**, 29 Market Place, Wantage OX12 8BG.
Tel: 01235–772207; fax: 01235–769044

**British Nutrition Foundation**, 52 High Holborn, London WC1V 6RQ.
Tel: 0171–404–6504; fax: 0171–404–6747

**Campden and Chorleywood Food Research Association**, Chipping Campden GL55 6LD.
Tel: 01386–840319; fax: 01386–841306

**Food and Drink Federation**, 6 Catherine Street, London WC2B 5JL.
Tel: 0171–836–2460

**Food Commission** and **National Food Alliance**, both at 5 Worship Street, London EC2A 2BH.
Tel: 0171–628–7774; fax: 0171–628–0817, Food Commission
Tel: 0171–628–2442, National Food Alliance

**Food Policy Research Unit**, Bradford University BD7 1DP.
Tel: 01274–385517

**Food Research Association at Leatherhead**, Randalls Road, KT22 7RY.
Tel: 01372–376761; fax: 01372–386228.

**Food Science and Technology Department**, Reading University. (The largest in the UK.)
Tel: 01734–318700

**Institute of Food Research** (Norwich and Reading), Media Inquiries, Catherine Reynolds, Institute of Food Research, Norwich Research Park, NR4 7UA.
Tel: 01603–255000; fax: 01603–507723

**Intervention Board**, King's Road, Reading RG1 3BU. Buys surplus food on Brussels's behalf.
Tel: 0118–939–1745/6; fax: 0118–939–3817

**Nestle UK**, St Georges House, Croydon CR9 1NR.
Tel: 0181–686–3333; fax: 0181–667–5033

**Northern Foods**, St Stephens Square, Hull HU1 3XG.
Tel: 01482–325432; fax: 01482–226136

## ADDITIVES

**Food Additives Industry Association**, Kings Buildings, Smith Square, London SW1P 3JJ.
Tel: 0171–834–3399; fax: 0171–834–8587

## ALCOHOL

**Alcohol Concern**, 32 Loman Street, London SE1 0EE.
Tel: 0171–928–7377; fax: 0171–928–4644

**Hope UK**, 25(f) Copperfield Street, London SE1 0EN.
Tel: 0171–928–0848; fax: 0171–401–3477

## BAKING

**Flour Advisory Bureau**, 21 Arlington Street, London SW1A 1RN.
Tel: 0171–493–2521; fax: 0171–493–6785

**National Association of Master Bakers**, 21 Baldock Street, Ware SG12 9DH.
Tel: 01920–468061; fax: 01920–461632

# BEER

**Bass plc**, 20 North Audley Street, London W1Y 1WE.
Tel: 0171–409–1919

**Bass Brewers**, 137 High Street, Burton on Trent.
Tel: 01283–511000

**British Institute of Innkeeping**, 80 Park Street, Camberley GU15 3PT.
Tel: 01276–684449; fax: 01276–23045

**Campaign for Real Ale**, 230 Hatfield Road, St Albans AL1 4LW.
Tel: 01727–867201; fax: 01727–867670

**Carlsberg-Tetley Brewing**, 2410 The Crescent, Birmingham Business Park B37 7YE.
Tel: 0121–606–0606; fax: 0121–606–4020

**Scottish & Newcastle**, 111 Holyrood Road, Edinburgh EH8.
Tel: 0131–556–2591; fax: 0131–558–1165

**Guinness**, 39 Portman Square, London W1H 0EE.
Tel: 0171–486–0288; fax: 0171–486–4968

**Whitbread**, Chiswell Street, London EC1Y 4SD.
Tel: 0171–606–4455

# CONFECTIONERY

**Biscuit, Cocoa, Chocolate and Confectionery Alliance**, London.
Tel: 0171–404–9111

**Cadbury**, PO Box 12, Bournville Lane, Bournville, Birmingham B30 2LU.
Tel: 0121–451–4455; fax: 0121–451–4192

**Mars**, Dundee Road, Slough SL1 4JX.
Tel: 01753–550055; fax: 01753–550111

# DAIRY PRODUCTS

**Baby Milk Action**, 23 St Andrews Street, Cambridge CB2 3AX.
Tel: 01223–464420; fax: 01223–464417

**Butter Council**, Tubs Hill House, London Road, Sevenoaks TN13 1BL.
Tel: 01732–460060

**Dairy Industry Federation**, 19 Cornwall Terrace, London NW1 4QP.
Tel: 0171–486–7244

**Milk Marque**, Worcester.
Tel: 01905–858500

**Unigate**, Wood Lane, London W12 7RP.
Tel: 0181–749–8888

## EGGS

**British Egg Information Service**, 126 Cromwell Road, London SW7 4ET.
Tel: 0171–370–7411; fax: 0171–373–3926

## FRUIT AND VEGETABLES

**Eurofruit Magazine**, Market Towers, New Covent Garden, London SW8 5NQ.
Tel: 0171–498–6711; fax: 0171–498–6472

**Fresh Fruit and Vegetable Information Bureau**, 126 Cromwell Road, London SW7 4ET.
Tel: 0171–373–7734; fax: 0171–373–3926

**Fresh Produce Consortium**, 103 Market Towers, Nine Elms Lane, London SW8 5NQ.
Tel: 0171–627–3391

**Geest**, White House Chambers, Spalding PE11 2AL.
Tel: 01775–761111

### *Bananas*

**Fyfe Group**, 12 York Gate, Regents Park, London NW1 4QJ.
Tel: 0171–487–4472

## ICE CREAM

**Ice Cream Alliance**, 5 Pelham Court, Pelham Road, Nottingham NG5 1AP.
Tel: 0115–985–8505; fax: 0115–985–7985

# MEAT AND POULTRY

**British Turkey Information Bureau**, 125 Old Brompton Road, London SW7 3RP.
Tel: 0171–244–7701; fax: 0171–244–8385

**National Federation of Meat and Food Traders**, 1 Belgrove, Tunbridge Wells TN1 1YW. Poultry merchants federation has the same address.
Tel: 01892–541412; fax: 01892–535462

**The Vegetarian Society**, Parkdale, Dunham Road, Altrincham WA14 4QG.
Tel: 0161–928–0793

# MUSHROOMS

**British Mushroom Group**, London.
Tel: 0171–379–8000

# NUTRITION

**Centre for Human Nutrition**, Northern General Hospital, Sheffield S5 7AU.
Tel: 0114–261–1531

**Dunn Nutritional Laboratory**, Downhams Lane, Milton Road, Cambridge CB4 1XJ.
Tel: 01223–426356

**Human Nutrition Unit**, London School of Hygiene, 2 Tavlton Street, London WC1.
Tel: 0171–380–0599

**Nutrition Department**, King's College, Campden Hill Road, London W8 7AH.
Tel: 0171–333–4268

# SAFETY

**Ministry of Agriculture Food Safety Press Desk**, 2 Whitehall Place, London SW1A 2HH.
Tel: 0171–270–8446/38; fax: 0171–270–8443/0

**Food Commission**, 5 Worship Street, London EC2A 2BH.
Tel: 0171–628–7774; fax: 0171–628–0817

**Institute for Environment and Health**, Leicester.
Tel: 0116–252–5530

**Institute of Food Research**.
Tel: 01603–255000, press

## *Listeria*

**Dr Dorothy Jones**, Microbiology, Leicester University.
Tel: 0116–252–2947

## *Overseas*

**Natural Resources Institute**, Central Avenue, Chatham Maritime ME4 4TB.
Tel: 01634–883129

# SOFT DRINKS

**British Soft Drinks Association**, 20 Stukeley Street, London WC2B 5LR.
Tel: 0171–430–0356; fax: 0171–831–6014

# SPIRITS

**Gin and Vodka Association of Great Britain**, Strangford Amport, Andover SP11 8AX.
Tel: 01264–773089

## *Pernod*

**Campbell Distillers**, 924 Great West Road, Brentford TW8 9DY.
Tel: 0181–568–4400; fax: 0181–568–2404

## *Rum*

**Main Rum Company**, 39 Roderick Road, London NW3 2NP.
Tel: 0171–284–1883 and

**43 Canning Street**, Liverpool L8 7NN.
Tel: 0151–709–8865

## *Whisky/gin*

**United Distillers**, Cherrybank, Perth PH2 0NG
Tel: 01738–621111; fax: 01738–452415

# SUGAR

**International Sugar Organization**, 1 Canada Square, Canary Wharf,
London E14 1XX.
Tel: 0171–513–1144

## *Beet*

**British Sugar**, PO Box 26, Peterborough PE2 9QU.
Tel: 01733–63171

## *Cane*

**E. D. and F. Man**, Sugar Quay, Lower Thames Street, London EC3R
6DU.
Tel: 0171–285–3000

**Tate & Lyle**, Sugar Quay, Lower Thames Street, London EC3R 6DQ.
Tel: 0171–626–6525

**World Sugar Research Organization**, Lyle Building, PO Box 68,
Reading RG6 2BX.
Tel: 01734–312059

# TEA

**Tea Brokers Association**, Sir John Lyon House, 5 High Timber Street,
Upper Thames Street, London EC4V 3LA.
Tel: 0171–236–3368

**Tea Council**, Sir John Lyon House, 5 Timber Street, Upper Thames
Street, London EC4V 3LA.
Tel: 0171–248–1024

## WINE

**English Vineyards Association**, 38 West Park, London SE9 4RH.
Tel: 0181–857–0452; fax: 0181–851–4864

**Institute of Masters of Wine**, 1 Queen Street Place, London EC4V 3AJ.
Tel: 0171–236–4427; fax: 0171–329–0298

## WORLD FOOD

**Food Security Unit**, Institute of Development Studies, Sussex
University, Brighton BN1 9RE.
Tel: 01273–606261

**Food Studies Group**, Queen Elizabeth House, 21 St Giles, Oxford OX1
3LA.
Tel: 01865–273600

**International Grains Council**, 1 Canada Square, Canary Wharf, London
E14 3PQ.
Tel: 0171–513–1122

**UN Food and Agriculture Organization**, Via delle Terme di Caracalla,
00100 Rome.
Tel: 00–39–6–522–53259; fax: 00–39–6–522–53699

**Wye College**, Professor Ian Carruthers, Ashford TN25 5AH.
Tel: 01233–812401

### *Food aid*

**Dr Ed Clay, Overseas Development Institute**, Portland House, Stag
Place, London SW1E 5DP.
Tel: 0171–393–1600; fax: 0171–393–1699

**Institute of Development Studies**, Sussex University, Falmer, Brighton
BN1 9RE.
Tel: 01273–606261

**World Food Programme**, Via Cristoforo Colombo 426, 00145 Rome, Italy.
Tel: 00–39–6–52251; fax: 00–39–6–57975652

## HEALTH

Try your local hospitals for medical experts. **The British Medical
Association Press Office** (tel: 0171–387–4499) is often able to suggest

names of doctors knowledgeable about medical subjects. You may have a BMA branch locally.

For the NHS, see Health Services, pages 79–86.

Journalists group: the **Medical Journalists Association** (tel: 01908–564623)

**Department of Health: Children, Drugs and Mentally Ill**, 79 Whitehall, London SW1A 2NS.
Tel: 0171–210–5231/5228/5375; fax: 0171–210–5433/4

**Biostatistics Unit** (MRC), Cambridge.
Tel: 0171–637–6011, MRC PR; fax: 0171–436–2665

**British Holistic Medical Association**, Rowland Thomas House, Royal Shrewsbury Hospital South SY3 8XF.
Tel: 01743–261155

**College of Health**, 21 Old Ford Road, London E2 9PL. Publishes *Guide to Hospital Waiting Lists*.
Tel: 0181–983–1225; fax: 0171–983–1553

**Health Education Authority**, Hamilton House, Mabledon Place, London WC1H 9TX.
Tel: 0171–383–3833; fax: 0171–387–0550

**Royal Society of Medicine**, 1 Wimpole Street, London W1M 8RE.
Tel: 0171–290–2900; fax: 0171–290–2909

**Wellcome Centre for Medical Science**, 183 Euston Road, London NW1.
Tel: 0171–611–8888; fax: 0171–611–8545

**World Health Organization**, 20 Ave Appia, 1211 Geneva 27, Switzerland.
Tel: 00–41–22–791–2111; fax: 00–41–22–791–0746


## ACUPUNCTURE

**British Acupuncture Association**, 34 Alderney Street, London SW1V 4EU.
Tel: 0171–834–1012

**British Medical Acupuncture Society**, Newton House, Newton Lane, Whitley, Warrington WA4 4JA.
Tel: 01925–730727; fax: 01925–730492


## AIDS

*National Aids Directory* (NAM Publications, 52 The Eurolink Centre, 49 Effra Rd, SW2 1BZ). Found in some libraries.

**AIDS Collaborating Centre**, UK National Institute for Biological Standards and Control, Blanche Lane, South Mimms EN6 3QG.
Tel: 01707–654753

**AIDS Care Education and Training** (ACET), PO Box 3693, London SW15 2BQ.
Tel: 0181–780–0400; fax: 0181–780–0450

**CRUSAID**, Livingstone House, 11 Carteret Street, London SW1H 9DJ.
Tel: 0171–976–8100

**St Mary's Hospital**, Paddington.
Tel: 0171–725–6666

**Terrence Higgins Trust**, 52 Gray's Inn Road, London WC1X 8JU.
Tel: 0171–831–0330; fax: 0171–242–0121

**Professor Robin Weiss,** Institute of Cancer Research, Fulham Road, London SW3 6JB.
Tel: 0171–352–8133; fax: 0171–352–3299

**MRC HIV Clinical Trials Centre**, UCL Medical School, Mortimer Market, London WC1E 6AU.
Tel: 0171–637–6011, MRC PR; fax: 0171–436–2665

**Positively Women**, 347 City Road, London EC1V 1LR.
Tel: 0171–713–0444

**Dr Peter Simmonds,** Medical Microbiology Medical School, Edinburgh EH8 9AG.
Tel: 0131–650–3161; fax: 0131–650–6531

**Professor Roy Anderson,** Zoology Department, Oxford University OX1 3PS.
Tel: 01865–271190; fax: 01865–310447

## *Drugs*

**Merck, Sharp and Dohme**, Hertford Road, Hoddesdon EN11 8BU.
Tel: 01992–467272

**Roche**, Broadwater, Welwyn.
Tel: 01707–366000

## *Immunity*

**Molecular Immunology Group**, John Radcliffe Hospital, Oxford OX3 9DU.
Tel: 01865–222336; fax: 01865–222502

# ALZHEIMER'S DISEASE

**The Alzheimer's Disease Society**, 10 Greatcoat Place, London SW1P 1PH.
Tel: 0171–306–0606

**Professor James Edwardson**, MRC Neurochemical Pathology Unit, Newcastle upon Tyne.
Tel: 0191–273–5251, ext. 126

**Institute of Human Ageing**, Liverpool University.
Tel: 0151–794–5074

# ANKYLOSING SPONDYLITIS

**National Ankylosing Spondylitis Society**, 5 Grosvenor Crescent, London SW1X 7ER.
Tel: 0171–235–9585; fax: 0171–235–5827

# ANOREXIA AND BULIMIA

**Eating Disorders Association**, Sackville Place, 44 Magdalen Street, Norwich NR3 1JU.
Tel: 01603–624310; fax: 01603–664915

# ARTHRITIS

**ARC Epidemiology Unit**, Stopford Building, Manchester University M13 9PT.
Tel: 0161–275–5046

**Arthritis and Rheumatism Council for Research**, Copeman House, St Mary's Court, St Mary's Gate, Chesterfield S41 7TD.
Tel: 01246–558033; fax: 01246–558007

**British Society for Rheumatology** and **British League against Rheumatism**, 41 Eagle Street, London WC1R 4AR.
Tel: 0171–242–3313; fax: 0171–242–3277

**Horder Centre for Arthritis**, St Johns Road, Crowborough TN6 1XP.
Tel: 01892–665577; fax: 01892–662142

**Professor Ian Haslock**, Centre for Biomedical Engineering, South Road, Durham DH1 3LE.
Tel: 0191–374–3932

## ARTIFICIAL LIMBS

**Queen Mary's Hospital**, Roehampton SW15 5PN.
Tel: 0181–789–6611

## ASTHMA

*Asthma and Outdoor Air Pollution* (HMSO publication)

**National Asthma Campaign**, Providence House, Providence Place, London N1 0NT. Can put inquirers in touch with medical experts.
Tel: 0171–226–2260; fax: 0171–704–0740

**Immunopharmacology**, School of Medicine, Southampton General Hospital SO16 6YD.
Tel: 01703–796960; fax: 01703–701771

## AUTISM

**National Autistic Society**, 276 Willesden Lane, London NW2 5RB.
Tel: 0181–451–1114; fax: 0181–451–5865

## BACK PAIN AND REPETITIVE STRAIN INJURY

**British Chiropractic Association**, Reading.
Tel: 01734–757557

**British Institute of Musculoskeletal Medicine**, 27 Green Lane, Northwood HA6 2PX.
Tel: 01923–820110; fax: 01923–820110

**British Orthopaedic Association**, 35 Lincolns Inn Fields, London WC2A 3PN.
Tel: 0171–405–6507

**British Osteopathic Association**, 8 Boston Place, London NW1 6QH.
Tel: 0171–262–5250

## BLOOD, BLOOD DISORDERS

**National Blood Authority**, Oak House, Reeds Crescent, Watford WD1 1QH.
Tel: 01923–212121

**Haematology Department**, Professor David Lynch, UCL, London
WC1E 6BT.
Tel: 0171–209–6221

## BLOOD PRESSURE

**MRC Blood Pressure Unit**, Western Infirmary, Glasgow.
Tel: 0171–637–6011, MRC PR

**Professor John Swales** and **Professor Herbert Thurston**, Medicine,
Leicester University LE1 7RH.
Tel: 0116–252–3182, Professor Swales; 0116–252–3188, Professor
Thurston

## BOWEL PROBLEMS

**British Colostomy Association**, 15 Station Road, Reading RG1 1LG.
Tel: 01734–391537; fax: 01734–569095

**Irritable Bowel Syndrome Network**, Centre for Human Nutrition,
Northern General Hospital, Sheffield S5 7AU.
Tel: 0114–261–1531 or
St Johns House, Hither Green Hospital, London SE13 6RU.
Tel: 0181–698–4611, ext. 8194

**National Association for Colitis and Crohn's Disease**, 98a London
Road, St Albans AL1 1NX.
Tel: 01727–844296

**St Mark's Hospital**, Watford Road, Harrow HA1 3UJ. (Specialist hospital formerly in City Road, London.)
Tel: 0181–235–4000

## BRAIN, STROKES

**Academic Unit of Neuroscience**, Charing Cross and Westminster
Medical School, London.
Tel: 0181–846–7598

**MRC Centre for Brain Repair**, Cambridge. Contact through MRC PR.
Tel: 0171–637–6011

**Headway National Head Injuries Association**, 7 King Edward Court,
King Edward Street, Nottingham NG1 1EW.
Tel: 0115–924–0800; fax: 0115–924–0432

**Stroke Association**, CHSA House, Whitecross Street, London EC1Y 8JJ.
Tel: 0171–490–7999; fax: 0171–490–2686

## CANCER

**BACUP** (British Association of Cancer United Patients), 3 Bath Place,
Rivington Street, London EC2A 3JR.
Tel: 0171–696–9003

**British Society for Clinical Cytology**, Central Research Laboratories,
Dawley Road, Hayes UB3 1HH.
Tel: 0181–606–2511; fax: 0181–606–2563

**Cancer Relief Macmillan Fund** (Macmillan Nurses), 15 Britten Street,
London SW3 3TZ.
Tel: 0171–351–7811; fax: 0171–376–8098

**Cancer Research Campaign**, 10 Cambridge Terrace, London NW1 4JL.
Tel: 0171–224–1333; fax: 0171–935–1546

**Imperial Cancer Research Fund**, 61 Lincoln's Inn Fields, London
WC2A 3PX.
Tel: 0171–242–0200; fax: 0171–269–3417

**ICRF Cancer Epidemiology Unit**, Oxford. Contact via ICRF press
office.
Tel: 0171–242–0200

**Institute of Cancer Research**, 17a Onslow Gardens, London SW7 3AL.
Tel: 0171–352–8133 and
15 Cotswold Road, Belmont SM2 5NG.
Tel: 0181–643–8901

**Wellcome-CRC Institute of Cancer**, Tennis Court Road, Cambridge
CB2 1QR.
Tel: 01223–334131

### Bowel cancer

**St Marks Hospital**, Watford Road, Harrow HA1 3UJ.
Tel: 0181–235–4000

### Breast cancer

**Breast Cancer Care**, 210 New Kings Road, London SW6 4NZ.
Tel: 0171–384–2984; fax: 0171–384–3387

## *Cervical cancer*

**Women's National Cancer Control Campaign**, 128 Curtain Road, London EC2A 3AR.
Tel: 0171–729–1735; fax: 0171–613–0771

## *Childhood*

**Childhood Cancer Research Group**, Paediatrics Department, 57 Woodstock Road, Oxford OX2 6HJ.
Tel: 01865–310030

## *Environment and cancer*

**Jack Birch Unit for Environmental Carcinogenesis**, Biology, York University YO1 5DD.
Tel: 01904–432029, PR

## *Skin*

**Photobiology Department**, St Thomas's Hospital, Lambeth Palace Road, London SE1 7EH.
Tel: 0171–928–9292; fax: 0171–922–8079

# CHILDBIRTH

**National Childbirth Trust**, Alexandra House, Oldham Terrace, London W3 6NH.
Tel: 0181–992–8637; fax: 0181–992–5929

**Royal College of Obstetricians and Gynaecologists**, 27 Sussex Place, London NW1 4RG.
Tel: 0171–262–5425; fax: 0171–723–0575
(Its research arm **WellBeing** is on 0171–723–9296)

# CHILD HEALTH

**Action for Sick Children**, 29 Euston Road, London NW1 2SD.
Tel: 0171–833–2041; fax: 0171–837–2110

**Child Health**, Postgraduate Medical Education, Warwick University, Coventry CV4 7AL.
Tel: 01203–523913; fax: 01203–524311

**Foundation for the Study of Infant Deaths**, 35 Belgrave Square, London SW1X 8QB.
Tel: 0171–235–0965; fax: 0171–823–1986

**Institute of Child Health**, 30 Guilford Street, London WC1.
Tel: 0171–242–9789; fax: 0171–831–0488

**Dr Sarah Stewart-Brown**, Health Service Research, Radcliffe Infirmary, Oxford OX2 6HE.
Tel: 01865–228414

## CREUTZFELDT-JAKOB DISEASE

**Lindsey French, Laurence Knight**, Department of Health.
Tel: 0171–210–5233/5223

## CYSTIC FIBROSIS

**CF Research Trust**, 5 Blyth Road, Bromley BR1 3RS.
Tel: 0181–464–7211

## DISEASE STATISTICS

**Communicable Disease Surveillance Centre**, 61 Colindale Avenue, London NW9 5HT.
Tel: 0181–200–1295; fax: 0181–200–7868

## DIABETES

**British Diabetic Association**, 10 Queen Anne Street, London W1M 0BD.
Tel: 0171–323–1531; fax: 0171–637–3644

**Diabetes Foundation**, 177a Tennyson Road, London SE25 5NF.
Tel: 0181–656–5467

## DRUG ABUSE

See also ALCOHOL, page 50.

**Home Office Press Desk for Drug Issues**, Queen Anne's Gate, London SW1H 9AT.
Tel: 0171–273–4640; fax: 0171–273–4660;
e-mail: commdir.ho@gtnet.gov.uk

**Association for Prevention of Addiction**, 67 Cowcross Street, London EC1M 6BT.
Tel: 0171–251–5860

**Drug Control Centre**, Kings College, Chelsea. Contact via college PR.
Tel: 0171–836–5454, ext. 3202

**Hope UK**, 25(f) Copperfield Street, London SE1 0EN.
Tel: 0171–928–0848; fax: 0171–401–3477

**ISDD** (Institute for Study of Drug Dependence), 32 Loman Street,
London SE1 0EE.
Tel: 0171–928–1211; fax: 0171–928–1771

**Standing Conference on Drug Abuse** (SCODA), 32 Loman Street,
London SE1 0EE.
Tel: 0171–928–9500; fax: 0171–928–3343

**US Drug Enforcement Agency.**
Tel: 00–1–202–307–7977

## Narcotic crops

**Colin Sage**, Wye College, Ashford TN25 5AH.
Tel: 01233–812401

**Catholic Institute for International Relations.**
Tel: 0171–354–0883

# DRUGS

**Association of the British Pharmaceutical Industry**, 12 Whitehall,
London SW1A 2DY. Produces a contacts directory.
Tel: 0171–930–3477

**Drug and Therapeutics Bulletin**, Consumers Association, 2 Marylebone
Road, London NW1 4DF. Edited by a leading commmentator, Dr Joe
Collier.
Tel: 0171 830–6000

**Glaxo Wellcome.**
Tel: 0171–493–4060

**Committee on the Safety of Medicines**, 1 Nine Elms Lane, London SW8
5NQ.
Tel: 0171–273–0451/2; fax: 0171–273–0453

**Zeneca Pharmaceuticals.**
Tel: 01625–582828

**Medicines Control Agency**, queries to the Department of Health.
Tel: 0171–210–5891

**Merck, Sharp and Dohme**, Hoddesdon EN11 8BU.
Tel: 01992–467272

**Proprietary Association of Great Britain**, Vernon House, Sicilian Avenue, London WC1A 2QH.
Tel: 0171–242–8331; fax: 0171–405–7719

**Roche**, Broadwater, Welwyn.
Tel: 01707–366000

**Smith Kline Beecham**, Brentford,
Tel: 0181–975–2000

**Strathclyde Institute for Drug Research**, G1 1XQ.
Tel: 0141–552–4400

**US Food and Drug Administration.**
Tel: 001–301–443–3170

## EAR, NOSE AND THROAT

**British Association of Otolaryngologists**, 35 Lincolns Inn Fields, London WC2A 3PN.
Tel: 0171–404–8373; fax: 0171–404–4200

**British Society of Hearing Therapists**, Hearing Centre, Yardley Green Hospital B9 5PX.
Tel: 0121–766–6611, ext. 2556

**Royal National Throat, Nose and Ear Hospital**, and Nuffield Hearing and Speech Centre, Grays Inn Road, London WC1.
Tel: 0171–837–8855

## ELDERLY

**Research into Ageing**, 15 St Cross Street, London EC1N 8UN.
Tel: 0171–404–6878; fax: 0171–404–6816

## ENVIRONMENT AND HEALTH

**Institute for Environment and Health**, PO Box 138, Lancaster Road, Leicester LE1 9HN.
Tel: 0116–252–5530

## EPIDEMIOLOGY

**Centre for Epidemiology of Infectious Disease**, Zoology Department, Oxford University OX1 3PS.
Tel: 01865–271190

# EPILEPSY

**British Epilepsy Association**, 40 Hanover Square, Leeds LS3 1BE.
Tel: 0113–243–9393; fax: 0113–242–8804

**National Society for Epilepsy**, Chalfont St Peter SL9 0RJ.
Tel: 01494–873991; fax: 01494–871927

# EQUIPMENT

**Bath Institute of Medical Engineering**, Wolfson Centre, Combe Park,
Bath BA1 3NG.
Tel: 01225–824103; fax: 01225–824111

# EYES

**Association of Optometrists**, 233 Blackfriars Road, London SE1 8NW.
Tel: 0171–261–9661; fax: 0171–261–0228

**British Council for Prevention of Blindness**, 12 Harcourt Street, London
W1H 1DS.
Tel: 0171–724–3716

**Eyecare Information Service**, PO Box 3597, London SE1 6DY.
Tel: 0171–357–7730; fax: 0171–357–7155

**Federation of Ophthalmic and Dispensing Opticians**, 113 Eastbourne
Mews, London W2 6LQ.
Tel: 0171–258–0240; fax: 0171–724–1175

**General Optical Council**, 41 Harley Street, London W1N 2DJ.
Tel: 0171–580–3898; fax: 0171–436–3525

**Institute of Ophthalmology**, Bath Street, London EC1V 9EL.
Tel: 0171–608–6800

**Institute of Vision Sciences**, Aston University, Birmingham B4.
Tel: 0121–359–3611

**Royal College of Ophthalmologists**, 17 Cornwall Terrace, London NW1
4QW.
Tel: 0171–935–0702; fax: 0171–935–9838

## *Contact lenses*

**European Centre for Contact Lens Research**, Manchester University
M13 9PL.
Tel: 0161–275–2112/4, PR office

**Award**, 3a Fleming Road, Kirkton Campus, Livingston (makes one-day lenses).
Tel: 01506–461622; fax: 01506–461623

## FEET

**Society of Chiropodists**, 53 Welbeck Street, London W1M 7HE.
Tel: 0171–486–3381; fax: 0171–935–6359

## FERTILITY, FAMILY PLANNING

**Abortion Law Reform Association**, 27 Mortimer Street, London W1N 7RJ.
Tel: 0171–637–7264

**Population Studies Centre**, London School of Hygiene, 99 Gower Street, London WC1E 6AZ.
Tel: 0171–388–3071

**Family Planning Association**, 27 Mortimer Street, London W1N 7RJ.
Tel: 0171–636–7866; fax: 0171–436–5723

**Human Fertilization and Embryology Authority**, 30 Artillery Lane, London E1 7LS.
Tel: 0171–377–5077

**International Planned Parenthood Federation**, Regent's College, London NW1 4NS.
Tel: 0171–486–0741; fax: 0171–487–7950; e-mail:
j.gizbert@ippf.attmail,com

**Issue** (National Fertility Association), 509 Aldridge Road, Great Barr, Birmingham B44 8NA.
Tel: 0121–344–4415; fax: 0121–344–4336

**MRC Reproductive Biology Unit**, 37 Chalmers Street, Edinburgh EH3 9EW. Contact via MRC PR.
Tel: 0171–637–6011; fax: 0171–436–2665

**Society for Protection of Unborn Children**, 7 Tufton Street, London SW1P 3QN.
Tel: 0171–222–5845; fax: 0171–222–0630

### *Chemicals' effect on male fertility*

**Institute for Environment and Health**, PO Box 138, Lancaster Road, Leicester LE1 9HN.

Tel: 0116–252–5530

## FIRST AID, RESUSCITATION

**British Red Cross**, 9 Grosvenor Crescent, London SW1X 7EJ.
Tel: 0171–235–5454; fax: 0171–245–6315

**Resuscitation Council** (doctors group), 9 Fitzroy Square, London W1P 5AH.
Tel: 0171–388–4678; fax: 0171–383–0773

**St John Ambulance**, 1 Grosvenor Crescent, London SW1X 7EF.
Tel: 0171–235–5231; fax: 0171–235–0796

## GENETICS

**Genetics Laboratory**, Dr Ian Craig, South Parks Road, Oxford OX1 3QU.
Tel: 01865–275327

**Institute of Molecular Medicine**, Professor Sir David Weatherall, John Radcliffe Hospital, Oxford OX3 9DU.
Tel: 01865–222359

**Nuffield Council on Bioethics**, Nuffield Foundation, 28 Bedford Square, London WC1B 3EG.
Tel: 0171–631–0566

## HAEMOPHILIA

**Haemophilia Society**, 123 Westminster Bridge Road, London SE1 7RW.
Tel: 0171–928–2020; fax: 0171–620–1416

**National Haemophilia Study**, ICRF Cancer Unit, Radcliffe Infirmary, Oxford OX2 6HE.
Tel: 0171–242–0200, ask for ICRF PR

## HEART PROBLEMS

**British Heart Foundation**, 14 Fitzhardinge Street, London W1H 4DH.
Tel: 0171–935–0185; fax: 0171–224–1868

**Coronary Artery Disease Research Association.**
Tel: 0171–349–8686

**Papworth Hospital.**
Tel: 01480–830541; fax: 01480–831147

**Dr Malcolm Mitchinson**, Pathology Department, Cambridge University.
Tel: 01223–333719/333690

*Heart problems and lifestyle*

**Dr T. M. Pollard**, Anthropology Department, 43 Old Elvet, Durham
DH1 3HN.
Tel: 0191–374–2841; fax: 0191–374–2870

## HOMEOPATHY

**British Homoeopathic Association**, 27A Devonshire Street, London
W1N 1RJ.
Tel: 0171–486–2957

**Homoeopathic Society**, 2 Powis Place, Great Ormond Street, London
WC1N 3HT.
Tel: 0171–837–9469

## HYPNOSIS

**Association of Qualified Curative Hypnotherapists**, 10 Balaclava Road,
Kings Heath, Birmingham B14 7SG.
Tel: 0121–441–1775

**British Hypnotherapy Association**, 1 Wythburn Place, London W1M
5WL.
Tel: 0171–723–4443

## IMMUNOLOGY

**British Society for Immunology**, Triangle House, Broomhill Road,
London SW18 4HX.
Tel: 0181–877–9920

**MRC Cellular Immunology Unit**, Oxford. Contact via MRC PR.
Tel: 0171–637–6011; fax: 0171–436–2665

## IMPLANTS

**IRC in Biomedical Materials**, Queen Mary and Westfield, Mile End Road, London E1 4NS. (Working on a new material for artificial hips.)
Tel: 0171–975–5285

**Professor Colin Humphreys**, Materials Science, Cambridge University.
Tel: 01223–334457/334300.

## INSECT-RELATED DISEASES

*Asthma, head lice, scabies etc.*

**Medical Entomology Centre**, Pembroke Street, Cambridge CB2 3DX.
Tel: 01223–312052

## INTERNATIONAL HEALTH

**Centre for International Health**, Queen Margaret College, Clerwood Terrace, Edinburgh EH12 8TS.
Tel: 0131–317–3491; fax: 0131–317–3465

## KIDNEY PROBLEMS

**National Kidney Federation**, 6 Stanley Street, Worksop S81 7HX.
Tel: 01909–487795; fax: 01909–481723

**Kidney Foundation**, Bridge Street, Rothwell, Northamptonshire.
Tel: 01536–712266

**Professor John Walls**, Medicine, Leicester University LE1 7RH.
Tel: 0116–252–5121

## LASERS

**National Medical Laser Centre**, UCL Medical School, London WC1E 6JJ
Tel: 0171–209–6136; fax: 0171–383–3780

## LEGIONNAIRES' DISEASE

**Professor Raj Bhopal**, Epidemiology, Newcastle University NE1 7RU.
Tel: 0191–222–7372

**Stuart Emslie**, Architecture, Strathclyde University, Glasgow G1 1XQ.
Tel: 0141–552–4400, ext. 3008

## LEUKAEMIA

**Institute of Child Health**, 30 Guilford Street, London WC1N 1EE.
Tel: 0171–242–9789; fax: 0171–831–0488

**Professor Steve Proctor**, Medicine, Newcastle University NE1 7RU.
Tel: 0191–222–7791

## LIVER

**Institute of Liver Studies**, King's College, London WC2R 2LS.
Tel: 0171–836–5454

## LUNGS

See also ASTHMA, page 60.

**British Lung Foundation**, 6th Floor, 78 Hatton Garden, London EC1N
8JR.
Tel: 0171–831–5831

## LUPUS

**Lupus UK**, 51 North Street, Romford RM1 1BA.
Tel: 01708–731251; fax: 01708–731252

## MENINGITIS

**National Meningitis Trust**, Fern House, Bath Road, Stroud GL5 3TJ.
Tel: 01453–751738; fax: 01453–753588

## MIGRAINE

**British Migraine Association**, 178A High Road, Byfleet KT14 7ED.
Tel: 01932–352468

**Migraine Trust**, 45 Great Ormond Street, London WC1N 3HD.
Tel: 0171–278–2676

*In children*

**Medical Paediatrics Department**, Royal Aberdeen Children's Hospital.
Tel: 01224–681818

## MOTOR NEURONE DISEASE

**Dr Alan McCruden** and **Professor Bill Stimson**, Immunology
Department, Strathclyde, Glasgow G1 1XQ.
Tel: 0141–552–4400; Dr McCruden, ext. 3749; Professor Stimson, ext.
3729

## MULTIPLE SCLEROSIS

**Dr Rachel Henderson**, Bioscience, Strathclyde University, Glasgow G1
1XQ.
Tel: 0141–552–4400, ext. 2468

## MUSCULAR DYSTROPHY

**Muscular Dystrophy Group**, 7 Prescott Place, London SW4 6BS
(research and welfare charity).
Tel: 0171–720–8055; fax: 0171–498–0670

## OBESITY

**Dr Celia McCrea**, Psychology Department, Leicester University LE1
7RH.
Tel: 0116–252–2161

**International Journal of Obesity**, Stockton Press, Houndmills,
Basingstoke RG21 2XS.
Tel: 01256–817245; fax: 01256–28339

## ORGAN TRANSPLANTS/DONORS

**Papworth Hospital.**
Tel: 01480–830541; fax: 831147

## OSTEOPOROSIS

**National Osteoporosis Society**, PO Box 10, Radstock BA3 3YB.
Tel: 01761–432472; fax: 01761–437903

**Professor John Currey**, Biology, York University, YO1 5DD.
Tel: 01904–432029, press office

## PARKINSON'S DISEASE

**Maudsley Hospital**, Denmark Hill, London SE5 8AZ.
Tel: 0171–919–2830; fax: 0171–703–7252

**Parkinson's Disease Society**, 22 Upper Woburn Place, London WC1H
0RA.
Tel: 0171–383–3513; fax: 0171–383–5754

## POISONS

**MRC Toxicology Unit**, Hodgkin Building, Leicester University, LE1
9HN.
Tel: 0171–637–6011, MRC PR; fax: 0171–436–2665

### *Poisons and snake bite*

**Professor Alan Harvey**, Strathclyde Institute for Drug Research,
Glasgow G1 1XQ.
Tel: 0141–552–4400, ext. 4155

## PSYCHIATRY AND PSYCHOLOGY

**British Association for Counselling**, 1 Regent Place, Rugby CV21 2PJ.
Tel: 01788–550899; fax: 01788–562189

**British Confederation of Psychotherapists**, 37 Mapesbury Road, London
NW2 4HJ.
Tel: 0181–830–5173

**British Psychological Society**, 48 Princess Road East, Leicester LE1
7DR.
Tel: 0116–254–9568; fax: 0116–247–0787

**Institute of Psychiatry**, De Crespigny Park, London SE5 8AF.
Tel: 0171–919–2830; fax: 0171–703–5796

**Manic Depression Fellowship**, 8 High Street, Kingston upon Thames
KT1 1EY.
Tel: 0181–974–6550; fax 0181–974–6600

**Maudsley Hospital**, Denmark Hill, London SE5 8AZ.
Tel: 0171–919–2830; fax: 0171–703–7252

**MENCAP** (Royal Society for Mentally Handicapped Children), 123
Golden Lane, London EC1 3PP.
Tel: 0171–454–0454

**MIND** (National Association for Mental Health), Granta House,
Broadway, London E15 4BQ.
Tel: 0181–519–2122

**MRC Applied Psychology Unit**, Cambridge.
Tel: 0171–637–6011, MRC PR; fax: 0171–436–2665

**Psychology Department, Goldsmiths' College**, Lewisham Way, London
SE14 6NW.
Tel: 0171–919–7870; fax: 0171–919–7873

**Psychology Department, Southampton University**, University Road,
Highfield SO17 1BJ.
Tel: 01703–592612; fax: 01703–594597

**Richmond Fellowship**, 8 Addison Road, London W14 8DL. Provides
hostels and care for former mental patients
Tel: 0171–603–6373; fax: 0171–602–8652

**Royal College of Psychiatrists**, 17 Belgrave Square, London SW1X 8PG.
Tel: 0171–235–2351

**School of Psychology**, University of Wales, PO Box 901, Cardiff CF1 3YG.
Tel: 01222–874000

**Society of Analytical Psychology**, 1 Daleham Gardens, London NW3
5BY. Based on Jung.
Tel: 0171–435–7696; fax 0171–431–1495

**Tavistock Institute**, 30 Tabernacle Street, London EC2A 4DE.
Concerned with psychology and human relations.
Tel: 0171–417–0407; fax: 0171–417–0566

**UK Council for Psychotherapy**, Regents College, Regents Park, London
NW1 4NS.
Tel: 0171–487–7554; fax: 0171–487–7554

## *Schizophrenia*

**Dr Tim Crow**, University Department of Psychiatry, Warneford Hospital, Oxford OX3 7JX.
Tel: 01865–226474/223909; fax: 01865–244990; e-mail:
timothy.crow@psychiatry.oxford.ac.uk

**Professor Glynn Harrison**, Psychiatry Department, McMillan House, Porchester Road, Nottingham. Has surveyed patients from Afro-Carribbean backgrounds.
Tel: 0115–952–9406; fax: 0115–985–6396

**Professor Shon Lewis**, Withington Hospital, Manchester M20 8LR.
Tel: 0161–447–4354; fax: 0161–447–4354; e-mail:
s_lewis@wph.fs1.man.ac.uk

**Professor Robin Murray**, Institute of Psychiatry, De Crespigny Park, London SE5 8AF.
Tel: 0171–703–6091; fax 0171–707–9044

**National Schizophrenia Fellowship**, 28 Castle Street, Kingston KT1 1SS.
Tel: 0181–547–3937; fax 0181–547–3862

**SANE**, 2nd Floor, 199 Old Marylebone Road, London NW1 5QP.
Campaigns on schizophrenia.
Tel: 0171–724–6520; fax: 0171–724–6502

## RADIOLOGY

**British Institute of Radiology**, 36 Portland Place, London W1N 4AT.
Tel: 0171–580–4085; fax: 0171–255–3209

**Royal College of Radiologists**, 38 Portland Place, London W1N 3DG.
Tel: 0171–636–4432

## RESEARCH

**Action Research**, Vincent House, North Parade, Horsham RH12 2DP.
Supports research in many fields.
Tel: 01403–210406; fax: 01403–210541

**Association of Medical Research Charities**, 29 Farringdon Road, London EC1M 3JB.
Tel: 0171–404–6454

**Medical Research Council**, 20 Park Crescent, London W1N 4AL.
Tel: 0171–637–6011; fax: 0171–436–2665, PR

**National Institute of Medical Research**, Ridgeway, London NW7 1AA.
Tel: 0181–959–3666; fax: 0181–906–4477

### Experiments on animals

**British Union for Abolition of Vivisection**, 16a Crane Grove, London
N7 8LB.
Tel: 0171–700–4888

**National Anti-Vivisection Society**, 261 Goldhawk Road, London W12
8EU.
Tel: 0181–846–9777

**Fund for Replacement of Animals in Medical Experiments**, 34 Stoney
Street, Nottingham NG1 1NB.
Tel: 0115–958–4740; fax: 0115–950–3570

## SKIN DISEASES

**British Association of Dermatologists**, 19 Fitzroy Square, London W1P
5HQ.
Tel: 0171–383–0266; fax: 0171–388–5263

**National Eczema Society**, 163 Eversholt Street, London NW1 1BU.
Tel: 0171–388–4097; fax: 0171–388–5882

## SLEEP

**Dr Chris Hanning**, Leicester University, LE1 7RH.
Tel: 0116–252–4141

## SMOKING

**Action on Smoking and Health**, 109 Gloucester Place, London W1H 4EJ.
Tel: 0171–935–3519; fax: 0171–935–3463

**British-American Tobacco**, Millbank, Knowle Green, Staines TW18
1DY.
Tel: 01784–460400

**FOREST**, 2 Grosvenor Gardens, London SW1W 0DH. Advocates smoking freedom.
Tel: 0171–823–6550; fax: 0171–823–4534

**Tobacco Manufacturers Association**, Glen House, Stag Place, London SW1E 5AG.
Tel: 0171–828–2041; fax: 0171–630–9638

## SPINA BIFIDA

**Association for Spina Bifida and Hydrocephalus**, 42 Park Road, Peterborough PE1 2UQ.
Tel: 01733–555988; fax: 01733–555985

## SURGERY

See under HEALTH SERVICES, page 84.

## TEETH

**Association of Dental Implantology**, 37 Halford Road, Richmond, TW10 6AW.
Tel: 0181–332–0321; fax: 0181–940–0337

**British Dental Association**, 64 Wimpole Street, London W1M 8AL.
Tel: 0171–935–0875; fax: 0171–487–3024

**British Dental Health Foundation**, Eastland Court, St Peters Road, Rugby CV21 3QP.
Tel: 01788–546365; fax 01788–546365

**British Orthodontic Society**, Eastman Hospital, Gray's Inn Road, London WC1X 8LD.
Tel: 0171–837–2193; fax: 0171–837–2193

**British Fluoridation Society**, Clinical Dental Sciences, Liverpool University, PO Box 147, L69 3BX. Promotes fluoridation of water to prevent tooth decay.
Tel: 0151–706–5216; fax: 0151–706–5845

**General Dental Practitioners Association**, Victoria House, Victoria Road, Barnsley S74 2BB.
Tel: 01226–299020

## TOURETTE SYNDROME

**Tourette Syndrome (UK) Association**, 27 Monkton Street, Ryde, Isle of Wight PO33 2BY.
Tel: 01983–568866; fax: 01983–565760

## TRAVELLERS' HEALTH

**Blood Care Foundation** – ships safe blood to travellers: can be contacted through MASTA, see below.

**Hospital for Tropical Diseases**, 4 St Pancras Way, London NW1 0PE.
Tel: 0171–387–4411

**MASTA** (Medical Advisory Services for Travellers Abroad), Keppel Street, London WC1E 6HJ.
Tel: 0171–631–4408

## TUBERCULOSIS

**MRC TB group**, London W12. Contact via MRC PR.
Tel: 0171–637–6011; fax: 0171–436–2665

## VIRUSES

**Virology Department**, Professor Richard Madeley, Newcastle University NE1 7RU.
Tel: 0191–222–6000, ext. 7628

## WOMEN'S HEALTH

**Association for Postnatal Illness**, 25 Jerdan Place, Fulham SW6 1BE.
Tel: 0171–386–0868

**WellBeing** (research arm of Royal College of Obstetricians).
Tel: 0171–723–9296

## HEALTH SERVICES

The National Health Service is run by the NHS Executive (press: 0113–254–6214/5606; fax: 0113–254–5800) whose regional offices co-exist with regional health authorities (see regional pages).

Family health services such as those offered by family doctors, chemists and dentists are overseen by local family health service authorities which consider any complaints.

The hospital service is divided between payers and providers. Local health authorities or commissions (boards in Scotland) plus some family doctors pay for patients from their districts or practices. Trusts provide hospital treatment and run ambulances. Local community health service councils represent patients' interests.

Public health is the responsibility of the district director of public health (a health service appointment) and the chief environmental health inspector (a local council appointment).

Reference: *The IHSM Health Services Year Book*. This lists family health service authorities, health authorities and commissions, fund-holding family doctors, hospital trusts, and (mainly national) health-related organizations.

*The Municipal Year Book* includes health authorities and hospital trusts.

**Department of Health**, 79 Whitehall, London SW1A 2NS.

**NHS Press Desks.**
Tel: 0171–210–5226/5229/5230/5222; fax: 0171–210–5433/4
**Public Health Press Desk**.
Tel: 0171–210–5233; fax: 0171–210–5433/4

**LSE Health**, London School of Economics, Houghton Street, London WC2A 2AE. **Professor Brian Abel-Smith** has been involved in studies of the NHS since the 1950s.
Tel: 0171–955–7540/6840; fax: 0171–955–6803

**Centre for Health Service Research**, Newcastle University, 21 Claremont Place, NE2 4AA.
Tel: 0191–222–7045; fax: 0191–222–6043

**Clinical Standards Advisory Group**. Ask NHS Press Desk above.

**Conservative Medical Society**, 32 Smith Square, London SW1P 3HH.
Tel: 0171–222–9000

**Health Service Ombudsman**, Church House, Great Smith Street, London SW1P 3BW.
Tel: 0171–276–2082; fax: 0171–276–2140

**Health Studies Institute**, Professor A.Alaszewski, University of Hull, HU6 7RX.
Tel: 01482–465895; fax: 01482–466306

**Institute for Health Policy Studies**, 129 University Road, Southampton SO17 1BL.
Tel: 01703–593394; fax: 01703–593177

**King's Fund**, 11 Cavendish Square, London W1M 0AN. Does health service research.
Tel: 0171–307–2400

**Socialist Health Association**, 16 Charles Square, London N1 6HP.
Tel: 0171–490–0057

## AMBULANCES

**Association of Professional Ambulance Personnel**, 6 Old Brewery, Shepton Mallet BA4 5QE.
Tel: 01749–344044; fax: 01749–342042

## CHEMISTS

**National Pharmaceutical Association**, 38 St Peter's Street, St Albans AL1 3NP. Independent retail chemists.
Tel: 01727–832161; fax: 01727–840858

**Pharmaceutical Services Negotiating Committee**, 47 Chase Side, London N14 5BP.
Tel: 0181–882–3888

**Royal Pharmaceutical Society**, 1 Lambeth High Street, London SE1 7JR.
Tel: 0171–735–9141; fax: 0171–735–7629

**School of Pharmacy**, Robert Gordon University, Schoolhill, Aberdeen AB9 1FR.
Tel: 01224–262500; fax: 01224–626559

## COMMUNITY HEALTH COUNCILS

**Association of Community Health Councils**, 30 Drayton Park, London N5 1PH.
Tel: 0171–609–8405; fax: 0171–700–1152

## DOCTORS

Reference: *Medical Directory*, a doctors' who's who.
Medical Register lists doctors authorized to practise.

**British Medical Association**, Tavistock Square, London WC1H 9JP. The doctors' trade union.
Tel: 0171–387–4499; fax: 0171–383–6403, press

**General Medical Council**, 44 Hallam Street, London W1N 6AE.
Registers doctors. Holds disciplinary hearings.
Tel: 0171–580–7642; fax: 0171–436–1383

**Medical Defence Union** (defends doctors and dentists in law suits), 3 Devonshire Place, London W1N 2EA
Tel: 0171–486–6181; fax: 0171–935–5503 and
192 Altrincham Road, Manchester M22 4NZ.
Tel: 0161–428–1234; fax: 0161–491–3301

**Royal College of General Practitioners**, 14 Princes Gate, London SW7 1PU.
Tel: 0171–581–3232; fax: 0171–225–3047


## HEALTH ECONOMICS

**Health Economics Research Unit**, Public Health Department, Aberdeen Medical School, AB9 2ZD.
Tel: 01224–681818, ext. 52764; fax: 01224–662994

**Office of Health Economics**, 12 Whitehall, London SW1A 2DY.
Tel: 0171–930–9203; fax: 0171–747–1419

**York Health Economics Consortium**, Heslington, York YO1 5DD.
Tel: 01904–433620; fax: 01904–433628


## HOSPITALS

**Hospital Doctors Association**, Old Court House, London Road, Ascot SL5 7EN.
Tel: 01344–26613

**Hospital Consultants and Specialists Association** (affiliated to the TUC), 1 Kingsclere Road, Overton, Basingstoke RG25 3JA.
Tel: 01256–771777; fax: 770999

**Intensive Care Society**, London.
Tel: 0171–383–2184

**Intensive Care World**, 85 Campden Street, London W8 7EN.
Tel: 0171–229–4552; fax: 0171–722–0744

## *Anaesthesia*

**Association of Anaesthetists**, 9 Bedford Square, London WC1B 3RA.
Tel: 0171–631–1650; fax: 0171–631–4352

**Royal College of Anaesthetists**, 48 Russell Square, London WC1B 4JY.
Tel: 0171–813–1900; fax: 0171–813–1876

## *Nurses*

**Institute of Nursing Studies**, Rob Newell, Hull University HU6 7RX.
Tel: 01482–465538

**Royal College of Nursing**, 20 Cavendish Square, London W1M 0AB.
Tel: 0171–409–2585; fax: 0171–408–0190

**Unison**, 1 Mabledon Place, London WC1H 9AJ.
Tel: 0171–388–2366, ext. 546; fax: 0171–387–6692

## *Occupational therapy*

**College of Occupational Therapists**, 6 Marshalsea Road, London SE1
1HL.
Tel: 0171–357–6480; fax: 0171–378–8095

## *Pathology*

**Institute of Biomedical Science**, 12 Coldbath Square, London EC1R
5HL.
Tel: 0171–636–8192; fax: 0171–436–4946

**Royal College of Pathologists**, 2 Carlton House Terrace, London SW1Y
5AF.
Tel: 0171–930–5861; fax: 0171–321–0523

## *Physiotherapy*

**Chartered Society of Physiotherapy**, 14 Bedford Row, London WC1R
4ED.
Tel: 0171–242–1941; fax: 0171–405–8252

## *Special hospitals*

Ashworth, Broadmoor, Rampton, see page 213.

## *Surgery*

**British Association of Day Surgery.**
Tel: 0171–405–3474; fax: 831–5741

**British Association of Aesthetic Plastic Surgeons.**
Tel: 0171–405–2234; fax: 430–1840

**British Association of Plastic Surgeons**
Tel: 0171–405–2234

All at 35 Lincolns Inn Fields, London WC2A 3PN.

**Royal College of Surgeons**, 35 Lincolns Inn Fields, London WC2A 3QQ.
Tel: 0171–405–3474

**Plastic and Reconstructive Surgery**, Professor Gus McGrouther,
University College London.
Tel: 0171–387–9300, ext. 5257

## MANAGEMENT

**Centre for Health Service Management**, Leicester Business School, LE1
9BH.
Tel: 0116–257–7222; fax: 0116–251–7548

**Health Service Management Centre**, 40 Edgbaston Park Road,
Birmingham B15 2RT.
Tel: 0121–414–7050; fax: 0121–414–7051

**Health Service Management Unit**, Devonshire House, Manchester M13
9PL.
Tel: 0161–275–2112/4, PR

**Institute of Health Service Management**, 39 Chalton Street, London
NW1 1JD. This has regional councils, listed in *IHSM Health Services
Year Book.*
Tel: 0171–388–2626; fax: 0171–388–2386

**National Association of Health Authorities and Trusts**, Birmingham
Research Park, Vincent Drive, Birmingham B15 2SQ. A rival of NHS
Trust Federation, see below.
Tel: 0121–471–4444; fax: 0121–414–1120

**NHS Trust Federation**, London.
Tel: 0171–633–0801

**Nuffield Provincial Hospitals Trust**, 59 New Cavendish Street, London

W1M 7RD. Aims to promote better NHS management.
Tel: 0171–485–6632; fax: 0171–485–8215

**Professor Calum Paton**, Health Planning and Management, Keele
University ST5 5BG.
Tel: 01782–583191

## NON-CONVENTIONAL TREATMENTS

**Institute for Complementary Medicine**, Unit 4, Tavern Quay, London
SE16 1AA.
Tel: 0171–237–5165

## PRIMARY HEALTH CARE

*Family doctors, nursing homes, care of elderly*

**Centre for Primary Health Care**, Dr Ruth Chambers, Keele University
ST5 5BG.
Tel: 01782–815555/716047

## PRIVATE HEALTH CARE

Reference: *Directory of Independent Hospitals and Health Services.*

**BUPA**, Provident House, Essex Street, London WC2R 3AX. Provides
insurance and operates hospitals.
Tel: 0171–353–5212; fax: 0171–353–0134

**Nuffield Hospitals**, 1 The Crescent, Surbiton KT6 4BN.
Tel: 0171–321–0362; fax: 0181–399–6726

## PUBLIC HEALTH

**Community Medicine Department**, University of Wales College of
Medicine, Heath Park, Cardiff CF4 4XW.
Tel: 01222–747747

**MRC Environmental Epidemiology Unit**, Southampton General
Hospital SO9 4XY.
Tel: 0171–637–6011, MRC PR

**Public Health Alliance**, 138 Digbeth, Birmingham B5 6DR.
Tel: 0121–643–4343, ext. 130; fax: 0121–643–4541

**Public Health Laboratory Service**, 61 Colindale Avenue, London NW9
5DF.
Tel: 0181–200–1295; fax: 0181–905–9729

**Public Health Engineering Unit**, Leeds University, LS2 9JT.
Tel: 0113–243–1751

**Public Health Medicine Department**, Leeds University, 20 Hyde
Terrace, LS2 9LN.
Tel: 0113–233–4860

# HOUSING

Surveyors, estate agents, builders and building society branches will tell
you about the local housing market. Housing associations have joined
councils in managing publicly-owned housing. Councils pay housing
benefit to those whose low incomes qualify them. This includes tenants in
privately owned homes.

Environmental health inspectors keep an eye on the condition of
houses, though slum clearance on any scale has long since ended. Councils
give improvement grants; and their social service departments help modify
the homes of older people.
Reference: *Housing Year Book* (includes aid and advice groups, housing
associations, building societies, builders).

## *National sources*

**Chartered Institute of Housing**, Coventry (keen on public-private
partnerships to build low-rent homes).
Tel: 01203–694433

**House Builders Federation**, 82 New Cavendish Street, London W1M
8AD.
Tel: 0171–580–5588; fax: 0171–323–1697

**Housing Corporation**, 149 Tottenham Court Road, London W1P 0BN.
Government agency which helps finance housing associations.
Tel: 0171–393–2093/5/6; fax: 0171–393–2099

**Incorporated Society of Valuers and Auctioneers**, 3 Cadogan Gate,
London SW1X 0AS.
Tel: 0171–235–2282

**Land Registry**, Lincoln's Inn Fields, London WC2A 3PH.
Tel: 0171–917–8894; fax: 0171–955–0110

**LSE Housing** (research group), LSE, London WC2A 2AE.
Tel: 0171–955–6872/7374

**National Association of Estate Agents**, 21 Jury Street, Warwick CV34 4EH.
Tel: 01926–496800; fax: 01926–403958

**National Federation of Housing Associations**, 175 Grays Inn Road,
London WC1X 8UX.
Tel: 0171–278–6571

**Royal Institution of Chartered Surveyors**, 12 Great George Street,
London SW1P 3AD.
Tel: 0171–222–7000; fax: 0171–222–9430

# CLEANING

**Soap and Detergent Industry Association**, PO Box 9, Hayes Gate
House, Hayes UB4 0JD.
Tel: 0181–573–7992; fax: 0181–561–5077

# HOME EQUIPMENT

**Mrs E. R. Davies**, Consumer Studies, Cardiff University.
Tel: 01222–874000, ext. 5794

**BFM** (British Furniture Manufacturers), 30 Harcourt Street, London
W1H 2AA.
Tel: 0171 724 0851; fax: 0171 706 1924

**British Aerosol Manufacturers Association**, Kings Buildings, Smith
Square, London SW1P 3JJ.
Tel: 0171–828–5111; fax: 0171–834–8436

**British Cutlery and Silverware Association**, 3 Melbourne Avenue,
Sheffield S10 2QJ.
Tel: 0114–266–3084; fax: 0114–267–0910

## *Microwave ovens*

**Engineering Science Department**, Oxford University, Parks Road,
Oxford OX1 3PJ.
Tel: 01865–273000

## HOMELESSNESS

**The Big Issue**, London.
Tel: 0171–418–0418

**Crisis**, 7 Whitechapel Road, London E1 1DU.
Tel: 0171–377–0489; fax: 0171–247–1525

**National Association for Voluntary Hostels**, Fulham Palace, Bishops Avenue, London SW6 6EA.
Tel: 0171–731–4205; fax: 0171–736–1292

**Shelter National Campaign for the Homeless**, 88 Old Street, London EC1V 9BB.
Tel: 0171–253–0202

### *Single homeless*

**Campaign for Single Homeless People**, 5 Cromer Street, London WC1H.
Tel: 0171–833–2071

**Stonham Housing Association**, 235 Union Street, London SE1 0LR.
Tel: 0171–401–2020

## SUBSIDENCE

**British Geological Survey**, Keyworth, Nottingham NG12 5GG.
Tel: 0115–936–3100; fax: 0115–936–3385, PR

## TENANTS AND LANDLORDS

**Association of Residential Letting Agents**, 18 Jermyn Street, London SW1Y 6HP.
Tel: 0171–734–0655; fax: 0171–352–2919

**Federation of Private Residents Associations**, 62 Bayswater Road, London W2 3PS.
Tel: 0171–402–1581

**Small Landlords Association**, 53 Werter Road, London SW15 2LL.
Tel: 0181–780–9954

# HUMAN RIGHTS

**Citizens' advice bureaux** are everywhere but tend to be overwhelmed with public inquiries. Many rights queries, about housing, for instance, can be taken up with the local council or with lawyers. There may be a local group of **Liberty** (see below) or a committee concerned with the police (who have a complaints system). Local ombudsmen (see under LOCAL GOVERNMENT, page 218) handle complaints of maladministration by councils.

## *National sources*

**Equal Opportunities Commission**, 36 Broadway, London SW1H 0XH.
Tel: 0171–222–1110/2818; fax: 0171–222–2771

**European Commission on Human Rights**, Council of Europe, 67006 Strasbourg Cedex, France.
Tel: 00–33–88–41–2000

**Human Rights Centre**, Essex University, Wivenhoe Hall, Colchester.
Tel: 01206–872568; fax: 01206–873428

**Liberty**, 21 Tabard Street, London SE1 4LA. Formerly the National Council for Civil Liberties.
Tel: 0171–403–3888

**National Association of Citizens' Advice Bureaux**, 115 Pentonville Road, London N1 9LP.
Tel: 0171–833–2181; fax: 0171–833–4371

## *Refugees*

**Asylum Aid**, 244a Upper Street, London N1 1RU.
Tel: 0171–359–4026

**British Refugee Council**, Bondway House, Bondway, London SW8 8BB.
Tel: 0171–582–6922

# INSURANCE

**Association of British Insurers**, 51 Gresham Street, London EC2V 7HQ.
Tel: 0171–600–3333

**British Insurance and Investment Brokers Association**, 14 Bevis Marks, London EC3A 7NT.
Tel: 0171–623–9043; fax: 0171–626–9676

**Chartered Insurance Institute**, 20 Aldermanbury, London EC2V 7HY. Professional body for insurance.
Tel: 0171–606–3835; fax: 0171–726–0131

**Chatset** (monitors Lloyd's), PO Box 661, London SW1W 8HY.
Tel: 0171–823–6980

**Commercial Union**, 1 Undershaft, London EC3P 3DQ.
Tel: 0171–283–7500

**Confederation of Insurance Trade Unions**, Whitehall College, Dane O'Coys Road, Bishops Stortford CM23 2JN.
Tel: 01279–755277

**Institute of Automotive Engineer Assessors**, 22 Bore Street, Lichfield WS13 6LP.
Tel: 01543–251346; fax: 01543–415804

**Institute of London Underwriters**, 49 Leadenhall Street, London EC3A 2BE. The insurance companies' underwriting organization.
Tel: 0171–240–2656; fax: 0171–836–7870

**Insurance Ombudsman Bureau**, 135 Park Street, London SE1 9EA.
Tel: 0171–928–7600

**Lloyd's**, 1 Lime Street, London EC3M 7HA.
Tel: 0171–623–7100

**Lloyd's Underwriters Association**, Lime Street, London EC3M 7HA.
Tel: 0171–626–9420

**London Insurance and Reinsurance Market Association**, Dexter House, Royal Mint Court, London EC3M 4QM.
Tel: 0171–480–5999

**Personal Investment Authority**, Canada Square, London E14 5AZ. Supervises life, endowment and pensions insurance, but not motor or house insurance.
Tel: 0171–538–8860

**Prudential**, 142 Holborn Bars, London EC1N 2NH.
Tel: 0171–548–3729; fax: 0171–548–3725

## REINSURANCE

**Alexander Howden Group** (brokers), 8 Devonshire Square, London EC2M 4YJ.
Tel: 0171–623–5500

**Global Reinsurance** (magazine), Hadleigh Business Centre, 351 London Road, SS7 2BT.
Tel: 01702–551556; fax: 01702–551511

**Lloyd's**, see above.

**Willis Corroon** (brokers), London EC3P 3AX.
Tel: 0171–488–8111

## MARRIAGE AND FAMILY

See also CHILDREN, page 26.

Reference: *The Government's Family Expenditure Survey.*
*British Household Panel Study*, tel: 01206–872938, press.

**Association of British Introduction Agencies**, 25 Abingdon Road, London W8 6AH.
Tel: 0171–937–2800

**Child Support Agency**, Quay House, Level Street, Brierley Hill, DY5 1XA.
Tel: 01384–574891/890/887; fax: 01384–574893

**Family Policy Studies Centre**, 231 Baker Street, London NW1 6XE.
Tel: 0171–486–8211; fax: 0171–224–3510

**Family Rights Group**, 18 Ashwin Street, London E8 3DL.
Tel: 0171–923–2628

**Family Welfare Associaton**, 501 Kingsland Road, London E8 4AA.
Helps families in difficulty.
Tel: 0171–254–6251

**National Council of One-parent Families**, 255 Kentish Town Road, London NW5 2LX.
Tel: 0171–267–1361

### *Divorce*

**Professor Rebecca Dobash**, Social and Administrative Studies, Cardiff University.
Tel: 01222–874086

### *Family poverty*

**Professor Hilary Graham**, Applied Social Studies, Warwick University CV4 7AL.
Tel: 01203–523173

## *Marriage guidance*

**Marriage Care**, 1 Blythe Mews, Blythe Road, London W14 0NW.
Formerly the Catholic Marriage Guidance Council.
Tel: 0171–371–1341; fax: 0171–371–4921

**Relate**, Herbert Gray College, Little Church Street, Rugby CV21 3AP.
Tel: 01788–573241; fax: 01788–535007

# MORTGAGES

**Building Societies Association/Council of Mortgage Lenders**, 3 Savile
Row, London W1X 1AF.
Tel: 0171–437–0655

**Building Societies Commission**, 30 Kingsway, London WC2B 6DS.
Tel: 0171–663–5360

**Building Societies Ombudsman**, 35 Grosvenor Gardens, London SW1.
Tel: 0171–931–0044

**Halifax Building Society**, Trinity Road, HX1 2RG.
Tel: 01422–333333

# RETIREMENT

Council social services departments have a responsibility for the welfare
of older people. There are many clubs and organizations for the retired
and the 50–plus. **Age Concern** (see below) and its local branches grew out
of the former Old People's Welfare Councils. Many voluntary groups and
care schemes offer help or outings for the elderly.

Most residential and nursing homes are now run privately or by voluntary organizations; but councils still run some, as well as inspecting the
rest. The government pays for residents but only if they cannot pay for
themselves.

## *National sources*

**Age Concern**, Astral House, 1268 London Road, London SW16 4ER.
Tel: 0181–679–8000

**Age Research Centre**, Manchester University M13 9PL.
Tel: 0161–275–2112/4, university PR

**Age Concern Institute of Gerontology**, King's College, London WC2R 2LS.
Tel: 0171–872–3033/3038

**Association of Retired People**, 3rd Floor, Greencoat House, Francis
Street, London SW1P 1DZ.
Tel: 0171–828–0500; fax: 0171–834–3829

**British Association for Services to the Elderly**, 119 Hassell Street,
Newcastle-under-Lyme ST5 1AX.
Tel: 01782–661033; fax 01782–712725

**Centre for Policy on Ageing**, 25 Ironmonger Row, London EC1V 3QP.
Tel: 0171–253–1787; fax: 0171–490–4206

**Help the Aged**, St James's Walk, London EC1R 0BE.
Tel: 0171–253–0253

**Professor Christopher Phillipson**, Applied Social Studies, Keele
University ST5 5BG.
Tel: 01782–584062

**Pre-Retirement Association**, Guildford.
Tel: 01483–301170

**Senior Studies Institute**, Lesley Hart, Strathclyde University, Glasgow
G1 1XQ.
Tel: 0141–552–4400, ext. 2492

**University of Third Age**, c/o Bassac, 13 Stockwell Road, London SW9 9AU.
Tel: 0171–737–2541

## HOMES

**Abbeyfield**, 53 Victoria Street, St Albans AL1 3UW.
Tel: 01727–857536; fax: 01727–846168

**British Federation of Care Home Proprietors**, 852 Melton Road,
Thurmaston LE4 8BN.
Tel: 0116–264–0095; fax: 0116–264–0141

**Methodist Homes for the Aged**, Epworth House, Stuart Street, Derby
DE1 2EQ.
Tel: 01332–296200; fax: 01332–296925

**National Care Homes Association**, 5 Bloomsbury Place, London WC1A.
Represents residential and nursing homes.
Tel: 0171–436–1871; fax: 0171–436–1193

## PENSIONS AND ANNUITIES

**Annuity Bureau**, 59 Upper Ground, London SE1 9PQ.
Tel: 0171–620–4090; fax: 0171–261–1888

**Annuity Direct**, 27 Paul Street, London EC2A 4JU.
Tel: 0171–588–9393

**Hermes** (formerly Postel), 21 Mansell Street, London E1 8AA.
Tel: 0171–702–0888; fax: 0171–702–9452

**National Association of Pension Funds**, 12 Grosvenor Gardens, London
SW1W 0EB.
Tel: 0171–730–0585

**National Pensioners Convention**, c/o TGWU, Smith Square, London
SW1P 3JB.
Tel: 0171–963–4520, TGWU press

**Occupational Pensions Board**, PO Box 2EE, Newcastle upon Tyne
NE99 2EE.
Tel: 0191–225–6414

**Pensions Ombudsman**, 11 Belgrave Road, London SW1V 1RB.
Tel: 0171–834–9144

**Society of Pension Consultants**, Ludgate House, Ludgate Circus,
London EC4A 2AB.
Tel: 0171–353–1688

## SEX

**Institute of Psychosexual Medicine**, 11 Chandos Street, Cavendish
Square, London W1N 9DE.
Tel: 0171–580–0631

### *Sexual disorders*

**Dr Desmond Dunleavy**, Psychology Department, Newcastle University
NE1 7RU.
Tel: 0191–222–7166

## HOMOSEXUALITY

**Albany Trust**, 26 Balham Hill, London SW12 9EB. Offers counselling.
Tel: 0181–675–6669

**Campaign for Homosexual Equality**, 38 Mount Pleasant, London WC1X
0AN.
Tel: 0171–833–3912

**Outrage**, London (group led by Peter Tatchell).
Tel: 0171–439–2381

**Stonewall**, 16 Clerkenwell Close, London EC1R 0AA.
Tel: 0171–336–8860; fax: 0171–336–8864

**Dr Didi Herman**, Law Department, Keele University ST5 5BG.
Tel: 01782–523225

## *Legal issues*

**Carl Stychin**, Law Department, Keele University ST5 5BG.
Tel: 01782–621111, ext. 7037

# SHOPS

Local shopkeepers often have a Chamber of Trade. Market stallholders
often have their own association. **USDAW** based in Manchester (tel:
0161–224–2804, fax 257–2566) is the shopworkers' union but tends to be
weak outside the co-operative movement. Many towns and cities have
shopping developments owned by large companies. Estate agents will
know about the local market for shops. Environmental health inspectors
oversee the healthiness of food shops.

**British Shops and Stores Association**, 2 Main Road, Middleton Cheney,
Banbury OX17 2TN.
Tel: 01295–712277; fax 01295–711665

**CWS**, PO Box 53, New Century House, Corporation Street, Manchester
M60 4ES.
Tel: 0161–827–5280; fax: 0161–832–2751

**Direct Marketing Association (UK)**, Haymarket House, 1 Oxendon
Street, London SW1Y 4EE.
Tel: 0171–321–2525; fax: 0171–321–0191

**Institute of Grocery Distribution**, Letchmore Heath, Watford WD2 8DQ.
Tel: 01923–857141; fax: 01923–852531

**Oxford Institute of Retail Management**, Dr Ross Davies, Templeton
College, OX1 5NY.
Tel: 01865–735422

**Retail Consortium**, 69 Fulham High Street, London SW6 3JW.
Grouping of large companies.
Tel: 0171–371–5177; fax: 0171–371–0529

**Retail Studies**, Manchester Business School.
Tel: 0161–275–6394/6333

# SOCIAL SERVICES AND SOCIETY

Council social-services departments (see *Social Services Yearbook*) are now responsible for the welfare of children, the disabled, the elderly and others in need. Social-security benefit, however, and other state payments for people in need, apart from housing benefit, are administered by local offices of the **Benefits Agency**. State pensions are administered by the **Department of Social Security** in Longbenton near Newcastle upon Tyne.
Reference: *Social Trends* (published annually by HMSO)
*British Social Attitudes*, see Social and Community Planning Research, page 97.
*Labour Force Survey* (quarterly survey of 60,000 households).
*Key Indicators of Local Authority Social Services.*

## *National sources*

**Centre for Analysis of Social Policy**, Social Science Department, Bath University BA2 7AY.
Tel: 01225–826826

**Centre on Microsocial Change**, Essex University, Colchester CO4 3SQ.
Carries out the annual British Household Panel Survey.
Tel: 01206–872938; fax: 01206–873151

**Economic and Social Research Council**, Polaris House, North Star Avenue, Swindon SN1 1UJ.
Tel: 01793–413117; fax: 01793–413130

**Joseph Rowntree Foundation**, The Homestead, 40 Water End, York YO3 6LP. Sponsors social research.
Tel: 01904–629241; fax: 01904–620072

**Policy Studies Institute**, 100 Park Village East, London NW1 3SR.
Leading research group on social issues and government.
Tel: 0171–387–2171; fax: 0171–388–0914

**Quality of Life Group**, Dr Robert Rogerson, Strathclyde University, Glasgow G1 1XQ.
Tel: 0141–552–4400, ext. 3037

**Social and Community Planning Research**, 35 Northampton Square, London EC1V 0AX. Publishes British Social Attitudes.
Tel: 0171–250–1866

**Social and Economic Research Department,** Glasgow University G12 8QQ.
Tel: 0141–339–8855; 0141–330–4240, press

**Social Policy Department**, Professor Michael Hill, Newcastle University.
Tel: 0191–222–7643

**Sociology Department**, Exeter University, Rennes Drive, EX4 4RJ.
Tel: 01392–263276

## ADVICE

**National Association of Citizens Advice Bureaux**, 115 Pentonville Road, London N1 9LP.
Tel: 0171–833–2181; fax: 0171–833–4371

## CARE

**Carers National Association**, 20 Glasshouse Yard, London EC1A 4JS.
Tel: 0171–490–8818; fax: 0171–490–8824

**Social Care Association**, 23a Victoria Road, Surbiton KT6 4JZ. For professional carers.
Tel: 0181–390–6831; fax: 0181–399–6183

## COMMUNITY DEVELOPMENT

**Association of Community Trusts and Foundations**, 52 High Holborn, London WC1V 6RL.
Tel: 0171–831–0033; fax: 0171–831–3881

**Community Development Foundation**, 60 Highbury Grove, London N5 2AG.
Tel: 0171–226–5375; fax: 0171–704–0313

**Community Matters** (National Federation of Community Organizations), 8 Upper Street, London N1 0PQ.
Tel: 0171–226–0189; fax: 0171–354–9570

**Lions Clubs International**.
Tel: 0121–441–4544

**National Council for Voluntary Organizations**, 8 All Saints Street,
London N1 9RL.
Tel: 0171–713–6161; fax: 0171–713–6300

**National Lottery Charities Board**, 7th Floor, 30 Orange Street, London
WC2H 7HH.
Tel: 0171–839–5371; fax: 0171–839–5369

**Rotary International**, Kinwarton Road, Alcester B49 6BP.
Tel: 01789–765411; fax: 01789–765570

**National Association of Round Tables**, Marches House, Embassy Drive,
Birmingham B15 1TP.
Tel: 0121–456–4402

**Women's Royal Voluntary Service**, 234 Stockwell Road, London SW9
9SP.
Tel: 0171–416–0146; fax: 0171–416–0148

# COMMUNITY DEVELOPMENT

See in SOCIETY, page 97.

# VOLUNTEERS

**Community Service Volunteers**, 237 Pentonville Road, London N1 9NJ.
Tel: 0171–278–6601

**National Association of Volunteer Bureaux**, 16 Waterloo Street,
Birmingham B2 5UG.
Tel: 0121–633–4555

**Volunteer Centre**, Carriage Row, 183 Eversholt Street, London NW1 1BU.
Tel: 0171–388–9888; fax: 0171–383–0448

## *School-leaver volunteers for overseas service*

**GAP Activity Projects**, 44 Queen's Road, Reading RG1 4BB.
Tel: 01734–594914

**Health Projects Abroad**, PO Box 24, Bakewell DE45 1ZW.
Tel: 01629–640051; fax: 01629–640054

**Project Trust**, Ballyhough, Isle of Coll PA78 6TE.
Tel: 01879–230444


# WOMEN

Towns have many groups for women: **Soroptimists**, **Business and Professional Women**, **Inner Wheel** (wives of Rotarians), **Ladies Circle** (wives of Round Table members), **Townswomen's Guild**.


## *National sources*

**British Federation of Women Graduates**, 4 Mandeville Court, 142 Battersea Park Road, SW11 4NB.
Tel: 0171–498–8037; fax: 0171–498–0173

**Business and Professional Women UK**, 23 Ansdell Street, London W8 5BN.
Tel: 0171–938–1729; fax: 0171–938–2037

**Equal Opportunities Commission**, 36 Broadway, London SW1H 0XH.
Tel: 0171–222–1110/2818; fax: 0171–222–2771

**National Women's Register**, Norwich.
Tel: 01603–406769; fax: 01603–765392

**Townswomen's Guilds**, 75 Harborne Road, Birmingham B15 3DA.
Tel: 0121–456–3435; fax: 0121–452–1890

**Women's National Commission**, Caxton House, Tothill Street, London SW1H 9NF.
Tel: 0171–261–8788

**Women's Nutritional Advice Service**, PO Box 268, Lewes BN7 2QN.
Tel: 01273–487366; fax: 01273–487576


# FEMINISM

Reference: *Encyclopaedia of Feminism*.

**Women: A Cultural Review** (journal), English Department, Birkbeck College, Malet Street, London WC1E 7HX.
Tel: 0171–631–6690

**Dr Didi Herman**, Law Department, Keele University ST5 5BG.
Tel: 01782–523225

**Sarah Franklin**, Sociology Department, Lancaster University LA1 4YW.
Tel: 01524–594187

## SEXUAL HARASSMENT

**Women's Studies Department**, Lancaster University.
Tel: 01524–65201; Dr Beverley Skeggs, ext. 2735; Dr Penny
Summerfield, ext. 2879

## VIOLENCE AGAINST WOMEN

**Refuge**, PO Box 855, London W4.
Tel: 0181–747–0133

**Professor Rebecca Dobash**, Social and Administrative Studies, Cardiff
University.
Tel: 01222–874086

## WORLDWIDE

**Centre for Cross-Cultural Research on Women**, Queen Elizabeth
House, 21 St Giles, Oxford OX1 3LA.
Tel: 01865–273600

**UN Development Fund for Women**, 3 Whitehall Court, London SW1A
2EL.
Tel: 0171–930–2931

**Womankind**, London W6 0LT.
Tel: 0181–563–8607/8; fax: 0181–563–8611

**Women's World Banking**, Nicola Armacost, 8 West 40th Street, New
York NY 10018.
Tel: 001–212–768–8513; fax: 001–212–768–8519

## YOUNG PEOPLE

### *Local sources*

County youth organizer, local youth organizer, local conference of youth
organizations, youth clubs, branches of national organizations listed
below.

## National sources

**Army Cadet Force and Combined Cadet Force**, E Block, Duke of York's HQ, London SW3 4RR.
Tel: 0171–730–9733

**Boys Brigade** (national office), Hemel Hempstead.
Tel: 01442–231681

**Catholic Youth Services.**
Tel: 0171–435–3596

**Commonwealth Youth Exchange Council**, 7 Lyon Yard, Tremadoc Road, London SW4 7NF. Supports group exchanges.
Tel: 0171–498–6151

**Demos Institute**, 9 Bridewell Place, London EC4V 6AP (has studied young people's lifestyles and views).
Tel: 0171–353–4479; fax: 0171–353–4481

**Duke of Edinburgh's Award**, Gulliver House, Madeira Walk, Windsor SL4 1EU.
Tel: 01753–810753; fax: 01753–810666

**Girl Guides Association**, 17 Buckingham Palace Road, London SW1W 0PT.
Tel: 0171–834–6242

**Girls Brigade**, Foxhall Road, Didcot OX11 7BQ.
Tel: 01235–510425; fax: 01235–510429

**Methodist Association of Youth Clubs**, 2 Chester House, Pages Lane, London N10 1PR.
Tel: 0181–444–9845; fax: 0171–365–2471

**NABC Clubs for Young People**, 369 Kennington Lane, London SE11 5QY.
Tel: 0171–793–0787; fax: 0171–820–9815

**Prince's Youth Business Trust**, 5 Cleveland Place, London SW1Y 6JJ.
Tel: 0171–925–2900

**Scouts Association**, BP House, Queens Gate, London SW7 5JS.
Tel: 0171–584–7030; fax: 0171–581–9953

**YMCA**, 640 Forest Road, Walthamstow, London E17 3EF.
Tel: 0181–520–5599

**Youth Hostels Association**, 8 St Stephens Hill, St Albans AL1 2DY.
Tel: 01727–855215

**Young Women's Christian Association**, 52 Cornmarket Street, Oxford OX1 3EJ.
Tel: 01865–726110; fax: 01865–204805

**Youth Clubs UK**, 11 St Bride Street, London EC4A 4AS.
Tel: 0171–353–2366; fax: 0171–353–2369

## FITNESS

**Professor Neil Armstrong**, Exeter University.
Tel: 01392–264812

## JOBS

**Dr Chris Murray**, Education Department, Manchester University M13 9PL.
Tel: 0161–275–2112/4, university PR

## SCHOOL-LEAVER VOLUNTEERS FOR OVERSEAS

See pages 100 and 101.

## TEENAGE PROBLEMS

**Psychiatric Social Work Department**, Manchester University M13 9PL.
Tel: 0161–275–2112/4, university PR

## YOUNG PEOPLE AND THE POLICE

**Professor Rebecca Dobash**, Social and Administrative Studies, Cardiff University.
Tel: 01222–874086

# 3 PEOPLE AT WORK

## COMPANIES

*Essential Finance for Journalists*, edited by Brian O'Kane and published by Oak Tree Press with Price Waterhouse in 1993, gives the basic facts about companies, their finance and the law concerning them.

It cautions journalists against jumping to conclusions from a quick reading of company accounts. There could be several reasons for a drop in sales, from new competition to a strike. The meaning of profit figures will vary according to whether buildings or other assets have been revalued: you need to read the notes to find out.

For similar reasons, the balance sheet showing assets and liabilities does not tell you what a company is worth. Accounts for groups tell you about the whole group, not about what money is where and whether it is available for spending.

O'Kane and his colleagues recommend journalists to read the whole of a company report and look out for inconsistencies and omissions. A glance at previous reports and statements may draw attention to these. Read the cash flow statement carefully: growing companies may not have the cash to meet their increased expenses and may have spent more than they can afford on new equipment. Ask also about the competition. If you are making a detailed investigation, go to see competitors, suppliers (do they get paid?) and customers.

Take opportunities to visit companies. You may not have the apparent ability of Sir John Harvey-Jones on TV to spot the crucial issues at a glance. But listen to what is said: even the best journalists need a hint from an insider if they are to produce an unusual story. Read documents handed to you: they may include important facts.

You can ask companies for their reports or look for them in larger libraries.

**Companies House** offers, at a small fee, a full public search service at its Cardiff and Edinburgh headquarters and in Birmingham, Glasgow, Leeds, London and Manchester. Normally you can obtain a company's last three years' returns and accounts, plus details of its directors. You can also inquire about people who are disqualified from being directors.

This is mundane stuff. But when investigative journalist Ray Fitzwalter followed up a hint that he should look into a firm called Open System Building, he found among its directors and former directors Reginald Maudling (then deputy leader of the Conservative Party), Dan Smith (PR man then prominent in the Labour Party on Tyneside), the clerk to the West Riding Council and a Coal Board divisional chairman; and the firm was based at the office of an architect, John Poulson. Fitzwalter thus identified five leading actors in the Poulson scandal (see page 369).

Apart from turning up at Companies House, you can make your inquiry by phone, fax, post or, via the **Mercury Data Network**, by computer. In Belfast, Northern Ireland information is given in paper form, usually within 48 hours.

**Companies House** addresses:

**Belfast:** 64 Chichester Street, BT1 4JX.
Tel: 01232–234488

**Birmingham Central Library**, Chamberlain Square, B3 3HQ.
Tel: 0121–233–9047; fax: 0121–233–9052

**Cardiff**: Crown Way, CF4 3UZ.
Tel: 01222–380801; fax: 380900

**Edinburgh**: 100 George Street, EH2 3DJ.
Tel: 0131–225–5774

**Glasgow**: 108 Bothwell Street, G2 7JP.
Tel: 0141–248–3315; fax: 0141–204–4534

**Leeds**: 25 Queen Street, LS1 2TW.
Tel: 01532–338338; fax: 01532–338335

**London**: 55 City Road, EC1Y 1BB.
Tel: 0171–253–9393; fax: 0171–608–0435

**Manchester**: 75 Mosley Street, M2 2HR
Tel: 0161–236–7500; fax: 0161–237–5258

If your office is well off, it may buy the *Hambro Company Guide* or the *Price Waterhouse Corporate Register*, giving details of stock market companies and their directors. The *Arthur Andersen Corporate Register* also lists directors, executives and shareholders of stock market companies.

The **British Library** operates a business information service from 25 Southampton Buildings, London WC2A 1AW (brief inquiry service tel: 0171–412–7454; charged on-line database search tel: 0171–412–7979).

Reference: *Stock Exchange Yearbook* (for listed companies).
*Kelly's Business Directory* (many small companies included).
*Macmillan's Unquoted Companies* – 20,000 not quoted on the Stock Exchange. What they do, who runs them.
*FT Smaller Companies Handbook.* Gives a page to each.
*Dun and Bradstreet's Key British Enterprises*
*Dun and Bradstreet's Who Owns Whom* (subsidiary companies)

**Department of Trade and Industry**, Companies Desk, 1 Victoria Street, London SW1H 0ET.
Tel: 0171–215–5974/2/1; fax: 0171–222–4382/233–7919

**Business History Unit**, London School of Economics, Houghton Street, London WC2A 2AE.
Tel: 0171–955–7109/7073

**Business in the Community**, 8 Stratton Street, London W1X 5FD.
Encourages firms to help their local community.
Tel: 0171–629–1600

**Business Link** – national network of business advice centres bringing together government, training councils and business.
Tel: 0171–215–0495, national press officer

**Industrial Common Ownership Movement**, 20 Central Road, Leeds LS1 6DE.
Tel: 0113–246–1738; fax: 0113 241 0002

**Institute of Directors**, 116 Pall Mall, London SW1Y 5EA.
Tel: 0171–839–1233

**ProShare**, 13 Basinghall Street, London EC2V 5BQ (promotes share ownership).
Tel: 0171–600–0984

**Stock Exchange**, Old Broad Street, London EC2N 1HP.
Tel: 0171–588–2355

**Unilever**, Blackfriars, London EC4.
Tel: 0171–822–5252

**Vickers**, Millbank, London SW1P 4RA.
Tel: 0171–828–7777; fax: 0171–828–6585

## BUSINESS STUDIES AND MANAGEMENT

**Business and Economic Studies**, Leeds University LS2 9JT.
Tel: 0113–233–4507

**Cardiff Business School.**
Tel: 01222–874000, ext. 6792

**Centre of Interdisciplinary Strategic Management Research**, Middlesex University Business School.
Tel: 0171–362–5920, PR

**Durham Business School**, Mill Hill Lane, DH1 3LB.
Tel: 0191–374–2211; fax: 0191–374–3748

**European Business School**, Regent's College, NW1 4NS.
Tel: 0171–486–0141

**Human Resources Magazine**, 103 Parkway, Regents Park, London NW1 7PP.
Tel: 0171–916–1880; fax: 0171–916–1881

**Institute of Management**, Corby NW17 1TT.
Tel: 01536–204222

**London Business School**, Sussex Place, Regent's Park, London NW1 4SA.
Tel: 0171–262–5050; fax: 0171–724–7875

**Management School**, Edinburgh University, EH8 9JY.
Tel: 0131–650–3814

**Manchester Business School.**
Tel: 0161–275–6333

**Warwick Business School**, Gibbet Hill Road, Coventry CV4 7AL.
Tel: 01203–524306; fax: 01203–523719

### Handwriting analysis

**International Graphoanalysis Society**, Stonedge, Dunkerton, Bath BA2 8AS.
Tel: 01761–437809; fax 01761–432572

## CORRUPTION

**Transparency International**, Heylstr. 33, D-10825 Berlin, Germany.
Tel: 00–49–30–787–5908; fax: 00–49–30–787–5707

**TI UK**, 1 George Street, Uxbridge UB8 1QQ.
Tel: 01895–274733; fax: 01895–256413

# FAMILY BUSINESS

**Centre for Family Enterprise,** Glasgow Caledonian University, Cowcaddens Road, G4.
Tel: 0141–331–3117; fax: 0141–331–3172

# MANAGEMENT BUY-OUTS AND BUY-INS

**3i** (Investors in Industry), 91 Waterloo Road, London SE1 8XP.
Tel: 0171–928–3131

**British Venture Capital Association**, 12 Essex Street, London EC2R 3AA.
Tel: 0171–240–3846; fax: 0171–240–3849

**Centre for Management Buy-Out Research**, Nottingham University.
Tel: 0115–951–5151; fax: 0115–951–3666

**CINVEN**, Hobart House, Grosvenor Place, London SW1X 7AD (venture capital company).
Tel: 0171–245–6911; fax: 0171–396–7173

**Management Buy-in Programme**, Touche Ross, Peterborough Court, Fleet Street, London EC4A 3JR. Experienced managers buy into firms seeking new management.

# MANAGEMENT CONSULTANTS

**Institute of Management Consultants**, 32 Hatton Gardens, London EC1N 8DL.
Tel: 0171–242–2140; fax: 0171–831–4597

**Management Consultancies Association**, 11 West Halkin Street, London SW1X 8JL.
Tel: 0171–235–3897; fax: 0171–235–0825

# MARKETING

See also MARKET RESEARCH, page 129.

**The Chartered Institute of Marketing**, Moor Hall, Cookham SL6 9QH.
Tel: 01628–524922; fax: 01628–531382

## MERGERS AND MONOPOLIES

**Monopolies and Mergers Commission**, 48 Carey Street, London WC2A 2JT.
Tel: 0171–324–1409/7, press; fax: 0171–324–1384; e-mail: mmc@gtnet.gov.uk

**Panel on Takeovers and Mergers**, Stock Exchange, Old Broad Street, London EC2N 1HP.
Tel: 0171–588–2355

**Ian Bradley**, Economics, Leicester University.
Tel: 0116–252–2901

## MULTINATIONALS

**Institute of Economics and Statistics**, St Cross Building, Manor Road, Oxford OX1 3UL.
Tel: 01865–271073; fax: 01865–271094

**Professor Neil Hood**, Strathclyde University, International Business Unit, Glasgow G1 1XQ.
Tel: 0141–552–4400, ext. 3245

**Professor John Stopford**, London Business School, Sussex Place, Regent's Park, London NW1 4SA.
Tel: 0171–262–5050; fax: 0171–724–7875

**Dr Robert Read**, Economics Department, Lancaster University.
Tel: 01524–594233

## SECURITY

**British Security Industry Association**, Barbourne Road, Worcester WR1 1RS.
Tel: 01905–21464; fax: 01905–613625

## SERVICE INDUSTRY

See also SHOPS, pages 95 and 96.

**Professor David Kirby**, Centre for Service Sector, Durham Business School, DH1 3LB.
Tel: 0191–374–2211; fax: 0191–374–3748

## SMALL BUSINESSES

**Centre for Small and Medium-sized Enterprises**, Warwick University, Coventry CV4 7AL.
Tel: 01203–524998

**Enterprise Development Centre**, Cranfield School of Management, Bedford MK43 0AL. Specially interested in small business overseas.
Tel: 01234–751122

**Federation of Small Business**, 140 Lower Marsh, London SE1 7AE.
Tel: 0171–401–2544, press

**Small Business Centre**, Durham University Business School, Mill Hill Lane, DH1 3LB.
Tel: 0191–374–2211; fax: 0191–374–3748

## WHISTLEBLOWERS

**Public Concern at Work**, 42 Kingsway, London WC2B 6EX. Advises people who think their company is acting wrongly.
Tel: 0171–404–6609; fax: 0171–404–6576

# COMPUTERS AND INFORMATION

**British Computer Society**, 1 Sanford Street, Swindon SN1 1HJ.
Tel: 01793–417417; fax: 01793–480270

**CCTA** (Government centre for information systems), St Andrews Business Park, Norwich NR7 0HS.
Tel: 01603–704831/614; fax: 01603–704817; e-mail: press@ccta.gov.uk

**Computing and Management School**, Sheffield Hallam University, 100 Napier Street, S11 8HD.
Tel: 0114–253–3117; fax: 0114–253–3161

**Edinburgh Supercomputer Unit.**
Tel: 0131–650–6438; fax: 0131–650–6555

**IBM.**
Tel: 0171–202–3744, press

**ICL**, High Street, London SW15 1SW.
Tel: 0181–788–7272

**National Computing Centre**, Oxford Road, Manchester M13 7ED.
Tel: 0161–228–6333; fax: 0161–228–2579

**PC Plus magazine**, 30 Monmouth Street, Bath BA1 2BW.
Tel: 01225–442244; fax: 01225–480325

## ARTIFICIAL INTELLIGENCE

**Professor Igor Aleksander**, Neural Systems, Imperial College,
Exhibition Road, SW7 2BT.
Tel: 0171–594–6189; fax: 0171–823–8125

**Centre for Neural Networks**, King's College, The Strand, WC2R 2LS.
Tel: 0171–873–2369; fax: 0171–836–1799

**Professor Aron Sloman**, Computer Science, Birmingham University,
Edgbaston B15 2TT.
Tel: 0121–414–4775; fax 0121–414–4281

## CHIPS

**IRC in Semi-conductors**, Bruce Joyce, Imperial College, London SW7
2BT.
Tel: 0171–594–6666

**NEC**, 1 Victoria Road, London W3 6UL. Biggest Japanese maker of
semiconductors.
Tel: 0181–993–8111

## COMPUTER CRIME

**Information Law and Technology**, A.J.Charlesworth, Hull University.
HU6 7RX.
Tel: 01482–466387; e-mail: a.j.charlesworth@law.hull.ac.uk

## DATA PROTECTION

**Data Protection Registrar**, Wycliffe House, Water Lane, Wilmslow SK9
5AF.
Tel: 01625–545700; e-mail: data@wycliffe.demon.co.uk

## MAINFRAMES

**Amdahl**, 137 Aldersgate Street, London EC1A 4JA.
Tel: 0171–600–0542

**Hitachi Data Systems**, Whitebrook Park, Lower Cookham Road, Maidenhead SL6 8YA.
Tel: 01628–585000; fax: 01628–778322

**IBM**.
Tel: 0171–202–3744, press

## MINIATURE PROCESSORS

**Toshiba Cambridge Research Centre**, 260 Science Park.
Tel: 01223–424666

## SECURITY

**Computer Security Research Centre**, Information Systems Department, LSE, London WC2A 2AE.
Tel: 0171–955–7641

## SOFTWARE

**Centre for Software Reliability**, City University, Northampton Square, London EC1V 0HB.
Tel: 0171–477–8421

**Computing Services Association**, 73 High Holborn, London WC1V 6LE.
Tel: 0171–405–2171; fax: 0171–404–4119

**Microsoft  PR:** Text 100, Network House, Wood Lane, London W12 7SL.
Tel: 0181–242–4100

### *Piracy*

**Business Software Alliance**, Leconfield House, Curzon Street, London W1Y 8AS.
Tel: 0171–491–1974

## VIRTUAL REALITY

**National Centre for Virtual Environments**, Salford University M5.
Tel: 0161–745–5000; fax: 0161–745–5999

**Virtuality**, Leicester (leading manufacturer).
Tel: 0116–233–7000

**Virtual Environment Research Centre**, Professor Graham Brookes, Hull
University HU6 7RX.
Tel: 01482–465696

**Virtual Manufacturing Project**, School of Mathematics, Bath University.
Tel: 01225–826826

## DESIGN AND TECHNOLOGY

Since 1987 the **Engineering and Physical Sciences Research Council** has
supported **Interdisciplinary Research Centres** (IRCs) at several universities. Most are included in the list below. Two are elsewhere in this
book.

**Advanced Technology Centre**, Warwick University (concerned with
manufacturing).
Tel: 01203–523102

**AEA Technology**, Harwell OX11 0RA. Commercial arm of UK Atomic
Energy Authority.
Tel: 01235–436581, press

**Association of Independent Research and Technology Organizations**,
PO Box 330, Cambridge CB5 8DU.
Tel: 01223–467831; fax: 462051

**British Technology Group**, 101 Newington Causeway, London SE1
6BU.
Tel: 0171–403–6666

**Central Research Laboratories** (Thorn EMI), Dawley Road, Hayes.
Works on a wide range of new ideas.
Tel: 0181–848–9779

**Cranfield University of Technology**, Bedford MK43 0AL. Leading
university in industrial research.
Tel: 01234–750111

**Engineering and Physical Sciences Research Council**, Polaris House,

North Star Avenue, Swindon SN2 1ET.
Tel: 01793–444147/313; fax: 444005

**Engineering Council**, 10 Maltravers Street, London WC2R 3ER.
Concerned with recruitment into engineering.
Tel: 0171–240–7891; fax: 0171–240–7517

**European Foundation for Technical Innovation**, Professor Ian
Mackintosh, UCL, Gower Street, London WC1E 6BT.
Tel: 0171–380–7049

**Institute of Mechanical Engineers**, 1 Birdcage Walk, London SW1H 9JJ.
Tel: 0171–222–7899; fax: 0171–222–4557

**Loughborough University of Technology**, LE11 3TU.
Tel: 01509–263171

**National Engineering Laboratory**, East Kilbride G75 0QU. Media
queries to DTI: see under INDUSTRY, page 124.

**Patent Office**, Cardiff Road, Newport NP9 1RH.
Tel: 01633–814666/813565; fax: 01633–813600

**Royal Academy of Engineering**, 29 Great Peter Street, London SW1P
3LW.
Tel: 0171–222–2688


# CATALYSTS AND CATALYITIC CONVERTERS

**IRC in Surface Science**, Professor Neville Richardson, Liverpool
University L69 3BX.
Tel: 0151–794–3543


# DESIGN

**Chartered Society of Designers**, 29 Bedford Square, London WC1B 3EG.
Tel: 0171–631–1510; fax: 0171–580–2338

**Design Council**, 1 Oxenden Street, London SW1Y 4EE.
Tel: 0171–208–2124; fax: 0171–839–6033

**Engineering Design Institute**, Loughborough University LE11 3TU.
Tel: 01509–223176; fax: 268013

**Royal College of Art**, Kensington Gore, London SW7 2EU.
Tel: 0171–584–5020

## FIBRE OPTICS

**IRC in Optoelectronics**, David Payne, Southampton University.
Tel: 01703–593155

**Professor E.W.Williams**, Electronics engineering, Keele University ST5
5BG.
Tel: 01782–583335

## LASERS

**Atomic and Laser Physics**, Professor Colin Webb, Dr Paul Ewart,
Clarendon Laboratory, Parks Road, Oxford OX1 3PU.
Tel: 01865–272340 (Ewart); 272210 (Webb); fax: 01865–272375; e-mail:
webb@vax.oc.ac.uk

**Professor Terry King**, Physics Department, Manchester University M13
9PL.
Tel: 0161–275–2112/4, university PR

## MATERIALS

**IRC in High-Performance Materials**, Mike Loretto, Birmingham
University, and also at Swansea.
Tel: 0121–414–5214

**Advanced Materials Research Laboratory**, North-East Wales Institute,
Wrexham.
Tel: 01978–290666

**Engineering Materials Department**, Sheffield University.
Tel: 0114–282–5467

**Institute of Materials**, 1 Carlton House Terrace, London SW1Y 5AF.
Tel: 0171–839–4071

**Materials Engineering Department**, University of Wales, Swansea.
Tel: 01792–205678

**Oxford Centre for Advanced Materials**, Dr B. Cantor, Parks Road,
OX1 3PH.
Tel: 01865–273652; fax: 01865–283333

**Professor Colin Humphreys**, Materials Science, Cambridge University.
Tel: 01223–334457/334300

*Smart materials*

**Cranfield University of Technology**, Shrivenham SN6 8LA.
Tel: 01793–782551

## MICROCOMPONENTS

**Daresbury Laboratory**, D.W.L.Tolfree. Precise components smaller than a pinhead.
Tel: 01925–603272; fax: 01925–603195; e-mail: d.w.l.tolfree@dl.ac.uk

## POLYMERS

**IRC in Polymer Science and Technology**, Durham University, South Road, DH1 3LF. Also at Bradford and Leeds Universities.
Tel: 0191–374–2576; fax: 0191–374–4651

**Professor Vernon Gibson**, Chemistry, Imperial College, London SW7 2AY.
Tel: 0171–594–5830; fax: 0171–594–5810; e-mail: v.gibson@ic.ac.uk

## PROCESS ENGINEERING

**IRC in Process Systems Engineering**, John Perkins, Imperial College, London SW7. Also at UCL.
Tel: 0171–594–6615

## ROBOTS

**Engineering Science Department**, Oxford University, Parks Road, OX1 3PJ.
Tel: 01865–273000

## SUPERCONDUCTIVITY

**IRC in Superconductivity**, Yao Liang, Cambridge University.
Tel: 01223–337077

**Professor Gordon Donaldson**, Physics, Strathclyde University, Glasgow G1 1XQ.
Tel: 0141–522–4400, ext. 3379

## WELDING

**Welding Institute**, Abington Hall, Cambridge CB1 6AL
Tel: 01223–891162; fax: 01223–892588

## ENERGY

Reference: *Digest of UK Energy Statistics.*

**Department of Trade and Industry**, Energy Press Desk, 1 Victoria Street, London SW1H 0ET.
Tel: 0171–215–6403/5377/5961; fax: 0171–222–4382

**County Natwest WoodMac**, 74 Queen Street, Edinburgh EH2 4NS.
Tel: 0131–225–8525

**EC Energy Monthly** (FT Newsletters), 149 Tottenham Court Road, London.
Tel: 0171–896–2222

**Energy and Environmental Research Programme**, Chatham House, 10 St James's Square, London SW1.
Tel: 0171–957–5700

**Energy Programme**, Science Policy Research Unit, Sussex University, Brighton BN1 9RF.
Tel: 01273–678758; fax: 01273–685865

**Oxford Institute of Energy Studies**, Robert Mabro, 57 Woodstock Road, OX2 6FA.
Tel: 01865–311377

**Sheffield Energy and Resources Information Service**, 103 Carterknowle Road, S7 2DY.
Tel: 0114–258–0448

**Dr Alex Henham**, Surrey University, Guildford GU2 5XH.
Tel: 01483–300800, ext. 2382

## COAL

**Coal Authority** (responsible for licensing of mines), 200 Lichfield Lane, Berry Hill, Mansfield NG18 4RG.
Tel: 01623–427162

**Coal Products**, Wingerworth Offices, Mill Lane, Chesterfield S42 6JT.
Tel: 01246–277001; fax: 01246–212212

**Coal UK** (FT Newsletters), 149 Tottenham Court Road, London.
Tel: 0171–896–2222

**RJB Mining**, Harworth Park, Blyth Road, Doncaster DN11 8BD.
Tel: 01302–751751

# ELECTRICITY

**Electricity Association**, 30 Millbank, London SW1P 4RD. Represents
the power industry.
Tel: 0171–963–5700; fax: 0171–963–5959

**GEC Alsthom**, 12 Dartmouth Street, London SW1H 9BJ.
Tel: 0171–233–2505

**National Grid**, Kirby Corner Road, Coventry CV4 8JY.
Tel: 01203–537777; fax: 01203–423678

**National Power**, Windmill Hill Business Park, Whitehill Way, Swindon
SN5 6PB.
Tel: 01793–877777; fax: 01793–892525

**OFFER** (Office of Electricity Regulation), Hagley House, Edgbaston
B16 8QG.
Tel: 0121–456–6208/6234; fax 454–7622

**PowerGen**, Westwood Way, Westwood Business Park, Coventry CV4
8LG.
Tel: 01203–424000; fax: 01203–425432

**Power UK**, FT Newsletters, 149 Tottenham Court Road, London.
Tel: 0171–896–2222

**Rolls-Royce**, 65 Buckingham Gate, London SW1E 6AT.
Tel: 0171–222–9020

## Gas turbines

**General Electric** (of USA), Hammersmith International Centre,
Shortlands, London W6.
Tel: 0181–741–9911

**PowerGen**, see above

## GAS

**British Gas**, Rivermill House, 152 Grosvenor Road, London SW1V 3JL.
Tel: 0171–821–1444

**British Gas Supply**, PGS (public gas supply), 17 London Road, Staines
TW18 4AE.
Tel: 01784–645000

**Gas Consumers Council**, 15 Wilton Road, London SW1V 2LT.
Tel: 0171–931–0977; fax: 0171–630–9934

**Gas Matters Newsletter**, and Gas Strategies, 82 Rivington Street,
London EC2A 3AY.
Tel: 0171–613–0087

**International Gas Report**, FT Newsletters, 149 Tottenham Court Road,
London.
Tel: 0171–896–2222

**OFGAS** (Office of Gas Supply), 130 Wilton Road, London SW1V 1LQ.
Gas industry regulator.
Tel: 0171–932–1606/7; fax: 0171–932–1664

**Society of British Gas Industries**, 36 Holly Walk, Leamington Spa.
Tel: 01926–334357; fax: 01926–450459

**Transco** (British Gas's pipeline division), 31 Homer Road, Solihull B91
3LT.
Tel: 0121–626–4431

## NUCLEAR

**British Energy**, Edinburgh (holding company for Nuclear Electric and
Scottish Nuclear). Ask Nuclear Electric (below).

**British Nuclear Fuels Ltd**, Risley, Warrington WA3 6AS.
Tel: 01925–834075/832146; fax: 01925–822711, press

**(Sellafield**, Seascale CA20 1PG. Tel: 019467–85839/6, press)

**British Nuclear Industry Forum**, 22 Buckingham Gate, London SW1E
6LB. Represents firms involved.
Tel: 0171–828–0116; fax: 0171–828–0110

**International Atomic Energy Agency**, Wagramerstr 5, PO Box 100, 1400
Vienna.
Tel: 00–43–1–206–02–1270/1275; fax: 00–43–1–234564

**National Radiological Protection Board**, Chilton, Didcot OX11 0RG.
Tel: 01235–822744, press; fax: 01235–833891

**Nuclear Electric**, Barnett Way, Barnwood, Gloucester GL4 7RS.
Tel: 01452–652443/855, press; fax: 01452–652750

**Nuclear Installations Inspectorate**, c/o Health and Safety Executive.
Tel: 0171–717–6700

**Science Policy Research Unit**, Professor Gordon MacKerron, Sussex
University, Brighton BN1 9RF.
Tel: 01273–686758

**UKAEA Fusion**, Culham, Abingdon OX14 3DB.
Tel: 01235–484190; fax: 01235–436899

**UK Nirex**, Curie Avenue, Harwell OX11 0RH. Nuclear waste disposal
company.
Tel: 01235–825515/06/01946–724880; fax: 01235–825547; e-mail:
response@nirex.co.uk

**Uranium Institute**, 12th Floor, 68 Knightsbridge, London SW1X 7LT.
Tel: 0171–225–0303; fax: 0171–225–0308


# OIL

**BP**, 1 Finsbury Circus, London EC2M 7BA.
Tel: 0171–496–5005; fax: 0171–496–4516

**College of Petroleum Studies**, 52 New Inn Hall Street, Oxford.
Tel: 01865–250521

**County Natwest WoodMac**, 74 Queen Street, Edinburgh EH2 4NS.
Tel: 0131–225–8525

**International Petroleum Exchange**, 58 Mark Lane, London EC3R 7NE.
Tel: 0171–481–2080

**Shell International**, Shell Centre, London SE1 7NA.
Tel: 0171–934–1234

**Texaco**, 1 Westferry Circus, Canary Wharf, London E14 4HA.
Tel: 0171–719–3000; fax: 0171–719–5104

## *North Sea*

**County Natwest WoodMac**, 74 Queen Street, Edinburgh EH2 4NS.
Tel: 0131–225–8525

**FT North Sea Letter**, FT Energy Publishing, 149 Tottenham Court Road, London W1P 9LL.
Tel: 0171–896–2222

**Internat Association of Underwater Engineering Contractors**, 177A High Street, Beckenham BR3 1AH.
Tel: 0181–663–3859; fax: 663–3860

**UK Offshore Operators Association**, 3 Hans Crescent, London SW1X 0LN.
Tel: 0171–589–5255; fax: 0171–589–8961


## RENEWABLE ENERGY/ENERGY FROM WASTE

**Association of Electricity Producers**, 41 Whitehall, London SW1A 2BX.
Tel: 0171–930–9390; fax: 0171–930–9391

**Energy Systems**, Strathclyde University, GI 1XQ.
Tel: 0141–552–4400, ext. 3788

**Engineering Department**, Professor Ali Sayigh, Reading University, Whiteknights, PO Box 225, RG6 2AY.
Tel: 01734–318588; fax: 01734–313835

**Friends of the Earth**, 26 Underwood Street, London N1 7JQ.
Tel: 0171–490–1555

**IT Power**, The Warren. Bramshill Road, Eversley RG27 0PR.
Tel: 01734–730073; fax: 01734–730820

**Renewable Energy Enquiries Bureau**, ETSU, Harwell, OX11 0RA.
Tel: 01235–432450

### *Solar power*

**BP Solar**, PO Box 191, Chertsey Road, Sunbury-on-Thames TW16 7XA.
Tel: 01932–779543; fax: 01932–762686

**Intersolar Group**, Cock Lane, High Wycombe HP13 7DE
Tel: 01494–452941

**Newcastle Photovoltaics Applications Centre**, Northumbria University NE1 8ST.
Tel: 0191–227–4595; fax: 0191–227–4561

**Solar Energy Society**, c/o CAT, Machynlleth SY20 9AZ.
Tel: 01654–703032; fax: 01654–702782

**Cardiff Engineering School**, Professor Brinkworth.
Tel: 01222–874797

## Tyres for power

**Elm Energy**, Sparklemore House, Biddings Lane, Coseley, Wolverhampton.
Tel: 01902–883555

## Water power

**Mott MacDonald** (consultants), 20 Wellesley Road, Croydon CR9 2UL.
Tel: 0181–686–5041

**Scottish Hydro-Electric**, 10 Dunkeld Road, Perth PH1 5WA.
Tel: 01738–455040; fax: 01738–455045

## Small scale water power

**National Association of Water Power Users**, The Rock, South Brent,
South Devon TQ10 9JL.
Tel: 01364–72185

## Wind

**British Wind Energy Association** (trade association), 42 Kingsway,
London WC2B 6EX.
Tel: 0171–404–3433; fax: 0171–404–3432; e-mail: bwea@gn.apc.org

**National Wind Power.**
Tel: 01628–532300; fax: 01628–531993

**Renewable Energy Systems**, Hemel Hempstead.
Tel: 01442–233444

**Vestas**, Smed Hansens Vej 27, DK-6940 Lem, Denmark. Biggest
European wind-turbine maker.
Tel: 00–45–97–34–11–88; fax: 00–45–97–34–14–84

## Wind battery chargers

**Marlec**, Rutland House, Trevithick Road, Corby NN17 1XY.
Tel: 01536–210588; fax: 01536–400211

## Wood, charcoal, biomass

**Biosphere Sciences Department**, King's College, Campden Hill Road,
London W8 7AH.
Tel: 0171–333–4317

## INDUSTRY

Local employers are likely to have a chamber of commerce. There may also be associations for particular trades. Government development corporations and regional offices, council planners, local partnerships and enterprise agencies are involved in industrial development.

Reference: *Business Monitors* (government reports) give production statistics.

### National sources

**Department of Trade and Industry Press Desk**, 1 Victoria Street, London SW1H 0ET.
Tel: 0171–215–5964/5847; fax: 0171–222–4382

**Association of British Chambers of Commerce**, 9 Tufton Street, London SW1P 3QB.
Tel: 0171–222–1555

**British Standards Institution**, 389 Chiswick High Road, London W4 4AL.
Tel: 0181–996–7378/4/2; fax: 0181–996–7400

**Centre for Industrial Policy and Performance**, Leeds University.
Tel: 0113–233–6699, press office

**Centre for Sustainable Industry**, The Rookery, Alderbury OX17 3NA.
Tel: 01993–811674

**Confederation of British Industry**, Centre Point, 103 New Oxford Street, London WC1A 1DU.
Tel: 0171–379–7400; fax: 0171–497–2596;
e-mail: 100647.3476@compuserve.com

**Foundation for Manufacturing and Industry**, 134 Buckingham Palace Road, London SW1W 9SA.
Tel: 0171–823–5360; fax: 0171–823–5361

**Industrial Society**, Robert Hyde House, 48 Bryanston Square, London W1H 7LN. Concerned with the human side of industry.
Tel: 0171–262–2401

**UNICE** (European employers association), Brussels.
Tel: 00–322–237–6511; fax: 00–322–231–1445

**Warwick Business School**, Coventry CV4 7AL. Includes industrial relations.
Tel: 01203–524306

*Premises*

**English Partnerships**, 16 Old Queen Street, London SW1H 9HP.
Tel: 0171–976–7070, press; fax: 0171–976–8017

**United Kingdom Science Park Association**, Aston Science Park, Love
Lane, Birmingham B7.
Tel: 0121–359–0981

# CERAMICS

**Ceram Research**, Queens Road, Stoke ST4 7LQ.
Tel: 01782–845431

**Design and Ceramics School**, Staffs University.
Tel: 01782–294000

**Engineering Materials Department**, Sheffield University.
Tel: 0114–282–5467

**Josiah Wedgwood and Sons**, Barlaston ST12 9ES.
Tel: 01782–204141

# CHEMICALS

**BASF**, 151 Wembley Park Drive, Wembley HA9 8HQ.
Tel: 0181–908–3188; fax: 0181–904–1173 and
PO Box 62, Seal Sands, Middlesbrough TS2 1TX.
Tel: 01642–546464; fax: 01642–546446

**Chemical and Biochemical Engineering**, Professor Alan Cornish, UCL,
Gower Street, London WC1E 6BT.
Tel: 0171–387–7050, ext. 3825; fax: 383–2348

**Chemical Engineering Department**, Cambridge.
Tel: 01223–332150

**Chemical Industries Association**, Kings Buildings, Smith Square,
London SW1P 3JJ.
Tel: 0171–834–3399; fax: 0171–834–4469

**Du Pont (UK)**, Gloucester.
Tel: 01452–633834

**Hoechst UK**, Salisbury Road, Hounslow TW4 6JH.
Tel: 0181–570–7712; fax: 0181–570–4634

**ICI**, 9 Millbank, London SW1P 3JF.
Tel: 0171–834–4444

**Rhone-Poulenc**, Oak House, Reeds Crescent, Watford WD1 1QH.
Tel: 01923–201518; fax: 01923–201920

**Shell Chemicals**, Heronbridge House, Chester Business Park, CH4 9QA.
Tel: 01244–685361; fax: 01244–685010

**Society of Chemical Industry**, 14 Belgrave Square, London SW1X 8PS.
Tel: 0171–235–3681

**Zeneca**, London.
Tel: 0171–304–5000

## *Hazards*

**Dr Rex Britter**, Engineering, Cambridge.
Tel: 01223–332643/332600

## CLOTHING AND TEXTILES

**British Association of Clothing Machinery Manufacturers**, 1st Floor, 159 Great Portland Street, London W1N 5FD.
Tel: 0171–631–5360; fax: 323–0096

**British Textile Machinery Association**, 20 Ralli Courts, West Riverside, Manchester M3 5FL.
Tel: 0161–834–2991

**British Textile Technology Group**, Didsbury, Manchester M20 8RX.
Tel: 0161–445–8141

**Northern Counties Textile Trades Federation**, 2A New Brown Street, Nelson BB9 7NY. Trade union grouping.
Tel: 01282–614055

**Transport and General Workers Union** (textiles), National House, Sunbridge Road, Bradford BD1 2QB. The National Association of Carpet Trade Unions has the same address.
Tel: 01274–725642; fax: 370282

## *Wool*

**Confederation of British Wool Textiles**, Merrydale House, Roydsdale Way, Bradford BD4.
Tel: 01274–652207

**Illingworth Morris** (Europe's largest wool processor), Fairweather Green, Thornton Road, Bradford BD8.
Tel: 01274–542255

## CRAFTS

**Crafts Council**, 44A Pentonville Road, London N1 9BY.
Tel: 0171–495–7040, PR Dobson Communications

## DYEING

**Colour Chemistry Department**, Leeds University, Leeds LS2 9JT.
Tel: 0113–243–1751; fax: 0113–233–6017

**Dr Arnie Peters**, Dyestuffs Research Group, Bradford University, BD7 1DP.
Tel: 01274–383789

## ENGINEERING

**Confederation of Shipbuilding and Engineering Unions**, 140 Walworth Road, London SE17 1JW.
Tel: 0171–703–2215; fax: 0171–252–7397

**Engineering Department**, Warwick University, CV4 7AL.
Tel: 01203–523877

**Engineering Employers Federation**, Broadway House, Tothill Street, London SW1H 9NQ.
Tel: 0171–222–7777; fax 0171–222–0792

**Engineering Industries Association**, 16 Dartmouth Street, London SW1H 9BL.
Tel: 0171–222–2367; fax: 0171–799–2206

**Engineering Training Authority**, 41 Clarendon Road, Watford WD1 1HS.
Tel: 01923–238441; fax: 01923–256086

**Foundry Trade International Magazine**, Queensway House, 2 Queensway, Redhill.
Tel: 01737–768611

**Machine Tool Technologies Association**, 62 Bayswater Road, London W2 3PS.
Tel: 0171–402–6671; fax: 0171–724–7250

**METCOM**, 235 Vauxhall Bridge Road, London SW1V 1EJ. Mechanical and metal trades confederation.
Tel: 0171–233–7011; fax: 0171–828–0667

**Perkins**, Frank Perkins Way, Peterborough.
Tel: 01733–67474; fax: 01733–582500

**Vickers**, Millbank Tower, Millbank, London SW1P 4RA.
Tel: 0171–828–7777; fax: 0171–331–3964

## FURNITURE

**BFM** (British Furniture Manufacturers), 20 Harcourt Street, London W1H 2AA.
Tel: 0171–724–0851; fax: 0171–706–1924

**National Federation of Furniture Trade Unions**, 22 Worple Road, London SW19 4DD.
Tel: 0181–947–3131; fax: 0181–944–6552

## HEALTH AND SAFETY

**Health and Safety Commission** (oversees Health and Safety Executive).
Tel: 0171–717–6000

**Health and Safety Executive**, 2 Southwark Bridge, London SE1 9HS.
Tel: 0171–717–6700, press; fax: 0171–928–6635
Bootle Press Office, Daniel House, Trinity Road, L20 3QY.
Tel: 0151–951–4000
Responsible for safety of industrial premises. It has offices throughout the country, see phone book.

**Institution of Occupational Safety and Health**, The Grange, Highfield Drive, Wigston LE18 1NN.
Tel: 0116–257–1399; fax: 0116–257–1451

**Robens Institute of Industrial and Environmental Health and Safety**, Surrey University GU2 5XH.
Tel: 01483–571281

**Sheffield Occupational Health Project**, 37 Exchange Street, S2 5TR.
Tel: 0114–755760

**Society of Occupational Medicine**, 6 St Andrews Place, Regents Park,
London NW1 4LB.
Tel: 0171–486–2641; fax: 486–0028

## *Stress*

**Professor Shirley Fisher**, Centre for Occupational and Health
Psychology, Strathclyde University, G1 1XQ.
Tel: 0141–552–4400, ext. 4245

## MARKET RESEARCH

**Federation of European Marketing Research Associations**, Studio 38,
Wimbledon Stadium Centre, SW17 0BA.
Tel: 0181–879–0709; fax: 947–2637

**Association of Market Survey Organizations**, Holford Mews, Cruikshank
Street, London WC1X 9HD.
Tel: 0171–837–1242; fax: 837–9445

## MATERIALS

See pages 116 and 117.

## PACKAGING AND PAPER

**Institute of Packaging**, Sysonby Lodge, Nottingham Road, Melton
Mowbray LE13 0NU.
Tel: 01664–500055; fax: 01664–64164

**British Paper and Board Industry Federation**, Rivenhall Road, Westlea,
Swindon SN5 7BD.
Tel: 01793–886086; fax: 0793–886182

**Pira International**, Randalls Road, Leatherhead KT22 7RU. Research in
paper, printing and packaging.
Tel: 01372–376161

## QUALITY

**Institute of Quality Assurance**, PO Box 712, 61 Southwark Street, London SE1 1SB.
Tel: 0171–401–7227; fax: 0171–401–2725

## RUBBER AND PLASTICS

See also POLYMERS, page 117.

**BP** (polyethylene), 1 Finsbury Circus, London EC2M 7BA.
Tel: 0171–496–5005; fax: 0171–496–4516

**British Plastics Federation**, 6 Bath Place, Rivington Street, London EC2A 3JE.
Tel: 0171–457–5000; fax: 0171–457–5045

**Malaysian Rubber Producers Research Association**, Brickendonbury, Hertford SG13 8NL.
Tel: 01992–584966

**Rapra Technology** (research), Shawbury, Shrewsbury SY4 4NR.
Tel: 01939–250383; fax: 01939–251118

## STEEL

**British Iron and Steel Producers Association**, 5 Cromwell Road, London SW7 2HX.
Tel: 0171–581–0231; fax: 0171–589–4009

**British Steel**, 9 Albert Embankment, London SE1 7XN.
Tel: 0171–735–7654; fax: 0171–587–1142

**CRU International**, 31 Mount Pleasant WC1X 0AD.
Tel: 0171–278–7788

**Meps** (Europe), Sheffield.
Tel: 0114–275–0570

**Metal Bulletin Research**, London.
Tel: 0171–827–9977

## JOBS AND TRAINING

**Job centres**, where people can learn about jobs on offer and also about such schemes as **Training for Work and Community Action**, are scattered through the country. There are also careers officers and school careers advisers.

Training and enterprise councils are locally organized bodies which act as the government's agent in providing money for youth training and other employment schemes, run commercially or by voluntary organizations or colleges. Towns also have many private employment agencies dealing particularly with secretarial and care work and, sometimes, with redundant executives.

Other local news sources: employers, unions.

Industrial tribunals hear allegations of unfair dismissal. Unemployment figures can be obtained from the regional office of the COI or the *Employment Gazette* (in local library).

Reference: *Labour Force Survey* (quarterly survey of 60,000 households).

## National sources

**Department of Education and Employment**, Sanctuary Buildings, Great Smith Street, London SW1P 3BT.
Fax: 0171–925–6979/80
**Jobs policy press desk**, tel: 0171–925–5107/5392
**Training**, tel: 0171–925–5361/5373/5499

**Association of Graduate Recruiters**, Sheraton House, Castle Park, Cambridge CB3 0AX.
Tel: 01223–356720; fax: 356720

**Employment Policy Institute**, South Bank House, Black Prince Road, London SE1 7SJ.
Tel: 0171–735–0777; fax: 0171–793–8192

**Equal Opportunities Commission**, 36 Broadway, London SW1H 0XH.
Tel: 0171–222–1110/2818; fax: 0171–222–2771

**Federation of Recruitment and Employment Agencies**, 36 Mortimer Street, London W1N 7RB.
Tel: 0171–323–4300; fax: 0171–255–2878

**Institute of Employment Consultants**, 6 Guildford Road, Woking GU22 7PX. Concerned with company recruitment.
Tel: 01483–766442

**Institute for Employment Studies**, Mantell Building, Sussex University, Brighton BN1 9RF.
Tel: 01273–686751; fax: 01273–690430

**Institute for Employment Research**, Warwick University CV4 7AL.
Tel: 01203–523514

**Institute of Personnel and Development**, Camp Road, London SW19 4UX.
Tel: 0181–971–9000

**Oxford Institute for Employee Relations**, John Purcell, Templeton College OX1 5NY.
Tel: 01865–735422; fax: 01865–736374

## *Employment protection*

**Central Office of Industrial Tribunals**, Southgate Street, Bury St Edmunds IP33 1AQ.
Tel: 01284–762300

**Institute of Employment Rights**, 112 Greyhound Lane, London SW16 5RN.
Tel: 0181–677–9644; fax: 0181–664–6822

## *Statistics*

**Office for National Statistics**, Great George Street, London SW1P 3AQ.
Tel: 0171–270–6192/6512, press; fax: 0171–270–6019

## *Training*

**Training and Enterprise National Council**, 10th Floor, 3 Albert Embankment, London SE1 7SX. National body for training and enterprise councils.
Tel: 0171–735–0010

## *Unemployed*

**Policy Studies Institute**, 100 Park Village East, London NW1 3SR (has done several studies).
Tel: 0171–387–2171; fax: 0171–388–0914

**Unemployment Unit**, 322 St John Street, London EC1V 4NT.
Tel: 0171–833–1222

**The TUC.** Runs 117 centres for unemployed people.
Tel: 0171–467–1248, press

# METALS, MINING AND MINERALS

**Earth Resources Department**, University of Wales, Swansea SA2 8PP.
Tel: 01792–205678

**International Mining Consultants**, Sutton-in-Ashfield NG17 2NS.
Tel: 01623–441444

**London Metal Exchange**.
Tel: 0171–264–5555

**Metal Bulletin Research**.
Tel: 0171–827–9977

**Metals Analyst**, Merrill Lynch, 25 Ropemaker Street, London EC2Y 9AS.
Tel: 0171–628–1000

**Mining Journal**, 60 Worship Street, London EC2A 2HD.
Tel: 0171–377–2020; fax: 0171–247–4100

**Roskill Information Services**, 2 Clapham Road, London SW9 0JA.
Tel: 0171–582–5155

**RTZ-CRA**, 6 St James's Square, London SW1Y 4LD.
Tel: 0171–930–2399; fax: 0171–930–3249

**School of Mines**, Camborne, Cornwall.
Tel: 01209–714866

# ALUMINIUM

**Aluminium Federation**, Broadway House, Calthorpe Road, Five Ways, Birmingham B15 1TN. Trade Association.
Tel: 0121–456–1103; fax: 456–2274

**Anthony Bird Associates**, 193 Richmond Road, Kingston on Thames KT2 5DD.
Tel: 0181–546–9045

**Billiton-Enthoven**, London.
Tel: 0171–488–3161

**International Primary Aluminium Institute**, 2 Cockspur Street, London SW1Y 5BQ.
Tel: 0171–930–0528

**Rudolf Wolff and Co.**, 31 Fenchurch Street, London EC3M 3DX.
Tel: 0171–626–8765

## COALMINING

See COAL, pages 118 and 119.

## COPPER

**Billiton-Enthoven**, London.
Tel: 0171–488–3161

## DIAMONDS

**De Beers**, 40 Holborn Viaduct, London EC1N 6RA.
Tel: 0171–404–4444

**Diamond International Newsletter**, c/o CRU, 31 Mount Pleasant,
London WC1X 0AD.
Tel: 0171–278–7788

**IDC Holdings** (merchants), 86 Hatton Garden, London EC1N 8QQ.
Tel: 0171–242–5303; fax: 0171–242–9406

## GEMS

**Gemmological Association**, 27 Greville Street, London EC1N 8SU.
Tel: 0171–404–3334; fax: 0171–404–8843

## GOLD

**Gold Fields Mineral Services**, Greencoat House, Francis Street, London
SW1P 1DH.
Tel: 0171–828–8040

**London Gold Market**, c/o N.M.Rothschild, New Court, St Swithin's
Lane, London EC4P 4DU.
Tel: 0171–280–5000

**Gold specialists, UBS**, 100 Liverpool Street, London EC2M 2RH.
Tel: 0171–901–3330

## LEAD

**Lead Development Association**, 42 Weymouth Street, London W1.
Tel: 0171–499–8422

# TIN

**Billiton-Enthoven**, London.
Tel: 0171–488–3161

**International Tin Research Institute**, Brunel Science Park, Uxbridge UX8 3PJ.
Tel: 01895–272406

# URANIUM

**Uranium Institute**, 68 Knightsbridge, London SW1X 7LT.
Tel: 0171–225–0303

# ZINC

**Zinc Development Association**, 43 Weymouth Street, London W1.
Tel: 0171–499–6636

# PAY

Reference: *New Earnings Survey.*
*Annual Abstract of Statistics.*

## National sources

**Incomes Data Services**, 193 St John Street, London EC1V 4LS.
Tel: 0171–250–3434

**Low Pay Unit**, 27 Amwell Street, London EC1R 1UN.
Tel: 0171–713–7616

**Sedgwick Noble Lowndes**, Norfolk House, Wellesley Road, Croydon CR9 3EB.
Tel: 0181–686–2466

## Management pay

**Towers Perrin**, Castlewood House, New Oxford Street, London WC1A 1DS. Advised Greenbury committee on top pay.
Tel: 0171–379–4000

## MINIMUM WAGE

**TUC** (press).
Tel: 0171–467–1248

**TGWU** (press).
Tel: 0171–963–4520

### *Economic effect*

**Economists at Barclay De Zoete Wedd**, Ebbgate House, Swan Lane, London EC4R 3TS.
Tel: 0171–956–4013, press; fax: 0171–956–4488

**Economists at Kleinwort Benson**, 20 Fenchurch Street, London EC3P 3DB.
Tel: 0171–623–8000

## SCIENCE

For journalists outside London, the best sources of information about new developments in science will probably be in their nearest university. On basic science, you will find books in your local library.

Buy the *New Scientist* if you can afford it or read it in your local library. *Nature* and other publications should be in a central library; librarians will tell you where to find them. For the really specialist magazines and back numbers to which informants may refer you, try a university library or the *Science Reference Library*.

Its **Physical Sciences Reading Room** is at 25 Southampton Buildings, off Chancery Lane, London WC2A 1AY, tel: 0171–412–7494; fax: 412–7495, and is worth visiting for its interest as a building alone. The Science Reference Library will photocopy articles for a fee. Computerized journalists can make on-line inquiries. The life, earth and medical sciences section is at 9 Kean Street (tel: 0171–412–7288: fax: 412–7217).

You can join the **Association of British Science Writers** (ABSW), Fortress House, 23 Savile Row, London W1X 1AB (tel: 0171–439–1205 Wednesdays and Thursdays only; fax 0171–973–3051).

ABSW arranges visits to laboratories and other sites round the country, holds lunches with distinguished speakers in London, and publishes a newsletter. Its activities are a useful pointer to ideas worth pursuing, even if they are not in themselves news.

The ABSW is a member of the **European Union of Science Journalists Associations**: secretary, Isabelle Riedinger, c/o ESF, 1 quai Lezay

Marnesia, F-67000 Strasbourg, France (tel: 00–33–88–76–71–34; fax: 00–33–88–36–69–45; e-mail: eusja@esf.c-strasbourg.fr.

The **CIBA Foundation** operates the Media Resource Service which suggests experts willing to answer questions on scientific subjects: 41 Portland Place, London W1N 4BN (tel: 0171–580–0100 or 0171–631–1634; fax: 637–2127).

The **British Association's** annual festival, held in different places round the country, is a valuable chance to meet scientists. It offers cheap rooms at the meet; and you can get free coffee and sandwiches and handouts galore at the press office.

Much government-sponsored research is funded through research councils, mainly based at Swindon. Press numbers:

**Biotechnology and Biological Sciences**, Polaris House, North Star Avenue, SN2 1UH.
Tel: 01793–413253/413301; fax: 01793–413382

**Economic and Social Research**, Polaris House, North Star Avenue, SN2 1UJ.
Tel: 01793–413000; fax: 01793–413001

**Engineering and Physical Sciences**, Polaris House, North Star Avenue, SN2 1ET.
Tel: 01793–444147/4313/05; fax: 01793–444005

**Medical Research Council**, 20 Park Crescent, London W1N 4AL.
Tel: 0171–637–6011; fax: 0171–436–2665, PR

**Natural Environment Research Council**, Polaris House, North Star Avenue, SN2 1EU.
Tel: 01793–411604/561; fax: 01793–411510, PR

**Particle Physics and Astronomy Research Council**, Polaris House, North Star Avenue, SN2 1SZ.
Tel: 01793–442012; fax: 01793–442002

The research councils have central laboratories which offer the use of large and expensive equipment to researchers: the **Rutherford Appleton Laboratory**, Chilton, Didcot OX11 0QX (tel: 01235–446482, press; fax: 446665; e-mail: jjch@ib.rl.ac.uk) and the **Daresbury Laboratory**, Warrington WA4 4AD (information, tel: 01925–603305; fax: 603100).

The trade union to which many government scientists belong is the **Institution of Professionals Managers and Specialists** (tel: 0171–928–9951; fax: 928–5996). Another active trade union is **Manufacturing Science Finance** (MSF), tel: 0181–871–2100; fax: 0181–887–1160.

Government policy has moved away from funding research budgets towards seeking bids for specific projects (whose scientific excellence does not necessarily have to have an immediate practical application) from research institutes, laboratories and universities. Government institutes have become semi-independent agencies, encouraged to find contracts where they can. Some, such as the **Plant Breeding Institute** at Cambridge, now **PBI International**, have been privatized.

There is an **Association of Independent Research and Technology Organizations** (tel: 01223–467831; fax: 01223–462051).

A directory *Current Research in Britain* is published by Cartermill International, Technology Centre, St Andrews (tel: 01334–477660; fax: 477180).

**British Association for Advancement of Science**, 23 Savile Row, London W1X 2NB.
Tel: 0171–973–3500; fax: 0171–973–3051

**British Society for Social Responsibility in Science**, 25 Horsell Road, London N5.
Tel: 0171–607–9615

**Central Laboratory for Research Councils**, Rutherford Appleton Laboratory, Chilton, Didcot OX11 0QX.
Tel: 01235–446482; fax: 01235–446665

**European Union: Science**, DG XII Rue de la Loi 200, B-1049, Belgium.
Tel: 00–32–2235–1111

**Imperial College of Science**, Exhibition Road, London SW7 2AZ.
Tel: 0171–589–5111; fax: 0171–584–7596

**Institute for Scientific Information**, 132 High Street, Uxbridge UB8 1DP.
Tel: 01895–230085

**Office of Science and Technology**, c/o DT1, 1 Victoria Street, London SW1H 0ET.
Tel: 0171–215–5962/1/5377, press; fax: 0171–222–4382

**Royal Society**, 6 Carlton House Terrace, London SW1Y 5AG. Has a science promotion section.
Tel: 0171–839–5561; fax: 0171–930–2170

**Save British Science Society**, PO Box 241, Oxford OX1 3QQ.
Tel: 01865–273407; fax: 01865–511370

**Science Photo Library.**
Tel: 0171–727–4712; fax: 0171–727–6041

**Science Policy Research Unit**, Sussex University, Brighton BN1 9RF.
Tel: 01273–686758

**Science and Technology Policy Department**, Manchester University, M13 9PL.
Tel: 0161–275–2112/4, press

## ASTRONOMY

**Armagh Planetarium**, College Hill.
Tel: 01861–523689; fax: 526187

**Blackett Laboratory**, Imperial College, Prince Consort Road, London SW7 2BZ.
Tel: 0171–594–7530; fax: 0171–594–7777

**British Astronomical Association**, Burlington House, Piccadilly, London W1V 0NL.
Tel: 0171–734–4145

**Professor George Efstathiou**, Physics Department, Oxford University, Keble Road OX1 3RH.
Tel: 01865–273300; fax: 01865–273390

**Jodrell Bank Science Centre**, Macclesfield SK11 9DL.
Tel: 01477–571874; fax: 01477–571875

**Royal Astronomical Society Press Officer**, Dr Jacqueline Mitton, Cambridge CB4 3QQ.
Tel: 01223–564914; fax: 01223–572892

**Royal Greenwich Observatory**, Madingley Road, Cambridge CB3 0HA.
Tel: 01223–374000; fax: 01223–374700

**Royal Observatory**, Blackford Hill, Edinburgh EH9 3HJ.
Tel: 0131–668–8100; fax: 0131–668–8264

**Rutherford Appleton Laboratory**, Didcot, OX11 02QX.
Tel: 01235–446482, press; fax: 01235–446665; e-mail: jjch@ib.rl.ac.uk

## BIOCHEMISTRY

**Biochemical Society**, 59 Portland Place, London W1N 3AJ.
Tel: 0171–580–5530; fax: 0171–637–7626

## BIODIVERSITY

**Royal Botanic Gardens**, Kew TW9 3AQ.
Tel: 0181–332–5000; fax: 332–5197

**Natural History Museum**, London SW7 5BD.
Tel: 0171–938–8779/8895, PR; fax: 9066

# BIOLOGY

**Institute of Biology**, 20 Queensbury Place, London SW7 2ZY.
Tel: 0171–581–8333

# BIOTECHNOLOGY

**Bioindustry Association**, 15 Belgrave Square, London SW1X 8PS.
Association of businesses working in bioscience.
Tel: 0171–245–9911; fax: 0171–235–4759

**Biotechnology and Biological Sciences Research Council**, Polaris House,
North Star Avenue, Swindon SN2 1UH.
Tel: 01793–413301; fax: 413382

**Celltech** (biotechnology company), 261 Bath Road, Slough.
Tel: 01753–534655; fax: 01753–536632

**Plant Biochemistry and Biotechnology Centre**, Leeds University LS2 9JT.
Tel: 0113–233–6699, PR; fax: 0113–233–6017

**Institute of Biotechnology**, Tennis Court Road, Cambridge CB2 1QT.
Tel: 01223–334160

**Dr Howard Chase**, Chemical Engineering, Cambridge.
Tel: 01223–332150

**Nuffield Council on Bioethics**, Bedford Square, London WC1B 3EG.
Tel: 0171–631–0566

## Biotechnology for pest control

**Virus Research Department**, John Innes Centre, Colney Lane, Norwich
NR4 7UH.
Tel: 01603–452571

## Controversy over patenting new varieties of plants

**Intermediate Technology Development Group**, 103 Southampton Row,
London WC1B 4HH.
Tel: 0171–436–9761; fax: 436–2013

**International Plant Genetic Resources Institute**, Via delle Sette Chiese 142, 00145 Rome, Italy.
Tel: 00–396–518–921

**Splice of Life** (bulletin of Genetics Forum).
Tel: 0171–638–0606

**Zeneca Seeds**, Tim Roberts, Jealott's Hill Research Station, Bracknell RG12 6EY.
Tel: 01344–414290; fax: 01344–413646

## *Risks of biotechnology*

**Dr Simon Shackley**, Lancaster University.
Tel: 01524–592673

## BOTANY/CROPS/FUNGI/PLANTS (see also page 188)

**British Mycological Society**, PO Box 30, Stourbridge DY9 9PZ.
Tel: 01562–887043; fax: 01562–887043

**British Society of Plant-Breeders**, Woolpack Chambers, Ely CB7 4ND.
Tel: 01353–664211

**International Mycological Institute**, Bakeham Lane, Egham TW20 9TY.
Tel: 01784–470111

**John Innes Centre**, Colney Lane, Norwich NR4 7UH.
Tel: 01603–452571

**Plant Breeding International**, Maris Lane, Trumpington, Cambridge.
Tel: 01223–840411; fax: 01223–845514

**Rothamsted Experimental Station**, Harpenden AL5 2JQ.
Tel: 01582–763133

**Royal Botanic Gardens**, Kew TW9 3AB.
Tel: 0181–332–5000; fax: 5310

## *Nitrogen fixation*

**Life Sciences Department**, Nottingham University NG7 2RD.
Tel: 0115–951–5151

**Nitrogen Fixing Laboratory**, Sussex University, Brighton BN1 9RQ.
Tel: 01273–678252

## CHEMISTRY

**Chemical Laboratories**, Cambridge University.
Tel: 01223–336300

**Government Chemist**, Queens Road, Teddington TW11 0LY. Media queries to DTI press office.
Tel: 0171–215–5961/5377

**Royal Society of Chemistry**, Burlington House, Piccadilly, London W1V 0BN.
Tel: 0171–437–8656; fax: 0171–734–8883

### *Carbon 60 – fullerene*

**Professor Harold Kroto**, School of Chemistry, Sussex University, Brighton BN1 9QJ.
Tel: 01273–678329

## EARLY MAN

**Biological Anthropology Department**, Downing Street, Cambridge CB2 3DZ.
Tel: 01223–335454

## FORENSIC SCIENCE

**Forensic Science Service**.
Tel: 0171–273–4610, press

**Metropolitan Forensic Laboratory**, New Scotland Yard, London SW1H.
Tel: 0171–230–3472, press

## GENETICS

See page 69.

## GEOLOGY

**British Geological Survey**, Keyworth, Nottingham NG12 5GG. Works overseas as well as at home.
Tel: 0115–936–3556/3497; fax: 0115–936–3385, PR

**Earth Sciences Department**, Cambridge University, Downing Street, Cambridge CB2 3BQ.
Tel: 01223–333400; fax: 01223–333450

**Earth Sciences Department**, Oxford University, Parks Road, Oxford OX1 3PR.
Tel: 01865–272000; fax: 01865–272072

**Geological Science**, Professor Claudio Vita-Finzi, UCL, London WC1E 6BJ.
Tel: 0171–380–7822; fax: 0171–387–1612

**Geological Society**, Burlington House, W1V 1RJ.
Tel: 0171–434–9944

## *Earthquakes*

**Earthquake Engineering Department**, Imperial College, Exhibition Road, London SW7 2AZ.
Tel: 0171–589–5111

**Geological Hazards Research Unit**, University of Wales, Natural Science Building, Swansea SA2 8PP.
Tel: 01792–295522

## *Volcanoes*

**Earth Sciences Department**, Leeds University, LS2 9JT.
Tel: 0113–233–5248

**Earth Sciences Department**, Open University, Milton Keynes MK7 6AA.
Tel: 01908–653949; fax: 01908–655151

**Geological Hazards Research Unit**, University of Wales, Natural Science Building, Swansea SA2 8PP.
Tel: 01792–295522

## INSECTS

**International Institute of Entomology**, 56 Queens Gate, London SW7 5JR.
Tel: 0171–584–0067

## NANOSCIENCE

Concerned with the use of tiny components, down to molecular size, principally for electronics. A nanometre is a billionth of a metre.

**Professor J. Fraser Stoddart**, School of Chemistry, Birmingham University B15 2TT.
Tel: 0121–414–4362

**Nanoelectronic Research Centre**, Glasgow University G12 8QQ.
Tel: 0141–339–8855

**EPSRC Nanotechnology Research Co-ordinator**, Bath.
Tel: 01225–866544; fax: 01225–868993

## NUCLEAR

**United Kingdom Atomic Energy Authority**, Harwell, Oxford OX11 0RA.
Tel: 01235–436900, press; fax: 01235–436899

**CERN** (European Centre for Nuclear Research), CH-1200 Geneva 23, Switzerland.
Tel: 00–41–22–767–4101, press; fax: 00–41–22–785–0247

**JET** (nuclear fusion experiment), Abingdon OX14 3EA.
Tel: 01235–464776, press

**National Radiological Protection Board**, Chilton, Didcot OX11 0RO.
Tel: 01235–822744, press; fax: 822746; e-mail: pressoffice@nrpb.org.uk

## PHYSICS

**Cavendish Laboratory**, Cambridge University, Madingley Road, CB3 0HE.
Tel: 01223–337200; fax: 01223–363263

**Clarendon Laboratory**, Parks Road, Oxford OX1 3PU.
Tel: 01865–272200; fax: 01865–272400

**Institute of Physics**, 47 Belgrave Square, London SW1X 8QX.
Tel: 0171–235–6111; fax: 0171–259–6002; e-mail: IOP @ UK.AC.ULCC

**National Physical Laboratory**, Queens Road, Teddington TW11 0LU.
Media queries to DTI.
Tel: 0171–215–5961/5377; fax: 0171–222–4382

# SEA

**Institute of Oceanographic Sciences**, Southampton University.
Tel: 01703–595000

**Scottish Association for Marine Science**, Dunstaffnage, Dunbeg, Oban.
Tel: 01631–562244

# SPACE

**Aerospace Engineering Department**, Glasgow University.
Tel: 0141–330–4240, press

**British National Space Centre**, 151 Buckingham Palace Road, London
SW1W 9SS.
Tel: 0171–215–0806/8, press; fax: 0171–215–0936

**European Space Agency**, 8 rue Mario Nikis, 75738 Paris, France.
Tel: 00–33–2–427–3771

**Mullard Space Science Laboratory** (UCL), Holmberg St Mary, Dorking
RH5 6NT.
Tel: 01483–274111; fax: 01483–278312

**Space Science Department**, Rutherford Appleton Laboratory, Chilton,
Didcot OX11 0QX.
Tel: 01235–446482; fax: 01235–446665

**Professor Ken Pounds and Colleagues**, Physics, Leicester University
LE1 7RH.
Tel: 0116–252–3509

## *Use of satellite data*

**Meteorology Department**, Reading University.
Tel: 01734–318954/2

# VIRUSES

**Institute of Virology and Environmental Microbiology**, Professor David
Bishop, Mansfield Road, Oxford OX1 3SR.
Tel: 01865–512361

# 4 PEOPLE AT PLAY

## ARTS

Try art gallery and museum curators, librarians, local arts and music societies, theatre managers, council arts or drama organizers, festival organizers. There may be local arts schools, colleges or university departments or local arts associations. See also regional headings, pages 242–308.

### *National sources*

**Department of National Heritage Arts Press Desk**, 2 Cockspur Street, London SW1Y 5DH.
Tel: 0171–211–6271/2; fax: 0171–211–6270

**Arts Council**, 14 Great Peter Street, London SW1P 3NQ.
Tel: 0171–333–0100; fax: 0171–973–6560, press

**National Campaign for the Arts**, Francis House, Francis Street, London SW1P 1DE.
Tel: 0171–828–4448; fax: 0171–931–9959

## ART AND ANTIQUES

**British Antique Dealers Association**, 20 Rutland Gate, London SW7 1BD.
Tel: 0171–589–4128; fax: 0171–581–9083

**Christies**, 8 King Street, London SW1Y 6QT. Has experts in art history.
Tel: 0171–839–9060

**Contemporary Art Society**, 20 John Islip Street, London SW1P 4LL.
Tel: 0171–821–5323; fax: 0171–834–0228

**Courtauld Institute of Art**, London University, Somerset House, The Strand WC2R 0RN.
Tel: 0171–872–0220

**National Art Collections Fund**, 7 Cromwell Place, London SW7 2JN.
Tel: 0171–225–4800; fax: 0171–225–4848

**National Artists Association**, 21 Steward Street, London E1 6AJ.
Tel: 0171–426–0911; fax: 0171–426–0282

**Philips** (auctioneers), 101 New Bond Street, London W1Y 0AS.
Tel: 0171–629–6602

**Sothebys**, 34 New Bond Street, London W1A 2AA. Has experts in art history.
Tel: 0171–493–8080; fax: 0171–409–3100

## *Art thefts*

**Art and Antiques Squad**, Scotland Yard.
Tel: 0171–230–2601, press

**Art Loss Register**, 13 Grosvenor Place, London SW1X 7HH.
Tel: 0171–235–3393; fax: 0171–235–1652

**Trace Magazine**, Philip Saunders, Plymouth. (Mr Saunders is also an expert on art stolen in the war.)
Tel: 01752–261996

**Council for Prevention of Art Theft**, 17 Whitcomb Street, London WC2H 7PL.
Tel: 0181–244–8445, secretary

## DANCE

**Ballroom Dancers Federation**, 9 Hazelwood Road, Cudham, Sevenoaks TN14 7QU.
Tel: 01689–855143; fax 01689–855143

**English Folk Dance and Song Society**, 2 Regents Park Road, London NW1 7AY.
Tel: 0171–485–2206; fax: 0171–284–0523

**Imperial Society of Teachers of Dancing**, Euston Hall, Birkenhead Street, London WC1H 8BE. Covers all forms of dancing.
Tel: 0171–837–9967; fax: 833–5981

**London City Ballet**, 71 Kingsway, London WC2B 6SX.
Tel: 0171–405–0044; fax: 0171–405–2050

**Place Theatre**, 17 Dukes Road, London WC1. Specializes in Indian and other overseas dance.
Tel: 0171–380–1268

**Rambert Dance Company**, 94 Chiswick High Road, London W4 1SH.
Tel: 0181–995–4246; fax: 0181–747–8323

**Royal Academy of Dancing**, 36 Battersea Square, London SW11 3RA.
Tel: 071–223–0091; fax: 0171–924–3129

## MUSIC

References: *New Grove Dictionary of Music and Musicians* (twelve volumes).
*Oxford Dictionary of Music* (one volume).
*Who's Who in Music.*

**British Association of Barbershop Singers**, 7 Northcote Road, Clifton, Bristol BS8 3HB.
Tel: 0117–973–6591; fax: 0227–973–6591

**Musicians Union**, 60 Clapham Road, London SW9 0JJ.
Tel: 0171–582–5566; fax: 0171–582–9805

**Royal Academy of Music**, Marylebone Road, London NW1 5HT.
Tel: 0171–873–7373; fax: 0171–873–7374

**Royal College of Music**, Prince Consort Road, London SW7 2BS.
Tel: 0171–589–3643; fax: 0171–589–7740

### *Brass bands*

**British Federation of Brass Bands.**
Tel: 01527–852485, secretary

### *British twentieth-century music*

**Dr Alain Frogley**, Music, Lancaster University, LA1 4YW.
Tel: 01524–593773

### *Elvis Presley, American jazz*

**Brian Ward**, History, Newcastle University NE1 7RU.
Tel: 0191–222–6490

## Overseas

**Centre of Music**, School of Oriental and African Studies, Russell Square, London WC1H 0XG.
Tel: 0171–637–2388

**Ethno-musicology Programme**, Edinburgh University, 27 George Square, EH9 3JT.
Tel: 0131–650–1000

## Pop

**Professor Simon Frith**, Logie Baird Centre, Strathclyde University, Glasgow G1 1XQ.
Tel: 0141–552–4400, ext. 3102

## *Recorded*

**BMG**, 69 Fulham High Street, London SW6 3JW.
Tel: 0171–973–0011; fax: 0171–371–9298

**British Phonographic Industry**, 25 Savile Row, London W1X 1AA.
Tel: 0171–287–4422; fax: 0171–287–2252

**Creation Records**.
Tel: 0171–722–8866

**EMI**.
Tel: 0171–605–5000

**International Federation of Phonographic Industries**, 54 Regent Street, London W1R 5PJ. Pursues pirates.
Tel: 0171–434–3521

**Phonographic Performance Ltd**, 14 Ganton Street, London W1V 1LB. Issues music licences.
Tel: 0171–437–0311; fax: 0171–734–2986

**PolyGram**, 1 Sussex Place, London W6 9XS.
Tel: 0181–910–5000

**Sony UK**.
Tel: 01932–816000

**Warner Music**, Baker Street, London W1M 1AJ.
Tel: 0171–486–1414

## THEATRE

Reference: *Who's Who in the Theatre.*
*Spotlight* (lists actors and their agents).

**Equity**, Guild House, Upper St Martin's Lane, London EC2H 9EG.
Tel: 0171–379–6000; fax 0171–379–7001

**English Touring Theatre**, New Century Building, Hill Street, Crewe CW1 1BX.
Tel: 01270–501800; fax 01270–501888

**Royal National Theatre**, SE1 9PX.
Tel: 0171–928–2033; fax: 0171–620–1197

**Royal Shakespeare Company**, Barbican, EC2Y 8BQ.
Tel: 0171–628–3351

**Theatrical Management Association**, Bedford Chambers, The Piazza, London WC2E 8HQ.
Tel: 0171–836–0971; fax: 0171–497–2543

### Minority theatre in Britain

**Talawa** (Afro-Caribbean theatre), 3rd Floor, 23 Great Sutton Street, London EC1V 0DN.
Tel: 0171–251–6644; fax: 0171–251–5969

**Tamasha**, Christine Landon-Smith.
Tel: 0181–889–6432

**Tara Arts** (Indian), 356 Garratt Lane, London SW18 4ES.
Tel: 0181–871–1458

### New plays

**Margaret Eddershaw**, Theatre Studies, Lancaster University.
Tel: 01524–594163

## BOOKS

**Whitaker's** (tel: 0171–836–8911, up to 4 p.m.) and the **Book Trust** (tel: 0181–870–9055) answer telephone inquiries about books and their publishers. Publishers supply brochures about forthcoming titles. Information about these also appears in *The Bookseller* (published weekly and also as an annual).

Books other than reference books published ten years or more ago can be hard to find. Westminster Libraries have more than most. If in reach of London try through **Westminster Reference Library** (tel: 0171–798–2036).

References: *Directory of Book Publishers.*
*Encyclopaedia of World Literature in the 20th Century.*
*Libraries in the United Kingdom and the Republic of Ireland* (Library Association).
*The Writers' and Artists' Yearbook.*
*Writers' Directory 1994–6* (American publication).

**British Library** (press), 96 Euston Road, London NW1 2DB.
Tel: 0171–412–7114/2; fax: 0171–412–7268

**Andre Deutsch**, 105 Great Russell Street, London WC1B 3LA.
Tel: 0171–580–2746; fax: 0171–631–3253

**Antiquarian Booksellers Association**, 40 Piccadilly, London W1V 9PA.
Tel: 0171–439–3118; fax: 0171–439–3119

**Authors Licensing and Collecting Society**, 74 New Oxford Street, London WC1A 1EF. Administers some rights.
Tel: 0171–255–2034; fax: 0171–323–0486

**Bodleian Library**, Broad Street, Oxford OX1 3BG (second largest in Britain).
Tel: 01865–227000

**Book Aid International**, 39 Coldharbour Lane, London SE5 9NR. Collects books for schools and universities overseas.
Tel: 0171–733–3577; fax: 0171–978–8006; e-mail: rls@gn.apc.org

**Booksellers Association**, 272 Vauxhall Bridge Road, London SW1V 1BA.
Tel: 0171–834–5477

**Book Trust**, 45 East Hill, London SW18 2QZ. Provides information; administers Booker Prize.
Tel: 0181–870–9055; fax: 0181–874–4790

**Butterworth-Heinemann**, Linacre House, Jordan Hill, Oxford OX2 8DP.
Tel: 01865–310366; fax: 01865–310898

**Cassell** (includes Gollancz), Wellington House, The Strand, London WC2.
Tel: 0171–420–5555

**Federation of Children's Book Groups**, 6 Bryce Place, Currie,

Edinburgh EH14 5LR.
Tel: 0131–449–2713

**Hamish Hamilton**, 27 Wrights Lane, London W8 5TZ.
Tel: 0171–416–3200; fax: 0171–416–3295

**HarperCollins**, Ophelia House, Fulham Palace Road, London W6 1AA.
Tel: 0181–741–7070

**HMSO** (review copies), St Crispins, Duke Street, Norwich NR3 1PD.
Publishes government reports.
Tel: 01603–695911/5895/4487; fax: 01603–695582

**Hodder Headline**, 338 Euston Road, London NW1 3BH.
Tel: 0171–873–6000

**Longman**, Burnt Mill, Harlow CM20 2JE.
Tel: 01279–426721/442601

**Macmillan**, 4 Little Essex Street, London WC2R 3LD and Houndmills, Basingstoke RG21 2XS. Includes Pan, Picador, Sidgwick and Jackson.
Tel: 0171–836–6633

**Michael Joseph**, 27 Wrights Lane, London W8 5TZ.
Tel: 0171–416–3200; fax: 0171–416–3293

**Oxford University Press**.
Tel: 01865–56767

**Penguin**, 27 Wrights Lane, London W8 5TZ.
Tel: 0171–416–3000; fax: 0171–416–3099

**Publishers Association**, 19 Bedford Square, London WC1B 2HJ.
Tel: 0171–580–6321/323–1548; fax: 0171–636–5375

**Random House UK**, 20 Vauxhall Bridge Road, London SW1V 2SA.
Includes Century, Chatto, Cape.
Tel: 0171–973–9000

**Orion Group** (includes Weidenfeld), Upper St Martins Lane, London WC2H 9EA.
Tel: 0171–240–3444

## DETECTIVE STORIES

**Sabine Vanacker**, Dutch Department, Hull University HU6 7RX.
Tel: 01482–465886

# LIBRARIES

**Library Association**, 7 Ridgmount Street, London WC1E 7AE.
Tel: 0171–636–7543; fax: 0171–436–7218

# NOVELS

**Romantic Novelists Association**, June Wyndham-Davies, PR and press.
Tel: 01628–521177

# POETRY

**The Poetry Society**, 22 Betterton Street, WC2H 9BU.
Tel: 0171–240–4810

# RUSHDIE AFFAIR

**Rushdie Defence Committee**, c/o ARTICLE 19, 33 Islington High
Street, London N1 9LH. Rushdie is published by Cape, see Random
House above.
Tel: 0171–278–9292

# WRITERS' FREEDOM

**International PEN**, 9 Charterhouse Buildings, London EC1M 7AT.
Tel: 0171–253–4308

# GAMBLING

**Bacta** (amusement machine association).
Tel: 0171–713–7144

**Bingo Association of Great Britain**, 4 St James Court, Wilderspool
Causeway, Warrington WA4 6PS.
Tel: 01925–234700; fax: 01925–234702

**Gaming Board for Great Britain**, 168 High Holborn, London WC1V
7AA. Overseas gaming, bingo, machines, many lotteries.
Tel: 0171–306–6200; fax: 0171–306–6266

**Gamblers Anonymous**, PO Box 88, London SW6 3DU.
Tel: 0171–384–3040

**Kunick** (largest fruit-machine supplier), Low Lane, Horsforth, Leeds
LS18 4ER.
Tel: 0113–239–0001; fax: 0113–259–0864

**National Council on Gambling**, London.
Tel: 0181–364–1376; also fax

## *Horse race betting*

**Horse Race Betting Levy Board**, 52 Grosvenor Gardens, London
SW1W 0AU.
Tel: 0171–333–0043; fax 0171–333–0041

**Horse Race Totalisator Board**, 74 Upper Richmond Road, London
SW15 2SU.
Tel: 0181–874–6411; fax 0181–874–6107

**Ladbroke Racing**, Imperial Drive, Harrow HA2 7JW.
Tel: 0181–868–8899

**National Association of Bookmakers**, 298 Ewell Road, Surbiton KT6
7AQ.
Tel: 0181–390–8222; fax: 0181–339–9940

**William Hill**, Station Road, London N22 4TP.
Tel: 0181–918–3600

## *National lottery*

**National Lottery** (Camelot), Watford.
Tel: 01923–425000

**National Lottery Charities Board**, 7th Floor, 30 Orange Street, London
WC2H 7HH.
Tel: 0171–839–5371; fax: 0171–839–5369

**National Heritage Memorial Fund**, 10 St James's Street, London SW1A
1EF. Distributes lottery money among heritage projects.
Tel: 0171–747–2030, press; fax: 0171–930–0968

**OFLOT** (Office of the National Lottery), 2 Monck Street, London
SW1P 2BQ.
Tel: 0171–227–2030/1; fax: 0171–227–2005

*Pools*

**Pool Promoters Association**, 100 Old Hall Street, Liverpool L3 9TD.
Tel: 0151–227–4181; fax: 0151–227–2584

**Littlewoods Pools**, Walton Hall Avenue, Liverpool.
Tel: 0151–525–3677

# GARDENS

**Garden Industry Manufacturers Association**, 225 Bristol Road,
Edgbaston B5 7UB.
Tel: 0121–446–6688; fax: 0121–446–5215

**Good Gardeners Association**, Pinetum Lodge, Churcham, Gloucester
GL2 8AD. Promotes organic methods.
Tel: 01452–750402; fax: 01452–750402

**Harlow Carr Gardens**, Harrogate.
Tel: 01423–565418; fax: 530663

**National Society of Allotment and Leisure Gardeners**, O'Dell House,
Hunters Road, Corby NN17 5JE.
Tel: 01536–266576

**Royal Horticultural Society**, 80 Vincent Square, London SW1P 2PB.
Tel: 0171–834–4333; fax: 0171–630–6060; Wisley  01483–224234

## GARDEN DESIGNS

**British Association of Landscape Industries**, Landscape House, Henry
Street, Keighley BD21 3DR.
Tel: 01535–606139; fax: 610269

**Society of Garden Designers**, 6 Borough Road, Kingston KT2 6BD.
Tel: 0181–974–9483; fax: 0181–974–9483

## LAWNMOWERS

**Atco**, Suffolk Works, Stowmarket.
Tel: 01449–612183

**Flymo**, Preston Road, Aycliffe Industrial Estate.
Tel: 01325–300303

## LEISURE

Your area will probably have local clubs and organizations operating in the fields set out below.

### *National sources*

**Leisure Studies Association**, Chelsea School Research Centre, Brighton University.
Tel: 01273–643741; fax: 01273–643704

**Oxford Centre for Tourism and Leisure Studies**, Oxford Brookes University.
Tel: 01865–483432

## BOATING

**British Marine Industries Federation**, Meadlake Place, Thorpe Lea Road, Egham TW20 8HE.
Tel: 01784–473377; fax: 01784–439678

## BRIDGE

**Bridge Magazine**, 369 Euston Road, London NW1 3AR.
Tel: 0171–388–2404

## CAMPING

**Camping and Caravanning Club**, Greenfields House, Westwood Way, Coventry CV4 8JH.
Tel: 01203–694995; fax: 01203–694886

## CHESS

**British Chess Federation**, 9a Grand Parade, St Leonards TN38 0DD.
Tel: 01424–442500

## COINS

**British Numismatic Trade Association**, PO Box 448, Bromley BR1 4EQ.
Tel: 0181–466–8501; fax: 0181–466–8502

# DARTS

**British Darts Organization**, 2 Pages Lane, London N10 1PS.
Tel: 0181–883–5544

# FIREWORKS

**British Pyrotechnists Association**, 1 Waterloo Way, Leicester LE1 6LP.
Tel: 0116–256–6000

**National Campaign for Firework Reform**, 118 Long Acre, London
EC2E 9PA.
Tel: 0171–836–6703

# PHOTOGRAPHY

**Royal Photographic Society**, The Octagon, Milsom Street, Bath.
Tel: 01225–462841

**Camera Club**, 16 Bowden Street, London SE11 4DS.
Tel: 0171–587–1809

# STAMP COLLECTING

**The Philatelic Traders Society**, 107 Charterhouse Street, London EC1M
6PT.
Tel: 0171–490–1005; fax: 0171–253–0414

# THEME PARKS

**Alton Towers.**
Tel: 01538–703344/702200

**British Association of Leisure Parks, Piers and Attractions**, 25 Kings
Terrace, London NW1 0JP.
Tel: 0171–383–7942; fax: 383–7925

**Disneyland Paris** (publicity), Beaumont House, Kensington Village,
Avonmore Road, W14 8TS;
Tel: 0171–605–2845; fax: 0171–605–2425

**Disney in United States**.
Tel: 0171–605–2829; fax: 605–2490

**Thorpe Park**, Staines Lane, Chertsey.
Tel: 01932–569393; fax: 566367

# WALKING

**Ramblers Association**, 1 Wandsworth Road, London SW8 2LX.
Tel: 0171–582–6878/6826

# SPORT

Every area has an array of sports clubs. Councils are involved as providers
of swimming baths and playing fields. They may have recreation organizers.
   Journalists group: the **Sports Writers Association of Great Britain**, 43
Lime Grove, New Malden KT3 3TP.
   National bodies and reference books are set out below. The **Sports
Council** produces an address book of governing bodies. There are corre-
sponding bodies in Scotland, Wales and Ireland.
Reference: *Radio 5 Sports Yearbook*.
*Guinness International Who's Who of Sport*.

## *National Sources*

**Central Council of Physical Recreation**, Francis House, Francis Street,
London SW1P 1DE.
Tel: 0171–828–3163; fax: 0171–630–8820

**Commonwealth Games Federation**.
Tel: 0181–871–2677

**Crystal Palace National Sports Centre**, Ledrington Road, London SE19
2BB
Tel: 0181–778–0131

**Institute of Groundsmanship**, 19 Church Street, The Agora, Wolverton
MK12 5LG.
Tel: 01908–312511; fax: 01908–311140

**Institute of Sport and Recreation Management**, 36 Sherrard Street,
Melton Mowbray LE13 1XJ.
Tel: 01664–65531; fax: 01664–501155

**Lilleshall Hall National Sports Centre**, Newport (Salop) TF10 9AT.
Tel: 01952–603003

**National Playing Fields Association**, 25 Ovington Street, London SW3 1LJ.
Tel: 0171–584–6445

**Sports Council**, 16 Upper Woburn Place, London WC1H 0QP.
Tel: 0171–273–1555; fax: 0171–383–0273

**Wembley Stadium** HA9 0DZ.
Tel: 0181–902–8833

## *Sport and society*

**Professor Eric Dunning** and **John Williams**, Leicester University LE1 7RH.
Tel: 0116–252–2736, Professor Dunning; 0116–252–2745, John Williams

## AMERICAN FOOTBALL

**British American Football Association**, 567 Kings Road, Stretford,
Manchester M32 8JQ.
Tel: 0161–864–1250

## ANGLING

**Anglers Conservation Association**, 6 Castlegate, Grantham, NG31 6SU.
Tel: 01476–61008

**Anglers Mail**, London SE1.
Tel: 0171–261–5778; fax: 261–6016

**Angling Times, Trout and Salmon Magazine**, both at Bretton Court,
Peterborough PE3 8DZ.
Tel: 01733–264666; fax 265515

**National Federation of Anglers**, Halliday House, Eggington Junction,
Derby DE65 6GU.
Tel: 01283–734735; fax: 01283–734799

**Environment Agency**, see under regions

## ARCHERY

**Grand National Archery Society**, 7th Street, National Agricultural.
Centre, Stoneleigh CV8 2LG.
Tel: 01203–696631; fax: 01203–4196662

## ATHLETICS

**Amateur Athletic Association of England**, 225A Bristol Road, Edgbaston, Birmingham B5 7UB.
Tel: 0121–440–5000; fax: 0121–440–0555

**Athletics Weekly**, Bretton Court, Peterborough PE3 8DZ.
Tel: 01733–264666; fax: 01733–265515

**British Athletics Federation**, 225A Bristol Road, Birmingham B5 7UB.
Tel: 0121–440–5000; fax: 0121–440–0555

## BADMINTON

**Badminton Association of England**, National Badminton Centre, Milton Keynes MK8 9LA.
Tel: 01908–568822; fax: 566922

## BASKETBALL

**English Basketball Association**, 48 Bradford Road, Stanningley LS28 6DF.
Tel: 0113–236–1166; fax: 0113–236–1022

## BOWLS

**Bowls International**, PO Box 100, Stamford PE9 1XQ.
Tel: 01780–55131; fax: 01780–57261

**English Bowling Federation**, 62 Frampton Place, Boston PE21 8EL.
Tel: 01205–366201

### *Crown green*

**British Crown Green Bowling Association**, 14 Leighton Avenue, Maghull, Liverpool L31 0AH.
Tel: 0151–526–8367

**Bowlers World**, 64 Greenfield Road, St Helens WA10 6SL.
Tel: 01744–731314; fax: 01744–27586

# BOXING

Reference: *British Boxing Yearbook.*

**Amateur Boxing Association**, Crystal Palace National Sports Centre, London SE19 2BB.
Tel: 0181–778–0251; fax: 0181–778–9324

**Boxing Monthly**, 24 Notting Hill Gate, London W11 3JE.
Tel: 0171–229–9944; fax: 0171–727–5442

**British Boxing Board of Control**, 52A Borough High Street, London SE1 1XW.
Tel: 0171–403–5879; fax: 0171–378–6670

## *Dangers*

**British Medical Association**.
Tel: 0171–387–4499, press

# CANOEING

**British Canoe Union**, John Dudderidge House, Adbolton Lane, West Bridgford NG2 5AS.
Tel: 0115–982–1100; fax: 0115–982–1797

# CAVING

**National Caving Association**, White Lion House, Ynys Uchaf, Ystradgynlais SA9 1RW.
Tel: 01639–849519

# CRICKET

Reference: *Wisden's Cricketers' Almanac* (includes previous season's Test matches anywhere in the world).
*Benson and Hedges Cricket Year* (Headline: £19.99).
*Cricketers' Who's Who.*
*Playfair Cricket Annual* (pocket-sized).

**Club Cricket Conference**, 361 West Barnes Lane, New Malden KT3 6JF.
Tel: 0181–949–4001; fax: 0181–336–0537

**Cricket Council**, Lords, London NW8 8QN.
Tel: 0171–286–4405

**Marylebone Cricket Club**, Lord's, St John's Wood Road, London NW8 8QN.
Tel: 0171–289–1611; fax: 0171–266–3459

**National Cricket Association**, Lord's, St John's Wood Road, London NW8 8QZ. Governing body for recreational cricket.
Tel: 0171–289–6098; fax: 0171–266–4022

**Test and County Cricket Board**, Lord's, St John's Wood Road, London NW8 8QN.
Tel: 0171–286–4405

**The Cricketer**, Beech Hanger, Ashurst TN3 9ST.
Tel: 01892–740256; fax: 01892–740588

**Women's Cricket Association**, Warwicks CCC, Edgbaston Road, Birmingham B5 7QX.
Tel: 0121–440–0520; fax: 0121–446–6344

**Wisden Cricket Monthly**, Down Road, Guildford GU1 2PY.
Tel: 01483–570358; fax: 01483–33153


## CROQUET

**Croquet Association**, Hurlingham Club, Ranelagh Gardens, London SW6 3PR.
Tel: 0171–736–3148; fax: 0171–736–3148


## CYCLING

See page 229.


## DRUGS AND SPORT

**Drug Control Centre**, King's, London.
Tel: 0171–836–5454, ext. 3202, PR

**Ivan Waddington**, Department of Sociology, Leicester University.
Tel: 0116–252–2735

# FENCING

**Amateur Fencing Association**, 33 Rothschild Road, London W4 5HT.
Tel: 0181–742–3032; fax: 0181–742–3033

# FIELD SPORTS

**British Field Sports Society**, 59 Kennington Road, London SE1 7PZ.
Tel: 0171–928–4742

**League Against Cruel Sports**, 83 Union Street, London SE1 1SG.
Tel: 0171–403–6155/407–0979

# FLYING

**British Microlight Aircraft Association**, The Bullring, Deddington,
Banbury OX15 0TT.
Tel: 01869–338888; fax: 337116

**Popular Flying Association**, Terminal Building, Shoreham Airport BN43
5FF.
Tel: 01273–461616; fax: 01273–463390

**Royal Aero Club**, and **British Gliding Association**, 47 Vaughan Way,
Leicester LE1 4SG.
Tel: 0116–253–1051; fax: 0116–251–5939

# GOLF

Reference: *The Royal and Ancient Golfers' Handbook.*
*Benson and Hedges Golf Year.*

**English Golf Union**, 1 Upper King Street, Leicester LE1 6XF.
Tel: 0116–255–3042; fax: 0116–247–1322

**Golf Foundation** (encourages young players), Hanbury Manor, Ware
SG12 0UH.
Tel: 01920–484044; fax: 01920–484055

**Golf Monthly**, King's Reach Tower, Stamford Street, London SE1 9LS.
Tel: 0171–261–7237; fax: 0171–261–7240

**Golf World Magazine**, 37 Millharbour, London E14 9TX.
Tel: 0171–538–1031; fax: 0171–538–4106

**Ladies Golf Union**, The Scores, St Andrews KY16 9AT.
Tel: 01334–475811; fax: 01334–472818

**Professional Golfers Association**, The Belfry, Sutton Coldfield B76 9PT.
Tel: 01675–470333

**PGA European Tour**, Wentworth, Surrey.
Tel: 01344–842881

**Royal and Ancient Golf Club**, 16 The Links, St Andrews KY16 9JD.
Governing body of golf and organizer of the Open.
Tel: 01334–472112

## GREYHOUND RACING

**National Greyhound Racing Club**, 24 Oval Road, London N21.
Tel: 0171–267–9256; fax: 0171–482–1023

## GYMNASTICS

**British Amateur Gymnastics Association**, Ford Hall, Lilleshall National
Sports Centre, Newport TF10 9NB.
Tel: 01952–820330; fax: 820326

## HANG GLIDING

**British Hang Gliding and Paragliding Association**, Loughborough Road,
Leicester LE4 5PJ.
Tel: 0116–261–1322; fax: 0116–261–1323

## HOCKEY

**All England Women's Hockey Association**, 51 High Street, Shrewsbury
SY1 1ST.
Tel: 01743–233572; fax: 01743–233583

**Hockey Association**, Norfolk House, 102 Saxon Gate West, Milton
Keynes MK9 2EP.
Tel: 01908–241100; fax: 241106

*Street hockey*

**British Skater Hockey Association**, Grammont, Chiddingley Road, Horam, Heathfield TN21 0JH.
Tel: 01435–32359

**Inline Hockey International**, 5n Peabody Buildings, Duchy Street, London SE1 8DS.
Tel: 0171–261–9878

# ICE HOCKEY

**British Ice Hockey Association**, 2nd Floor, 517 Christchurch Road, Bournemouth BH1 4AG.
Tel: 01202–303946; fax: 01202–398005

# ICE SKATING

**National Ice Skating Association of UK**, 15 Gee Street, London EC1V 3RE.
Tel: 0171–253–3824; fax: 0171–490–2589

# JUDO

**British Judo Association**, 7a Rutland Street, Leicester LE1 1RB.
Tel: 0116–255–9669; fax: 0116–255–9660

# KABADDI (INDIAN FIELD GAME)

**National Kabaddi Association**, 7 Holling Mill Close, Edgbaston, Birmingham B5 7OO.
Tel: 0121–446–4642; fax: 0121–446–4410

# KARATE

**British Karate Federation**, Kilgetty, Dyfed.
Tel: 01834–813776

**English Karate Governing Body**, 58 Bloomfield Drive, Bath BA2 2BG.
Tel: 01225–834008

## MOTOR CYCLING

**Auto-Cycle Union**.
Tel: 01788–540519; fax: 573585

**Speedway Control Board**, Wood Street, Rugby, CV21 2YX
Tel and fax: 01788–540960

## MOTOR SPORT

**British Touring Car Championship**.
Tel: 01280–706866

**FIA** (Federation Internationale de l'Automobile), Paris.
Tel: 00–331–43–12–44–71, press

**Formula One Constructors Association**, 6 Princes Gate, London SW7 1QJ.
Tel: 0171–584–6668

**McLaren**, Woking Business Park.
Tel: 01483–728211

**RAC Motor Sports Association**, Riverside Park, Colnbrook SL3 0HG.
Tel: 01753–681736; fax: 01753–682938

**Williams Grand Prix Engineering**, Basil Hill Road, Didcot.
Tel: 01235–815161

## MOUNTAINEERING

**British Mountaineering Council**, 177 Burton Road, West Didsbury,
Manchester M20 2BB.
Tel: 0161–445–4747; fax: 0161–445–4500

## NETBALL

**All England Netball Association**, 9 Paynes Park, Hitchin SG5 1EH.
Tel: 01462–442344; fax: 01462–442343

## OLYMPICS

**British Olympic Association**, Church Row, Wandsworth Plain, London
SW18 1ES.
Tel: 0181–871–2677/870–3690; fax: 0181–871–9104

## PARACHUTING

**British Parachute Association**, 5 Wharf Way, Glen Parva, Leicester LE2 9TF.
Tel: 0116–278–5271; fax: 0116–247–7662

## PIGEON RACING

**Royal Pigeon Racing Association**, The Reddings, Cheltenham GL51 6RN.
Tel: 01452–713529; fax: 01452–857119

**Rod Adams**, Newcastle University NE1 7RU.
Tel: 0191–222–6000, ext. 7008

## POLO

**Hurlingham Polo Association**, Winterlake, Kirtlington, Kidlington OX5 3HG.
Tel: 01869–350044; fax: 01869–350625

## POOL

**English Pool Association**, 44 Jones House, Penkridge Street, Walsall WS2 8JX.
Tel: 01922–35587

## RACING

Reference: *Racehorses of the Year.*
*Horses in Training.*
*Directory of the Turf.*

**British Horse Racing Board**, 42 Portman Square, London W1H 0EN.
Tel: 0171–396–0011

**The Jockey Club**, 42 Portman Square, London W1H 0EN.
Tel: 0171–486–4921/935–5984

**Thoroughbred Breeders Association**, Stanstead House, The Avenue, Newmarket CB8 9AA.
Tel: 01638–661321; fax: 01638–665621

## REAL TENNIS

**Tennis and Rackets Association**, Queen's Club, Palliser Road, West Kensington, London.
Tel: 0171–386–3448; fax: 0171–385–7424

## RIDING

**Association of British Riding Schools**, Old Brewery Yard, Penzance TR18 2SL.
Tel: 01736–69440/51390

**British Horse Society** (also the **Pony Club**), Stoneleigh Park, Kenilworth CV8 2LR.
Tel: 01203–696697; fax: 01203–696867

**British Show Jumping Association**, British Equestrian Centre, Stoneleigh CV8 2LR.
Tel: 01203–696516; fax: 696685

## ROLLER SKATING

**Federation of Roller Skating**, Lilleshall National Sports Centre, Newport (Salop) TF10 9AT.
Tel: 01952–825253; fax: 01952–825228

### *Rollerblading*

**British Inline Skating Association**.
Tel: 0171–384–2233

## ROWING

**Amateur Rowing Association**, 6 Lower Mall, London W6 9DJ.
Tel: 0181–748–3632; fax: 0181–741–4658

## RUGBY LEAGUE

Reference: *Rothman's Rugby League Yearbook* (Headline: £16.99).

**Rugby Football League**, Redhall House, Redhall Lane, Leeds LS17 8NB.
Tel: 0113–232–9111

# RUGBY UNION

Reference: *Rothman's Rugby Union Yearbook* (Headline: £16.99).

**Rugby Football Union**, Rugby Road, Twickenham TW1 1DZ.
Tel: 0181–892–8161; fax: 0181–892–9816

**Rugby World Magazine**, 17 College Avenue, Maidenhead SL6 6BX.
Tel: 01628–776433

# SAILING

**Royal Yachting Association**, Romsey Road, Eastleigh SO50 9YA.
Tel: 01703–629962; fax: 01703–629924

# SHOOTING

**British Association for Shooting and Conservation**, Marford Mill,
Rossett, Wrexham LL12 0HL.
Tel: 01244–570881; fax: 01244–571678

**National Rifle Association**, Bisley, Brookwood, Woking GU24 0PB.
Tel: 01483–797777; fax: 01483–797285

**National Small-Bore Rifle Association**.
Tel: 01483–476969; fax: 476392

## Clay pigeon shooting

**Clay Pigeon Shooting Association**, 107 Epping New Road, Buckhurst
Hill IG9 5TQ.
Tel: 0181–505–6221/2; fax: 0181–506–0739

# SKI-ING

**British Association of Ski Instructors**, Aviemore.
Tel: 01479–861717

**British Ski Federation**, 258 Main Street, East Calder EH53 0EE.
Tel: 01506–884343; fax: 01506–882952

**Erna Low Consultants**, 9 Reece Mews, SW7 3HE (represents seventeen French resorts).
Tel: 0171–584–2841; fax: 0171–589–9531

## SNOOKER

**Snooker Scene Magazine**, 202 Hagley Road, Edgbaston B16 9PQ.
Tel: 0121–454–2931; fax: 0121–452–1822

**World Professional Billiards and Snooker Association**, 27 Oakfield Road, Clifton, Bristol BS8 2AT.
Tel: 0117–974–4491; fax: 974–4931

## SOCCER

Reference: *Official Football Association Yearbook* (published by Macmillan: useful for addresses and phone numbers).
*Rothman's Football Yearbook* (Headline, £16.99) lists managers and gives details of all English League clubs and players and Scottish, European and non-league football.
*Endsleigh Football Club Directory.*
*World Soccer*, Guy Oliver.
*News of the World Football Annual* and *Playfair Football Annual* (both pocket-sized).

**Centre for Football Research**, Leicester University LE1 7RH.
Tel: 0116–252–2731, Patrick Murphy; 0116–252–2745, John Williams

**FA Women's Football Co-ordinator**, 9 Wyllyotts Place, Potters Bar EN6 2JD.
Tel: 01707–651840; fax: 01707–644190

**Football Association**, 16 Lancaster Gate, London W2 3LW.
Tel: 0171–262–4542; fax: 0171–402–0486

**Football League**, 319 Clifton Drive South, Lytham St Anne's FY8 1JG.
Tel: 01253–729421; fax: 01253–724786

**World Soccer Magazine**, Kings Reach Tower, Stamford Street, London SE1 9LS.
Tel: 0171–261–6488

# SPORTS MEDICINE

**British Association of Sport and Medicine**, c/o John Clegg, 67 Springfield Lane, Eccleston, WA10 5HB.
Tel: 01744–28198; fax: 01744–28198

**Institute of Sports Medicine**, Burlington House, Piccadilly, London W1V 0LG.
Tel: 0171–287–5269

# SWIMMING

**Amateur Swimming Federation of Great Britain**, Harold Fern House, Derby Square, Loughborough LE11 0AL.
Tel: 01509–230431; fax: 610720

**Royal Life Saving Society UK**, Mountbatten House, Studley, Warwicks B80 7NN. Trains lifeguards.
Tel: 01527–853943; fax: 01527–854453

# TABLE TENNIS

**English Table Tennis Association**, 3rd Floor, Queensbury House, Havelock Road, Hastings TN34 1HF.
Tel: 01424–722525; fax 422103

# TENNIS

Reference: *ITA Official Handbook.*
*World of Tennis.*

**All-England Lawn Tennis and Croquet Club**, Church Road, London SW19 5AE.
Tel: 0181–946–2244

**Lawn Tennis Association**, Queens Club, Barons Court, London W14 9EG.
Tel: 0171–381–7000; fax: 0171–381–5965

# VOLLEYBALL

**English Volleyball Association**, 27 South Road, West Bridgford, Nottingham NG2 7AG.
Tel: 0115–981–6324; fax: 0115–945–5429

## WATER SKI-ING

**British Water Ski Federation**, 390 City Road, London EC1V 2QA.
Tel: 0171–833–2855; fax: 0171–837–5879


## WEIGHTLIFTING

**British Amateur Weight Lifters Association**, 3 Iffley Turn, Oxford OX4
4DU.
Tel: 01865–778319; fax: 01865–778319


## WINDSURFING

**RYA Windsurfing**, RYA House, Romsey Road, Eastleigh SO50 9YA.
Tel: 01703–627962; fax: 01703–629924


## WRESTLING

**British Amateur Wrestling Association (and English Olympic)**, 41 Great
Clowes Street, Salford M7 9RQ.
Tel: 0161–832–9209; fax: 833–1120


# TOURISM, TRAVEL, HOTELS

**HVS International**, 34 Brooks Street, W1Y 1YA. Publishes tourism
studies.
Tel: 0171–495–5056

**Professor Kit Jenkins**, Scottish Hotel School, Strathclyde University,
Glasgow G1 1XQ.
Tel: 0141–522–4400, ext. 3940

**Oxford Centre for Tourism and Leisure Studies**, Oxford Brookes
University, Oxford.
Tel: 01865–483432

**World Travel and Tourism Council**, 4 Suffolk Place, Haymarket,
London SW1Y 4BS.
Tel: 0171–222–1955; fax 0171–222–4983

# HOLIDAYS IN BRITAIN

**British Resorts Association**, Southport.
Tel: 0151–934–2286

**British Tourist Authority** and **English Tourist Board**, Thames Tower,
Black's Road, London W6 9EL.
Tel: 0181–563–3037/5; fax: 563–3029;
e-mail: 101512.2651@compuserve.com

**Holidays One-Parents**, 51 Hampshire Road, Droylesden, Manchester
M43 7PH.
Tel: 0161–370–0337

# HOTELS

**Best Western Hotels**, 143 London Road, Kingston upon Thames KT2
6NA.
Tel: 0181–541–0050; fax: 0181–546–1638

**Hilton International**, Rhodes Way, Watford WD2 4YW.
Tel: 01923–231333; fax: 01923–233358

**Hotel and Catering Management School**, Oxford Brookes University,
Oxford.
Tel: 01865–483800

**Hotel and Catering Training Company**, International House, High
Street, London W5 5SA.
Tel: 0181–579–2400

**Hotel, Catering and Institutional Management Association**, 191 Trinity
Road, London SW17 7HN.
Tel: 0181–672–4251; fax: 0181–682–1707

**Scottish Hotel School**, Strathclyde University, Glasgow G1 1XQ.
Tel: 0141–552–4400; fax: 0141–552–1576

# TOUR OPERATORS

**Federation of Tour Operators**.
Tel: 01273–477722

**Saga Holidays**, Middleburg Square, Folkestone CT20 1AZ.
Tel: 01303–711111; fax: 01303–220391

**Thomson Holidays**, Greater London House, Hampstead Road, London NW1 7SD.
Tel: 0171–387–9321

## TRAVEL AGENTS

**ARTAC** (Alliance of Independent Travel Agents), Herlington, Orton Malbourne PE2 5PR.
Tel: 01733–390900; fax: 01733–390997

**Association of British Travel Agents**, 55 Newman Street, London W1P 4AH.
Tel: 0171–637–2444

## TRAVEL TO DISTANT PLACES

**Abercrombie and Kent**, Sloane Square House, Holbein Place, London SW1W 8NS.
Tel: 0171–730–9600

**Centre for Advancement of Responsive Travel**, 70 Dry Hill Park Road, Tonbridge TN10 3BX.
Tel: 01732–352757

**Dr Tim Forsyth**, Geography, London School of Economics, London WC2A 2AE.
Tel: 0171–955–6061; e-mail: t.forsyth@lse.ac.uk.

**Tourism Concern**, Southlands College, Wimbledon Parkside, London SW19 5NN.
Tel: 0181–944–0464

### *Ecological tourist-volunteers*

**Earthwatch**, Belsyre Court, Observatory Street, Oxford.
Tel: 01865–516366

### *Health*

**Medical Advisory Service for Travellers Abroad** (MASTA), Keppel Street, WC1E 6HJ.
Tel: 0171–631–4408; fax: 0171–323–4547

# 5 THE COUNTRYSIDE

## ANIMALS

**Animal Ecology Research Group**, Zoology, South Parks Road, Oxford OX1 3PS.
Tel: 01865–271190; fax: 01865–310447

**British Hedgehog Preservation Society**, Knowbury House, Knowbury, Ludlow SY8 3LQ.
Tel: 01584–890287

**Fauna and Flora International.**
Tel: 01223–461471

**Mammal Society**, 15 Cloisters Business Centre, 8 Battersea Park Road, London SW8 4BG.
Tel: 0171–498–4358; fax: 0171–498–4459

**Zoological Society of London**, Regents Park, London NW1 4RY.
Tel: 0171–722–3333

## ANIMAL HEALTH

**British Small Animals Veterinary Association**, Church Lane, Shurdington, Cheltenham GL51 5TQ.
Tel: 01242–862994; fax: 01242–863009

**British Veterinary Association**, 7 Mansfield Street, London WIM 0AT.
Tel: 0171–636–6541

**Clinical Veterinary Department**, Cambridge University.
Tel: 01223–337600

**Institute for Animal Disease Research**, Houghton, Huntingdon PE17 9XX.
Tel: 01480–464176

**Institute for Animal Health**, Ash Road, Pirbright GU24 0NF.
Tel: 01483–232441; fax: 01483–232448

**Royal Veterinary College**, London.
Tel: 0171–468–5000

## ANIMAL POWER

**Draught Animal News**, Centre for Tropical Veterinary Medicine, Easter
Bush, Roslin EH25 9RG.
Tel: 0131–650–6216

## ANIMAL WELFARE

**The Royal Society for the Prevention of Cruelty to Animals** has local
inspectors throughout the country.

**Advocates for Animals**, 10 Queensferry Street, Edinburgh EH2 4PG.
Tel: 0131–225–6039; fax: 0131–220–6377

**Animal Concern**, 62 Old Dumbarton Road, Glasgow G3 8RE.
Tel: 0141–334–6014; fax: 0141–445–6470

**Cats Protection League**, 17 Kings Road, Horsham RM13 5PN.
Tel: 01403–261947; fax: 01403–218414

**International Fund for Animal Welfare**, Tubwell House, New Road,
Crowborough TN6 2QH.
Tel: 01892–663374

**National Canine Defence League.**
Tel: 0171–837–0006

**Royal Society for the Prevention of Cruelty to Animals**, The Causeway,
Horsham RH12 1HG.
Tel: 01403–264181

**Universities Federation for Animal Welfare**, 8 Hamilton Close, South
Mimms, Herts EN6 3QD. Seeks to improve conditions of animals.
Tel: 01707–658202; fax: 01707–649279

# APES

**Biological Anthropology**, Dr Phyllis Lee, Downing Street, Cambridge
CB2 3DZ.
Tel: 01223–335459/54

# CATS

**Cat Fancy**, 4 Penel Orlieu, Bridgwater TA6 3PG.
Tel: 01278–427575

# DEER

**British Deer Society**, Church Farm, Lower Basildon, Reading RG8
9NH.
Tel: 01734–844094

# DOGS

**Crufts**, 1 Clarges Street, London W1Y 8AB.
Tel: 0171–493–7838

**Dogs Monthly**, Ascot House, High Street, Ascot SL5 7JG.
Tel: 01784–431599; fax: 01784–471538

# ELEPHANTS

**Zoology Department**, Dr Keith Eltringham, Cambridge University.
Tel: 01223–334455/336600

**World Wide Fund for Nature**, Panda House, Weyside Park, Godalming
GU7 1XR.
Tel: 01483–426444

# HORSES

**British Equine Veterinary Association**, Hartham Park, Corsham SN13
0QB.
Tel: 01249–715723; fax: 01249–701026

## PETS

**Pet Trade and Industry Association**, Bedford Business Centre, 170 Mile End Road, MK42 9TW.
Tel: 01234–273933; fax: 01234–273550

## WHALES AND DOLPHINS

**Environmental Investigation Agency**, 15 Bowling Green Lane, London EC1R 0BD.
Tel: 0171–490–7040

**Whale and Dolphin Conservation Society**, 19A James St West, Bath.
Tel: 01225–334511; fax: 01225–480097

## BIRDS

Reference: *Handbook of Birds of Europe, Middle East and North Africa.*

### *National sources*

**British Ornithologists Union**, c/o Zoological Museum, Tring HP23 6AP.
Tel: 01442–890080

**British Trust for Ornithology**, The Nunnery, Nunnery Place, Thetford IP24 2PU. (Bird watchers' organization.)
Tel: 01842–750050; fax: 01842–750030.

**Hawk and Owl Trust**, c/o Zoological Society, London NW1 4RY.
Tel: 0171–722–3333

**International Council for Bird Preservation**, 32 Cambridge Road, Girton CB3 0PJ.
Tel: 01223–277318

**Royal Society for the Protection of Birds**, The Lodge, Sandy SG19 2DL. Regional offices are listed in regional pages.
Tel: 01767–680551

## BIRD TRADE

**Environmental Investigation Agency**, 15 Bowling Green Lane, London EC1R 0BD.
Tel: 0171–490–7040

## ENVIRONMENT

Local planning officers oversee local use of land. Public inquiries may be held into appeals against councils' planning decisions. Inspectors for these are appointed by the **Planning Inspectorate**, Bristol (press calls to the **Department of Environment**, tel: 0171–890–4607/8).

**Friends of the Earth** (see below) publishes The *A to Z of Local Pollution: Who to Contact Action Guide.*

Reference: *The World Directory of Environmental Organisations* is published by the California Institute of Public Affairs, fax: 00–1–916–442–2478.

*Who's Who in the Environment.*

### *National sources*

**Department of Environment**, Environment Press Desk, Eland House, Stag Place, London SW1E 5DU.
Tel (air quality): 0171–890–4621/2; fax: 0171–890–4619; tel (water and land): 0171–890–4631/3; fax: 890–4639

**Ministry of Agriculture**, Environment Press Desk, 3 Whitehall Place, London SW1A 2HH.
Tel: 0171–270–8094/8436; fax: 0171–270–8443/8440

**Biosphere Sciences Department**, King's College, Campden Hill Road, London W8 7AH.
Tel: 0171–333–4317

**Botanic Gardens Conservation Secretariat**, 199 Kew Road, Richmond, Surrey TW9 3BW.
Tel: 0181–948–8827

**British Ecological Society**, 26 Blades Court, Deodar Road, Putney, London SW15 2NU.
Tel: 0181–871–9797; fax: 871–9779

**Centre for Environmental Technology**, Imperial College, London SW7 2PE.
Tel: 0171–594–9283; fax: 0171–581–0245; e-mail: v.james@ic.ac.uk

**Durrell Institute of Conservation and Ecology**, Kent University, Canterbury CT2 7NX.
Tel: 01227–451805, university PR

**Conservation Foundation**, 1 Kensington Gore, London SW7 2AT.
Tel: 0171–823–8842

**Environment Agency** (new agency to administer rivers, pollution, waste).
Tel: 0171–276–4109/4369/0504

**Environment Council**, 21 Elizabeth Street, SW1W 9RH. Independent forum.
Tel: 0171–824–8411

**Environmental Investigation Agency**, 15 Bowling Green Lane, London EC1R 0BD.
Tel: 0171–490–7040

**Environmental Resources Management**, 166 Gloucester Place, London W1H 3DB.
Tel: 0171–465–7200

**Environmental Resources**, Salford University, Manchester M5 4WT.
Tel: 0161–745–5221

**Environmental Science Department**, Professor M. Seaward, Bradford University, Richmond Road, BD7 1DP.
Tel: 01274–384212; fax: 01274–305340

**Environmental Science Institute**, Lancaster University, LA1 4YQ.
Tel: 01524–593838; fax: 01524–843854

**Friends of the Earth**, 26 Underwood Street, London N1 7JQ.
Tel: 0171–490–1555

**Gaia Foundation**, 18 Well Walk, London NW3 1LD.
Tel: 0171–435–5000; fax: 0171–431–0551

**Global Security Programme**, Free School Lane, Cambridge CB2 3RQ.
Tel: 01223–334509

**Greenpeace**, Canonbury Villas, London N1 2PN.
Tel: 0171–354–5100

**Institute of Terrestrial Ecology**, Monks Wood, Abbots Ripton PE17 2LS.
Tel: 01487–773381

**Institute of Terrestrial Ecology**, Bush Estate, Penicuik, Midlothian EH26 0QB.
Tel: 0131–445–4343; fax: 0131–445–3943

**International Institute for Environment and Development**, 3 Endsleigh Street, London WC1H 0DD.
Tel: 0171–388–2117; fax: 0171–388–2826

**Royal Commission on Environmental Pollution**, Church House, Great Smith Street, London SW1P 3BL. Produced Transport and Environment (Cmmnd number 2674, HMSO £25.60).
Tel: 0171–276–2080

**UK Ecolabelling Board**, 7th Floor, 30 Albert Embankment, London SE1 7TL.
Tel: 0171–820–1199; fax: 0171–820–1104


## ACID RAIN

**Dr Sarah Metcalfe** and **Dr J.D.Whyatt**, Geography, Hull University.
Tel: 01482–466341, Dr Metcalfe; 01482–465352, Dr Whyatt; e-mail: j.d.whyatt@uk.ac.hull.geo

**Professor David Littlejohn**, Chemistry, Strathclyde University, Glasgow G1 1XQ.
Tel: 0141–552–4400, ext. 2067


## CLIMATE/GLOBAL WARMING

Reference: Sir John Houghton: *Global Warming* (Lion: £12.99).

**Atmospheric, Oceanic and Planetary Physics**, Professor Fred Taylor, Clarendon Laboratory, Parks Road, Oxford OX1 3PU.
Tel: 01865–272903

**Centre for Global Atmosphere Modelling**, Dr Mike Blackburn, Reading University RG6 2AU.
Tel: 01734–318327

**Centre for Social and Economic Research on Global Environment**, East Anglia University, Norwich NR4 7TJ.
Tel: 01603–592840; fax: 250588

**Centre for Study of Environmental Change**, Lancaster LA1 4YN.
Tel: 01524–592655

**Climate Change Secretariat**, 11 chemin des Anemones, POB 76, CH-1219 Chatelaine.
Tel: 00–41–22–979–9111; fax: 00–41–22–797–3420

**Climate Research Unit**, East Anglia University, Norwich NR4 7TJ.
Tel: 01603–592722; fax: 01603–507784

**Energy and Environmental Research Programme**, Chatham House, 10 St James's Square, London SW1.
Tel: 0171–957–5700

**Environmental Change Unit**, 1A Mansfield Road, Oxford OX1 3TB.
Tel: 01865–281180

**European Medium Range Weather Forecast Centre**, Shinfield Park, Reading.
Tel: 01734–876000

**Global Environmental Change Programme**, Wye College, Ashford, Kent TN25 5AH.
Tel: 01233–812401; fax: 01233–813187

**Global Environment Research Office**, Polaris House, North Star Avenue, Swindon SN2 1EU.
Tel: 01793–411734; fax: 0793–411691

**Meteorological Office**, London Road, Bracknell RG12 2SZ.
Tel: 01344–854629/856255, press; fax: 01344–856087;
e-mail: metpress@meto.gov.uk

**Meteorology Department**, Reading University, Whiteknights RG6 2AU.
Tel: 01734–318954

**TIGER Programme**, Institute of Hydrology, Wallingford OX10 8BB.
Tel: 01491–692211; fax: 01491–692430; e-mail: tiger@ioh.ac.uk.

## *Politics*

**Dr Ian Rowlands, Development Studies Institute**, LSE, Houghton Street, London WC2A 2AE.
Tel: 0171–955–7479

## COASTS

**Dr Chris Frid, Marine Sciences**, Newcastle.
Tel: 0191–252–4850

## DESERTIFICATION/DRY LANDS

**Centre for Arid Zone Studies**, University of Wales, Bangor LL57 2UW.
Tel: 01248–351151

**Centre for International Drylands Research**, Professor David Thomas, Sheffield University.
Tel: 0114–282–4763

**Professor A. Millington**, Geography, Leicester University.
Tel: 0116–252–3830

## LAW

**Environmental Law Association**, Steven Tromans, Simmons and Simmons, 21 Wilson Street, EC2M 2TX.
Tel: 0171–628–2020; fax: 2070

**Environmental Law Committee of Law Society.**
Tel: 0171–320–5810, press

## NOISE

**Association of Noise Consultants**, 6 Trap Road, Guilden Morden, near Royston SG8 0JE.
Tel: 01763–852958

## OZONE

**Chemical Laboratories**, Cambridge University.
Tel: 01223–336300; fax: 01223–336362

**Institute of Environmental Sciences**, Lancaster University LA1 4YQ.
Tel: 01524–65201, ext. 5828

### CFC substitutes

**ICI Klea**, PO Box 11, The Heath, Runcorn WA7 4QF.
Tel: 01928–513213; fax: 01928–511418

### Low-level ozone and health

See AIR POLLUTION, page 201.

### Stratospheric ozone

**European Ozone Research**, Cambridge.
Tel: 01223–311772.

Also **British Antarctic Survey**, Madingley Road, Cambridge CB3 0ET.
Tel: 01223–251414, PR; fax: 01223–302093

### Effect on plants

**Dr Peter Lumsden**, Applied Biology, University of Central Lancashire, Preston PR1 2HE.
Tel: 01772–893510

## PESTS

**British Pest Control Association**, 3 St James' Court, Friar Gate, Derby DE1 1ZU.
Tel: 01332–294288; fax: 295904

**Rentokil**, Felcourt, East Grinstead RH19 2JY.
Tel: 01342–833022; fax: 01342–326229

## POLLUTION

**Environment Agency for England and Wales**, London SE1 7TJ.
Tel: 0171–840–6143, press; fax: 0171–582–8240

### Air

See page 201.

### North Sea

**Jane Hunt**, Lancaster University.
Tel: 01524–592677

## RECYCLING

**Recycling Council**, 56 Front Street East, Bedlington NE22 5AB.
Tel: 01670–530770; fax: 01670–530014

**Waste Watch** (national agency for recycling).
Tel: 0171–248–1818

**James Donaldson, Waste Exchange Services**, 70 Brunswick Street, Stockton-on-Tees. Organizes re-use of industrial waste.
Tel: 01642–677169; fax: 01642–603726

## SCIENCE AND ENVIRONMENTAL POLICY

**Jane Hunt**, Lancaster University.
Tel: 01524–592677


## WASTE

**Packaging and Industrial Films Association**, The Fountain Precinct, 1 Balm Green, Sheffield S1 3AF.
Tel: 0114–276–6789

**Waste and Environment Today Magazine**, AEA Technology, Building 7.12, Harwell OX11 0RA.
Tel: 01235–433484

**Waste Management International**, 3 Shortlands, London W6 8DA. British branch of US firm.
Tel: 0181–563–7000


## FARMING

The National Farmers Union has county branches, and the farm advisory service, ADAS, has local representatives. Farmers often join in co-operatives to buy supplies or to sell produce. Also important for livestock farmers are local auction markets and breed societies.

You may have an agricultural college in your area.


### *National sources*

**ADAS**, Oxford Spires Business Park, Kidlington OX5 1NZ. National farm advice service.
Tel: 01865–842742; fax: 01865–845030

**Centre for Agricultural Strategy**, University, 1 Earley Gate, Reading RG6 2AT.
Tel: 01734–318152/150; fax: 0734–353423

**Farming Information Centre**, National Farmers Union, Agriculture House, London SW1X 7NU. Has picture library.
Tel: 0171–235–5077

**National Institute of Agricultural Botany**, Huntingdon Road, Cambridge CB3 0LE. Offers seed services.
Tel: 01223–276381; fax: 01223–277602

**Royal Agricultural Society**, Stoneleigh.
Tel: 01203–696969

**Cranfield University**, Silsoe MK45 4DT.
Tel: 01525–863000

**Wye College**, Ashford, Kent TN25 5AH.
Tel: 01233–812401

## BEES

**Bees for Development**, Troy, Monmouth NP5 4AB.
Tel: 01600–713648; fax: 01600–716167

**British Bee-Keepers Association**, National Agricultural Centre,
Stoneleigh CV8 2LZ.
Tel: 01203–696679

**Dr William Kirk**, Biological sciences, Keele University, ST5 5BG.
Tel: 01782–621111, ext. 7091

## CROPS

See also page 141.

**Home Grown Cereals Authority**, Highgate Hill, N19 5PR.
Tel: 0171–263–3391; fax: 0171–561–6231

**Institute of Arable Crops Research, Broomsbarn**, Suffolk.
Tel: 01284–810363

**Long Ashton**, BS18 9AF.
Tel: 01275–392181

**Scottish Crop Research Institute**, Invergowrie, Dundee DD2 5DA.
Tel: 01382–562731; fax: 01382–562426

## DAIRY FARMING

**Centre for Dairy Research**, Agriculture, Reading University.
Tel: 01734–318471

**Holstein Friesian Society**, Scotsbridge House, Rickmansworth WD3 3BB.
Tel: 01923–774241; fax: 01923–770003

# ECONOMICS

**Agricultural Economics Department**, Manchester University, M13 9PL.
Tel: 0161–275–2112/4, university PR

**Agriculture, Economics and Management Department**, Reading
University, 4 Earley Gate, PO Box 237, Reading RG6 2AR.
Tel: 01734–875123, ext. 4028/9; fax: 352421

**Touche Ross**, Vincent Hedley Lewis, Peterborough Court, Fleet Street,
London EC4A 3JR.
Tel: 0171–936–3000

# FARM ANIMALS

For health, see pages 177 and 178.

**Ministry of Agriculture Animal-Welfare**, 2 Whitehall Place, London
SW1A 2HH. Also handles queries for Central Veterinary Laboratory.
Tel: 0171–270–8446/37/38, press; fax: 0171–270–8447

**Humane Slaughter Association**, 34 Blanche Lane, South Mimms, Herts
EN6 3PA.
Tel: 01707–659040; fax: 01707–649279

**Institute of Grassland and Environmental Research**, Plas Gogerddan,
Aberystwyth SY23 3EB.
Tel: 01970–828255; fax: 01970–828357

**Livestock Auctioneers Association**, Surveyor Court, Westwood Way,
Coventry CV4 8JE.
Tel: 0171–334–3832

**Meat and Livestock Commission**, Snowdon Drive, Winterhill, Milton
Keynes MK6 1AX.
Tel: 01908–677577

**Respect for Animals**, PO Box 500, Nottingham.
Tel: 0115–952–5440

## *Ducks*

**Cherry Valley Farms**, Rothwell, Lincolnshire. PR: Harris and Hunter.
Tel: 0181–892–2720; fax: 0181–892–2130

## *Export of live animals*

**Animal Transport Association**, PO Box 251, Redhill RH1 5FU.
Tel: 01737–822249; fax: 01737–822954

**Compassion in World Farming**, 5A Charles Street, Petersfield GU32 3EH.
Tel: 01730–268863; fax: 01730–260791; e-mail: @ciwf.win-uk.net

## *Feed*

**UKASTA**, 3 Whitehall Court, London SW1A 2EQ.
Tel: 0171–930–3611; fax: 0171–930–3952

## *Mad cow disease* (see also pages 177–8)

**Institute for Animal Health**, Pirbright GU24 0NF.
Tel: 01483–232441; fax: 01483–232448

**Professor Frank Owen**, Biological Sciences, Manchester University M13 9PL.
Tel: 0161–275–2112/4, press

## *Poultry*

**British Poultry Breeders and Hatcheries Association**, 52 High Holborn, London WC1V 6SX.
Tel: 0171–242–4683

**Lincolnshire College of Agriculture**, Caythorpe Court, Grantham NG32 3EP.
Tel: 01400–272521

## *Rare breeds*

**Rare Breeds Survival Trust**, National Agricultural Centre, Stoneleigh CV8 2LG.
Tel: 01203–696969

## *Turkeys*

**Bernard Matthews PLC**, Great Witchingham Hall.
Tel: 01603–872611

## FERTILIZERS

**Fertilizer Manufacturers Association**, Greenhill House, Thorpe Wood, Peterborough PE3 6GF.
Tel: 01733–331303; fax: 333617

**Soil Science Department**, University of Reading.
Tel: 01734–318911

# FRUIT

**Apple and Pear Research Council**, East Malling Research Station, ME19 6DZ.
Tel: 01732–844828; fax: 01732–844828

**Common Ground**, 41 Shelton Street, London WC2H 9HJ. Runs Save our Orchards campaign.
Tel: 0171–379–3109

**English Apples and Pears**, Brogdale Farm, Faversham.
Tel: 01795–530666

**English Fruit Company**, River House, Stour Street, Canterbury.
Tel: 01227–762200; fax: 01227–762210

# MARKETING

**Professor Christopher Ritson**, Agriculture Economics and Food Marketing, Newcastle University NE1 7RU.
Tel: 0191–222–6909

**Farm Shop and Pick-Your-Own Association**, SW1X 7NU.
Tel: 0171–235–5077, ext. 281

# ORGANIC FARMING

**British Organic Farmers and Organic Growers**, and **Soil Association**, 86 Colston Street, Bristol BS1 5BB.
Tel: 0117–929–0661; fax: 925–2504

**Henry Doubleday Research Association**, Ryton-on-Dunsmore CV8 3LG.
Tel: 01203–303517; fax: 01203–639229

# OSTRICHES

**British Domesticated Ostrich Association**, 14 Bank Street, Carlisle.
Tel: 01228–34423; fax: 01228–818022

# PEST CONTROL

**International Pesticide Directory**, Publications of London, 222 Maylands Avenue, Hemel Hempstead HP2 7TD.

**British Crop Protection Council**, 49 Downing Street, Farnham GU9 7PH.
Tel: 01252–733072; fax: 01252–727194

**Centre for Pest Management**, Imperial College, Silwood Park, Ascot SL5 7PY.
Tel: 01344–23911; fax: 01344–20094

**ICI Agrochemicals**, Fernhurst, Haslemere GU27 3JE.
Tel: 01428–655880, press

**International Institute of Biological Control**, Silwood Park, SL5 7TA.
Tel: 01344–872999; fax: 01344–872901

**Monsanto** (weedkiller manufacturer).
Tel: 01494–474918

**Pesticides Trust**, Eurolink Centre, 49 Effra Road, London SW2 1BZ (opposes pesticides).
Tel: 0171–274–8895

**Scottish Crop Research Institute**, Invergowrie, Dundee DD2 5DA.
Tel: 01382–562731; fax: 01382–562426


## PIGS

**Dr J.Chadwick**, Agriculture, Newcastle University.
Tel: 0191–222–6901

**Pig Farming Magazine**, 245 Blackfriars Road, London SE1 9UY.
Tel: 0171–921–5000


## TRACTORS

**Massey-Ferguson**, Banner Lane, Coventry CV4 9GF.
Tel: 01203–694400


## WHEAT

**John Innes Centre**, Colney Lane, Norwich NR4 7UJ.
Tel: 01603–452571


## YOUNG FARMERS

**National Federation of Young Farmers Clubs**, YFC Centre, National Agriculture Centre, Kenilworth CV8 2LG.
Tel: 01203–696544; fax: 696559

# FISH AND FISHING

**MAFF** (Ministry of Agriculture), Fisheries Press Desk, 2 Whitehall Place, London SW1A 2HH.
Tel: 0171–270–8025; fax: 0171–270–8447

**Hull University International Fisheries Institute**, Dr Keith Haywood, Hull HU6 7RX.
Tel: 01482–466420; fax: 01482–471835

**MacAlister Elliott and Partners**, 56 High Street, Lymington SO41 9AH.
Tel: 01590–679016

**Marine Laboratory**, PO Box 101, Victoria Road, Aberdeen AB9 8DB.
Tel: 01224–876544

**Nautilus Consultants**, 30 Elbe Street, Edinburgh EH6 7HW.
Tel: 0131–555–0660

**Renewable Resources Assessment Group**, Imperial College, London SW7.
Tel: 0171–589–5111

# FISH FARMING

**British Trout Association**, 10 Barley Mow Passage, London W4 4PH.
Tel: 0181–994–6477; fax: 0181–742–3080

**Institute of Aquaculture**, Stirling University FK9 4LA.
Tel: 01786–473171

## *Pollution from fish farms*

**Dr Ray Goulder**, Applied Biology, Hull University, HU6 7RX.
Tel: 01482–465161

# FORESTRY

**Association of Professional Foresters**, 7 West Street, Belford NE70 7QA.
Tel: 01668–213937; fax: 01668–213555

**Booker Countryside**, White Hall, Coppingford Road, Sawtry PE17 5XT.
Tel: 01487–832211; fax: 01487–831666

**British Christmas Tree Growers Association**, 12 Lauriston Road, Wimbledon SW19 4TQ.
Tel: 0181–946–2695; fax: 0181–947–0211

**Forestry Commission**, 231 Corstorphine Road, Edinburgh EH12 7AT.
Tel: 0131–334–0303; fax: 0131–334–4473

**Institute of Chartered Foresters**, 7A St Colme Street, Edinburgh EH12 6AA.
Tel: 0131–225–2705; fax: 0131–220–6128

**International Tree Foundation**, Sandy Lane, Crawley Down RH10 4HS.
Tel: 01342–712536; fax: 01342–712536

**Timber Growers Association**, 5 Dublin Street Lane South, Edinburgh EH1 3PX.
Tel: 0131–538–7111; fax: 0131–538–7222


## AGROFORESTRY

**Agricultural and Forest Sciences Department**, University of Wales, Bangor LL57 2UW.
Tel: 01248–351151


## FOREST SCIENCE AND RESEARCH

**Agricultural and Forest Sciences Department**, University of Wales, Bangor LL57 2UW.
Tel: 01248–351151

**Edinburgh Centre for Tropical Forests**, Darwin Building, Mayfield Road, Edinburgh EH9 3JU.
Tel: 0131–662–0752

**Forest Authority**, Forest Research Station, Alice Holt Lodge, Wrecclesham GU10 4LH.
Tel: 01420–22255

**Forestry Department**, Aberdeen University, St Machar Drive, Old Aberdeen AB9 2UD.
Tel: 01224–272670

**Oxford Forestry Institute**, South Parks Road, Oxford OX1 3RB.
Tel: 01865–275103/5000, press

# HORTICULTURE

**Professor Geoffrey Dixon, Scottish Agricultural College**, Auchencruive.
Tel: 01292–520331

**Horticulture and Landscape Department**, Reading University.
Tel: 01734–318071

**Horticulture Research International**, Wellesbourne, Warwick CV35 9EF.
Tel: 01789–470382; fax: 01789–470552

# MICROPROPAGATION OF PLANTS

**Professor Andy Roberts**, Life Sciences, University of East London, E15
4LZ.
Tel: 0181–590–7700

# NATURE

**British Reedgrowers Association**, Old Bank of England Court, Queen
Street, Norwich NR2 4TA.
Tel: 01603–629871

**British Trust for Conservation Volunteers**, 36 St Mary's Street,
Wallingford OX10 0EU. Has many local  groups.
Tel: 01491–839766; fax: 01491–839646

**Centre for Population Biology**, Imperial College, London SW7. Studies
plant and animal populations.
Tel: 0171–589–5111

**English Nature**, Northminster House, Peterborough PE1 1UA.
Tel: 01733–455000

**European Wildlife Division**, Department of Environment, Room 105,
Tollgate House, Houlton Street, Bristol BS2 9DJ.
Tel: 0117–987–8628

**Joint Nature Conservation Committee (for UK)**, Monkstone House,
City Road, Peterborough PE1 1JY.
Tel: 01733–62626; fax: 555948

**Natural History Museum**, Cromwell Road, London SW7 5BD. It
researches widely and is the British authority on identifying and classifying
wildlife. The plant conservation charity **Plantlife** is based at the museum.
Tel: 0171–938–8779/8895, press; fax: 0171–938–9066

**Royal Society for Nature Conservation**, Wickham Park, Waterside South, Lincoln LN5 7JR. National body for wildlife trusts.
Tel: 01522–544400; fax: 01522–511616

**World Wide Fund for Nature**, Godalming GU7 1XR.
Tel: 01483–426444

## BIODIVERSITY

**Royal Botanic Gardens**, Kew TW9 3AB.
Tel: 0181–332–5000

### *In Madagascar*

**Dr David Du Puy**
Tel: 0181–332–5237; M. Maunder, tel: 0181–332–5583

## BUTTERFLIES

**World Conservation Monitoring Centre**, 219 Huntingdon Road, Cambridge CB3 0DL.
Tel: 01223–277314; fax: 01223–277136

## CROCODILES

**World Conservation Monitoring Centre**, see above.

## INSECTS

**Entomology Department**, Natural History Museum, Cromwell Road, London SW7 5BD.
Tel: 0171–938–9451

**International Institute of Entomology**, 56 Queens Gate, London SW7 5JR.
Tel: 0171–584–0067

# RURAL AREAS

The countryside is a scene of growing controversy both over building and the lack of building as people from towns seek to live and work there.

Many local organizations are interested: parish councils, district (borough) councils, county councils and their planners, Ramblers Association branches, Women's Institutes, community councils.

## National sources

**ACRE** (Action with Communities in Rural England), Somerford Road, Cirencester GL7 1TW. An umbrella body for rural community councils.
Tel: 01285–653477; fax: 01285–654537

**Council for the Protection of Rural England**, 25 Buckingham Palace Road, London SW1W 0PP.
Tel: 0171–976–6433

**Country Landowners Association**, 16 Belgrave Square, London SW1X 8PQ.
Tel: 0171–235–0511

**Countryside Commission**, John Dower House, Crescent Place, Cheltenham GL50 3RA.
Tel: 01242–521381; fax: 01242–584270

**National Trust**, 36 Queen Anne's Gate, London SW1H 9AS. Regional offices are listed in regional pages.
Tel: 0171–222–9251; fax: 0171–222–5097

**Commons, Open Spaces and Footpaths Society**, 25a Bell Street, Henley RG9 2BA.
Tel: 01491–573535

**Ramblers Association**, 1 Wandsworth Road, London SW8 2LX.
Tel: 0171–582–6876/6826

**Rural Development Commission**, 19 Dacre Street, London SW1H 0DH.
Tel: 0171–340–2906/7, press; fax: 0171–340–2910

# WATER

See also regional pages.

**British Waterways**, Willow Grange, Church Road, Watford WD1 3QA.
Tel: 01923–201292/361; fax: 01923–201300

**Chartered Institute of Water and Environmental Management**, 15 John Street, London WC1N 2EB.
Tel: 0171–831–3110; fax: 0171–405–4967

**Hydraulics Research**, Wallingford OX10 8BA.
Tel: 01491–835381

**Institute of Freshwater Ecology**, Windermere Laboratory, Ferry House, Far Sawrey LA22 0LP.
Tel: 01539–442468; fax: 446914

**Institute of Hydrology**, Wallingford OX10 8BB.
Tel: 01491–838800

**OFWAT** (Office of Water Services), 7 Hill Street, Birmingham B5 4UA.
Tel: 0121–625–1416/1342, press; fax: 0121–625–1346

**Water Companies Association**, 1 Queen Anne's Gate, London SW1H 9BT. Represents smaller water companies.
Tel: 0171–222–0644

**Water Research Centre**, PO Box 16, Marlow SL7 2DH.
Tel: 01491–571531; fax: 01491–579094

**Water Services Association of England and Wales**, 1 Queen Anne's Gate, London SW1H 9BT. Represents privatized water companies.
Tel: 0171–957–4567; fax: 0171–957–4666

## DESALINATION

**Weir Westgarth**, contact via Weir Pumps Office, Cathcart, Glasgow G44 4EX.
Tel: 0141–637–7141, press

## FLOODS

**Flood Hazard Research Centre**, Middlesex University.
Tel: 0181–362–5920, press

**Professor George Fleming**, Civil Engineering, Strathclyde University, Glasgow G1 1XQ.
Tel: 0141–552–4400, ext. 3771

**Institute of Hydrology**, see above.

# GROUNDWATER IN BRITAIN

**British Geological Survey**, Keyworth NG12 5GG.
Tel: 0115–936–3556/3497; fax: 0115–936–3385, PR

# RIVERS

**Environment Agency for England and Wales**, 20 Albert Embankment,
London SE1 7TLJ.
Tel: 0171–840–6143; fax: 0171–582–8240

# 6 CITIES AND TOWNS

**British Urban Regeneration Association**, 33 Great Sutton Street, London EC1V 0DX
Tel: 0171–253–5054; fax: 0171–490–8735

**City and Regional Planning Department**, University of Wales, PO Box 906, Cardiff CF1 3YN.
Tel: 01222–874308

**Civic Trust**, 17 Carlton House Terrace, London SW1Y 5AW.
Tel: 0171–930–0914; fax: 0171–321–0180

**English Partnerships** (urban regeneration agency), 16 Old Queen Street, SW1H 9HP.
Tel: 0171–976–7070, press; fax: 0171–976–8017

**Professor Peter Hall**, The Bartlett, University College London.
Tel: 0171–387–7456; fax: 0171–380–7453; e-mail: p.hall@ucl.ac.uk

**Royal Town Planning Institute**, 26 Portland Place, London W1N 4BE.
Tel: 0171–636–9107; fax: 0171–323–1582

**School for Advanced Urban Studies**, Rodney Lodge, Grange Road, Bristol BS8 4EA.
Tel: 0117–974–1117; fax: 0117–973–7308

**Tidy Britain Group**, The Pier, Wigan WN3 4GX.
Tel: 01942–824620

**Town and Country Planning Association**, 17 Carlton House Terrace, London SW1Y 5AS.
Tel: 0171–930–8903

**Town and Regional Planning**, Sheffield University.
Tel: 0114–282–6180/6304

## AIR POLLUTION

**Centre for Environmental Technology**, Imperial College London SW7 2BX.
Tel: 0171–589–5111

**Environmental Medicine Department**, Aberdeen University.
Tel: 01224–272000

**Dr Nick Hewitt, Environmental Science**, Lancaster Univeristy.
Tel: 01524–593931

**Dr Peter Lucas, Biological Science**, Lancaster University.
Tel: 01524–65201, ext. 3534

**Environment Agency for England and Wales**, 20 Albert Embankment, London SE1 7TJ.
Tel: 0171–840–6143; fax: 0171–582–8240

## TOURISM

**Great British Cities**, c/o City Council, 24 Castle Gate, Nottingham NG1 7AT.
Tel: 0181–742–3388, PR; fax: 0181–995–2374

## URBAN DEPRIVATION

**Professor Michael Pacione**, Geography, Strathclyde University, Glasgow G1 1XQ.
Tel: 0141–552–4400, ext. 3793

## BROADCASTING, FILM AND VIDEO

See also MEDIA, pages 218–22.

Reference: *Blue Book of British Broadcasting.*
*BFI Film and TV Handbook.*
*A Biographical Dictionary of Film*, David Thomson (Deutsch: £14.99).
*Broadcasting in the United Kingdom*, Barrie Macdonald.
*Directors' Guild Directory.*

*Directory of British Film and TV Producers* (Producers Alliance for Cinema and Television).
*Halliwell's Film Guide*, and Ephraim Katz's *International Encyclopaedia of Film*. These have synopses of films with assessments of quality.

**Advertising Film and Videotape Association**, 26 Noel Street, London W1V 3RD.
Tel: 0171–434–2651; fax: 0171–434–9002.

**BBC**, Broadcasting House, London W1A 1AA.
Tel: 0171–580–4468; fax: 0171–637–1630

**BBC TV Centre**, Wood Lane, London W12 7RJ.
Tel: 0181–743–8000

**BBC World Service**, PO Box 76, London WC2B 4PH.
Tel: 0171–240–3456

**BBC Worldwide TV**, 80 Wood Lane, London W12 0TT.
Tel: 0181–743–5588

**British Academy of Film and TV Arts** (BAFTA), 195 Piccadilly, London SW1P 3NQ.
Tel: 0171–734–0022; fax: 0171–734–1792

**Broadcasters Audience Research Board**, Glenthorne House, Hammersmith Grove, W6 0ND
Tel: 0181–741–9110; fax: 0181–741–1943

**Broadcasting Complaints Commission**, 35 Grosvenor Gardens, London SW1W 0BS.
Tel: 0171–630–1966; fax: 0171–828–7316

**Broadcasting Entertainment Cinematograph and Theatre Union** (BECTU), 111 Wardour Street, London W1V 4AY.
Tel: 0171–437–8506; fax: 0171–437–8268

**Broadcasting Standards Council**, 5 The Sanctuary, London SW1P 3JS.
Tel: 0171–233–0544; fax: 0171–233–0397

**Commonwealth Broadcasting Association**, Room 312, 152 Great Portland Street, London W1N 6AJ.
Tel: 0171–765–5144

**Directors' Guild of Great Britain**, 15 Great Titchfield Street, London W1P 7FB.
Tel: 0171–436–8626

**Federation of Entertainment Unions**, 1 Highfield, Twyford, Southampton SO21 1QR.
Tel: 01962–713134

**National Museum of Photography, Film and TV**, Pictureville, Bradford
BD1 1NQ.
Tel: 01274–727488; fax: 01274–723155

**Producers Alliance for Cinema and TV**, Gordon House, Greencoat
Place, London SW1P 1PH. Independent producers.
Tel: 0171–233–6000; fax: 233–8935

**Voice of the Listener and Viewer**, 101 King's Drive, Gravesend DA12
5BQ. Independent consumer body.
Tel: 01474–352835

**Women in Film and Television**, Garden Studio, Betterton Street,
London WC2H 9BP.
Tel: 0171–240–4875

# FILM

**British Board of Film Classification**, 3 Soho Square, London W1V 6HD.
Tel: 0171–439–7961; fax: 0171–287–0141

**British Film Commission**, 70 Baker Street, London W1 1DJ.
Government agency to promote film production.
Tel: 0171–224–5000; fax: 0171–224–1013

**British Film Institute**, 21 Stephen Street, London W1P 2LN.
Tel: 0171–957–8919/20; fax: 0171–436–0439

**Film Education**, 41 Berners Street, London W1P 3AA. Promotes film
studies in schools.
Tel: 0171–637–9932; fax: 0171–637–9996

# RADIO

**Association of Independent Radio Companies**, 46 Westbourne Grove,
London W2 5SH.
Tel: 0171–727–2646; fax: 0171–229–0352

**Radio Authority**, 14 Great Queen Street, London WC2B 5DG.
Tel: 0171–430–2724; fax: 0171–405–7064, press

**Radio Society of Great Britain**, Lambda House, Cranborne Road,
Potters Bar EN6 3JE.
Tel: 01707–659015; fax: 01707–645105

## TELEVISION

Reference: *ITC Factfile*, see ITC below.

**Channel Four**, 124 Horseferry Road, London SW1P 2TX.
Tel: 0171–396–4444, press

**Channel Five Broadcasting**.
Tel: 0171–550–5555

**GMTV**, Upper Ground, London SE1 9TT.
Tel: 0171–827–7000; fax: 7002

**Guild of Local Television**, 16 Fountain Road, Edgbaston B17 8NL.
Tel: 0121–429–3706; fax: 0121–429–3706

**Independent Television Commission**, 33 Foley Street, London W1P
7LB. Oversees ITV and cable.
Tel: 0171–306–7746/4; fax: 0171–306–7800;
e-mail: 100731.3515@compuserve.com

**ITV Network Centre** (and **ITV Association**), 200 Grays Inn Road,
London WC1X 8HF. Responsible for ITV networking.
Tel: 0171–843–8000; fax: 0171–843–8158

**ITN**, 200 Grays Inn Road, London WC1X 8XZ.
Tel: 0171–833–3000

**Royal Television Society**, 100 Gray's Inn Road, London WC1X 8AL
(discussion forum).
Tel: 0171–430–1000; fax: 0171–430–0924

### Effects of TV viewing

**Dr Andrew Colmans**, Psychology, Leicester University.
Tel: 0116–252–2167

### Satellite and cable

**British Sky Broadcasting**, 6 Centaurs Business Park, Grant Way,
Isleworth TW7 5QD.
Tel: 0171–705–3000

**Cable Communications Association**, 5th Floor, Artillery House,
Artillery Row, SW1P 1RT.
Tel: 0171–222–2900; fax: 0171–385–1874

**Satellite and Cable Broadcasters Group**, 34 Grand Avenue, London
N10 3BP.
Tel: 0181–444–4891; fax: 0181–444–6473

**Super Channel**, 3 Shortlands, London W6 8BX.
Tel: 0181–600–6100

## VIDEO

**British Video Association**, 167 Great Portland Street, London W1N 5FD. Trade association for video cassettes.
Tel: 0171–436–0041

## BUILDING/CONSTRUCTION

### Local sources.

Architects, builders, civil-engineering contractors, consultant engineers (who may open a local office for a big project), council building inspectors and planners, unions.

### National sources

**Asbestos Removal Contractors Association**, 6 Parkway, Chelmsford CM2 9DD.
Tel: 01245–259744; fax: 01245–490722

**Bovis**, Northolt Road, Harrow HA2 0EE
Tel: 0181–422–3488

**Building Employers Confederation**, 82 New Cavendish Street, London W1M 8AD.
Tel: 0171–580–5588; fax: 0171–631–3872

**Building Research Establishment**, Bucknalls Lane, Garston, Watford WD2 7JR.
Tel: 01923–664083/80; fax: 01923–664010

**Concrete Society**, 3 Eatongate, 112 Windsor Road, Slough SL1 2JA.
Tel: 01753–693313

**Construction Industry Council**, 26 Store Street, London WC1E 7BT.
Tel: 0171–637–8692

**National Council of Building Material Producers**, 26 Store Street, London WC1E 7BT.
Tel: 0171–323–3770; fax: 0171–323–0307

**Construction Industry Training Board**, Bircham Newton, Kings Lynn PE31 6RH.
Tel: 01553–776677; fax: 01553–692226

**Construction Management and Engineering Department**, Reading
University.
Tel: 01734–318201

**Construction Safety Campaign**, 225 Poplar High Street, London E14.
Tel: 0171–537–7220

**European Construction Institute**, Loughborough University.
Tel: 01509–222620; fax: 01509–610231

**Laing**, Page Street, London NW7 2ER.
Tel: 0181–959–3636

**Tarmac**, Wolverhampton.
Tel: 01902–307407

**Taylor Woodrow.**
Tel: 0181–813–0813

**UCATT** (construction workers union), 177 Abbeville Road, London
SW4 9RL.
Tel: 0171–622–2362/2442; fax: 0171–498–5272

**Wimpey**, London W6 7EN.
Tel: 0181–846–3343, press


# ARCHITECTS

Reference: *Architectural Review.*
*Architects Journal.*

**Royal Institute of British Architects**, 66 Portland Place, London W1N
4AD.
Tel: 0171–580–5533; fax: 0171–255–1541


## *Contemporary architecture*

**Dr N. Whiteley**, Visual Arts, Lancaster University.
Tel: 01524–65201, ext. 3171


# BUILDING MATERIALS

**Brick Development Association**, Woodside House, Winkfield, Windsor
SL4 2DX.
Tel: 01344–885651; fax: 01344–890129

**British Cement Association**, Telford Avenue, Crowthorne RG11 6YS.
Tel: 01344–762676; fax: 01344–761214

**Jewson** (builders' merchant), PO Box 90, Cringleford, Norwich.
Tel: 01603–456133

## CIVIL ENGINEERING

**W.S.Atkins**, Woodcote Grove, Ashley Road, Epsom KT18 5BW.
Tel: 01372–726140

**Civil Engineering Department**, Strathclyde University, John Anderson
Building, 107 Rottenrow, Glasgow G4 0NG.
Tel: 0141–552–4400

**Federation of Civil Engineering Contractors**, 6 Portugal Street, London
WC2A 2HJ.
Tel: 0171–404–4020

**Halcrow**, London W6 7BY.
Tel: 0171–602–7282; fax: 0171–603–0095 and
Burderop Park, Swindon SN4 0QD.
Tel: 01793–812479

**Institution of Civil Engineers**, 1 Great George Street, London SW1P
3AE.
Tel: 0171–222–7722; fax: 0171–222–0973

## GLASS

**Glass and Glazing Federation**, 44 Borough High Street, London SE1 1XB.
Tel: 0171–403–7177; fax: 0171–357–7458

## HEATING AND VENTILATION

**Heating and Ventilating Contractors Association**, 34 Palace Court,
London W2 4JG.
Tel: 0171–229–2488; fax: 0171–727–9268

## PAINT

**British Coatings Federation**.
Tel: 01372–360660

**Paint Research Association**, 8 Waldegrave Road, Teddington TW11 8LD.
Tel: 0181–977–4427; fax: 0181–943–4705

## ROOFS

**British Flat Roofing Council**, 36 Bridlesmith Gate, Nottingham NG1 2GQ.
Tel: 0115–950–7733; fax: 0115–950–4122

**National Federation of Roofing Contractors**, 24 Weymouth Street,
London W1N 4LX.
Tel: 0171–436–0387; fax: 0171–637–5215

## SICK BUILDING SYNDROME

**Dr Nick Baker**, Architecture, Cambridge University.
Tel: 01223–332981

## WOOD

**Timber Research and Development Association**, Stocking Lane,
Hughenden Valley, HP14 4ND.
Tel: 01494–563091

## CRIME AND PUNISHMENT

Newspapers make regular calls on local police and on police press officers.
The **Crown Prosecution Service** has lawyers operating in every local criminal court. There are local victim-support schemes and neighbourhood
watches. Some places have watchdog committees keeping an eye on the
police and crime.

### *National sources*

**Home Office Police Press Desk**, Queen Anne's Gate, London SW1H 9AT.
Tel: 0171–273–4610; fax: 0171–273–4660;
e-mail: commdir.ho@gtnet.gov.uk

**Criminal Justice, Young Offenders Press Desk.**
Tel: 0171–273–4600
The Home Office has an information and library service.

**Centre for Criminology and Justice**, Professor Keith Bottomley, Hull University HU6 7RX.
Tel: 01482–465790

**Centre for Police and Criminal Justice Studies**, Exeter University.
Tel: 01392–411263

**Centre for the Study of Public Order**, Leicester University, Salisbury Road LE1 7QT.
Tel: 0116–252–2458; fax: 0116–252–3944

**Crown Prosecution Service** (CPS), 50 Ludgate Hill, London EC4M 7EX. The CPS can be hard to contact locally; but CPS lawyers can easily be approached in court.
Tel: 0171–273–8105/3; fax: 0171–329–8377

**Institute for the Study and Treatment of Delinquency**, King's College, London WC2R 2LS
Tel: 0171–873–2822

**Institute of Criminology**, Cambridge University.
Tel: 01223–335360

**National Criminal Intelligence Service**, 2 Citadel Place, Spring Gardens, London SE11 5EF. Analyses organized crime, drug trafficking, etc.
Tel: 0171–238–8248/8431, press; fax: 238–8446

## CORRUPTION

**Transparency International UK**, 1 George Street, Uxbridge UB8 1QQ.
Tel: 01895–274733; fax: 01895–256413

## COUNTERFEITING

**Anti-Counterfeiting Group**, PO Box 578, High Wycombe HP13 5FY.
Tel: 01494–449165; fax: 01494–465052

## DRUGS

See pages 64 and 65.

## FORENSIC SCIENCE

**Forensic Science Service**, Priory House, Gooch Street North, Birmingham B5 6QQ.
Tel: 0171–273–4610, Home Office PR

## FRAUD

**Serious Fraud Office**, Elm House, Elm Street, London WC1X 0BJ.
Tel: 0171–239–7002/3, press; fax: 0171–837–1173

**Fraud Squad**, Metropolitan Police.
Tel: 0171–230–2601, press

**Fraud Investigation Unit**, KPMG Peat Marwick, 1 Puddle Dock,
London EC4V 3PD.
Tel: 0171–236–8000; fax: 0171–248–6552

**Kroll Associates**, 25 Savile Row, London W1X 0AL.
Tel: 0171–396–0000; fax: 0171–396–9966

**Network Security Management**, Hambros, 41 Tower Hill, London EC3N
4HA.
Tel: 0171–480–5000

### *International*

**Commercial Crime Bureau**, International Chamber of Commerce, 14
Belgrave Square, London SW1X 8PX.
Tel: 0171–823–2811

**Dr Barry Rider**, Jesus College, Cambridge CB5 8BL.
Tel: 01223–311690/339339

## INDUSTRIAL ESPIONAGE

**Carratu International**, Athene House, Shoe Lane, London EC4A 3BQ.
Tel: 0171–353–3800

**Peter Sommer**, LSE, London WC2A 2AE.
Tel: 0171–955–6197/0181–340–4139; e-mail: p.m.sommer@lse.ac.uk.

## MONEY LAUNDERING

**National Criminal Intelligence Service**, 2 Citadel Place, Spring Gardens,
London SE11 5EF.
Tel: 0171–238–8248/8431, press; fax: 238–8446

**Dr Barry Rider**, see above.

## PIRACY

**International Maritime Bureau**, Maritime House, 1 Linton Road,
Barking IG11 8HG.
Tel: 0181–591–3000; fax: 0181–594–2833

**NUMAST** (ships officers union), 750 High Road, London E11 3BB.
Tel: 0181–989–6677; fax: 0181–530–1015

## *Recordings*

**International Federation of Phonographic Industries**, 54 Regent Street, London W1R 5PJ.
Tel: 0171–434–3521

## *Software*

**Business Software Alliance**, Leconfield House, Curzon Street, London W1Y 8AS.
Tel: 0171–491–1974

## POLICE

**Association of Chief Police Officers**, 67 Buckingham Gate, London SW1E 6BE.
Tel: 0171–230–7184; fax: 0171–230–7212

**Metropolitan Police Press Bureau**.
Tel: 0171–230–2171

**Police Complaints Authority**, 10 Great George Street, London SW1P 3AE.
Tel: 0171–273–6483; fax: 0171–273–6421

**Police Federation**, 15 Langley Road, Surbiton KT6 6LP.
Tel: 0181–399–2224

**Police Superintendents Association**, 67A Reading Road, Pangbourne RG8 7JD.
Tel: 01734–844005; fax: 01734–845642

**Police Review**, South Quay Plaza 2, 183 Marsh Wall, London E14 9FZ.
Tel: 0171–537–2575; fax: 0171–537–2560

**Statewatch**, PO Box 1516, London N16 0EW. Bimonthly about police, prisons, security, immigration.
Tel: 0181–802–1882

## PRISONS/PRISONERS

**Apex Trust**, St Alphage House, Wingate Annexe, 2 Fore Street, EC2Y

5DA. Deals with prisoners' employment.
Tel: 0171–638–5931

**Howard League for Penal Reform**, 708 Holloway Road, London N19 3NL.
Tel: 0171–281–7722

**NACRO** (National Association for the Care and Rehabilitation of Offenders), 169 Clapham Road, London SW9 0PU.
Tel: 0171–582–6500

**Penal Affairs Consortium**, Office F6B, Kingsgate Business Centre, Kingston KT2 5AA.
Tel: 0181–546–5355; fax: 546–9978

**Prison Officers Association**, 245 Church Street, London N9 9HW.
Tel: 0181–803–0255; fax: 0181–803–1761

**Prison Service**, Cleland House, Page Street, London SW1P 4LN.
Tel: 0171–217–6633; fax: 0171–828–8692

**Prison Reform Trust**, 2nd Floor, Old Trading House, 15 Northburgh Street, London EC1V 0AH.
Tel: 0171–251–5070

**BM-PROP** (National Prisoners Movement), London WC1N 3XX.
Tel: 0181–542–3744


## PROBATION

Probation officers work for local magistrates, producing reports on and providing services for offenders and seeking to encourage them not to offend again. They work with people released on licence from youth custody or on parole from prison. They operate community service.

**Association of Chief Officers of Probation**, 20 Lawefield Lane, Wakefield WF2 8SP.
Tel: 01924–361156; fax: 01924–372837


## RAPE

**Rape Crisis Centre**, PO Box 69, London WC1X 9NJ.
Tel: 0171–916–5466

**Rape Crisis Centre**, Edinburgh.
Tel: 0131–556–9437

**Women Against Rape**, London WC1X 0AN.
Tel: 0171–837–7509

## SECURITY

**British Security Industry Association**, Barbourne Road, Worcester WR1
1RS.
Tel: 01905–21464; fax: 01905–613625

## SPECIAL HOSPITALS

**Special Hospitals Service Authority**, 375 Kensington High Street,
London W14 8QH. Manages Ashworth, Broadmoor, Rampton.
Tel: 0171–605–9730, press; fax: 0171–605–9714

## VICTIMS

**Criminal Injuries Compensation Board**, Morley House, Holborn
Viaduct, London EC1A 2BP.
Tel: 0171–936–3476

**Victim Support**, 39 Brixton Road, London SW9 6DZ.
Tel: 0171–735–9166; fax: 0171–582–5712

## WOMEN AND CRIME

**Professor Pat Carlen**, Criminology, Keele University.
Tel: 01782–583082

# DEVELOPMENT AGENCIES

The Government has set up development corporations to organize development in many areas, often run-down parts of cities. For many areas it
has also set up government offices (London, Merseyside etc.) for local
liaison.

Many councils have departments devoted to promoting local development. Some have set up partnerships with local firms. Many towns and

districts have local enterprise agencies. For organizations like these, see regional pages 238–311.

## National sources

**British Coal Enterprise**, Edwinstowe, Nottinghamshire (set up to promote jobs in former mining areas).
Tel: 01623–826833

**British Steel (Industry)**, Sheffield S3 8HS (set up to promote jobs near former steelworks).
Tel: 0114–273–1612

**Centre for Local Economic Strategies**, Professor Brian Robson, Manchester University M13 9PL.
Tel: 0161–275–3636

**Professor Kevin Morgan**, European Regional Development, Cardiff University.
Tel: 01222–874851

## JUSTICE

Magistrates' clerks will keep you right about magistrates' courts. Coroners should tell the press when they are holding inquests. The local civil courts are the county courts which may also have small claims courts. Solicitors can easily be approached in court, but they will also have a local **Law Society**. The **Solicitors and Barristers Directory** (Waterlow) includes all the courts in England and Wales.

People accused of more serious offences are committed by the magistrates to a crown court which may be some distance away. Finding the date and time of a hearing may require ringing the court daily. Phone numbers for crown courts are listed in *The Guardian Media Guide*.
Reference: *Law Reports.*
*Halsbury's Statutes.*

## National sources

**Legal Secretariat to the Law Officers**, 9 Buckingham Gate, London SW1E 6JP.
Tel: 0171–233–7524; fax: 0171–233–9206

**Justice**, London (concerned with mistakes in administration of justice).
Tel: 0171–329–5100

**Law Commission** (produces proposals to revise the law).
Tel: 0171–453–1220, press

**Legal Business Magazine**, 28 Cato Street, London W1H 5HS. Surveys
legal earnings.
Tel: 0171–396–9292

**Legal Services Ombudsman**.
Tel: 0161–236–9532, press

**Lord Chancellor's Department** (media), 54 Victoria Street, SW1E 6QW
(concerned with courts and legal aid).
Tel: 0171–210–8511/8692; fax: 0171–210–8633

**Society of Black Lawyers**, 444 Brixton Road, London SW9 8EJ.
Tel: 0171–737–1060; fax: 0171–737–1060


## ARBITRATION

**Centre for Dispute Resolution**, 100 Fetter Lane, London EC4A 1DD
(mediator for commercial disputes).
Tel: 0171–430–1852

**School of International Arbitration**, Queen Mary and Westfield College.
Tel: 0171–975–5555


## BARRISTERS

**Bar Council**, 1 Dean's Yard, SW1P 3NR.
Tel: 0171–222–2525, press

**Family Law Bar Association**, Queen Elizabeth Building, Temple,
London EC4Y 9BS.
Tel: 0171 797–7837; fax: 0171–352–5422


## INVESTIGATORS

**Association of British Investigators**, 10 Bonner Hill Road, Kingston
KT1 3EP. Private investigators.
Tel: 0181–546–3368; fax: 0181–546–7701

**Institute of Professional Investigators**, 31a Wellington Street, St John's,
Blackburn BB1 8AF. Includes investigators of all kinds.
Tel: 01254–680072; fax: 59276

## SOLICITORS

**Association of Women Solicitors**, 50 Chancery Lane, London WC2A 1SX.
Tel: 0171–320–5793

**Law Society**, 113 Chancery Lane, London WC2A 1PL.
Tel: 0171–320–5810/11/5884, press

**Solicitors Complaints Bureau**, 8 Dormer Place, Leamington Spa.
Tel: 01926–822042; 01926–831532

# LOCAL GOVERNMENT

Councils employ public relations officers, besides a wide range of chief officers who can speak to journalists. Some councillors work for their council more or less full time.

The heyday of local councils ended in the 1970s when the Callaghan government found it could no longer afford their continued expansion, and new council dwellings in London were costing over £100,000 each to build. Since then, Conservative Governments have curbed both the powers and the money-raising of councils and created non-elected local government bodies such as development corporations and training and enterprise councils. Colleges and some schools are now outside council control

But councils still spend large sums and appoint directors of this and that at mouth-watering salaries while threatening to sack teachers and dinner ladies. Councils affect everyone's life. Even well-to-do families call in the 'social services' when Grandma needs help.

Local government has probably never been adequately covered in the press which cannot afford locally the time and money it devotes to national politics. In the north-east in the 1960s, for example, we who were then at *The Northern Echo* failed to notice the series of contracts awarded to John Poulson (see pages 369 and 370).

But local affairs can be more complex than national. John Authers has written in the *Financial Times*: 'Local government finance has for many years been one of the UK's most impenetrable mysteries'.

The task of the journalist is hard but has been made easier by the **Local Government (Access to Information) Act**. The local **reference library** and **town hall** will know what documents are open to the public. But a journalist still needs to know what document to look for. The key questions are four:

1 How do council decisions affect people?
2 Are the wide powers of councils and their officials used properly and not oppressively?
3 Is money being spent to the best advantage?
4 Is money properly used?

Reports by the **Audit Commission** (the councils' auditor) and other bodies show wide variations in spending from council to council, the cumulative result of past decisions but also of differing situations.

Councillors do not in the main have much personal control over spending decisions, so buying re-election is normally not possible. There can, however, be abuses, particularly where one political party is more or less permanently in power.

Part of London local government's problem is that it is only thinly covered in the daily press. Large sums are spent without anyone really noticing.

Newspapers have a responsibility to look into and publicize what is going on in their areas, particularly if there is no effective local political opposition. Besides councils, the responsibility covers the many other bodies which take part in local government: health authorities, training and enterprise councils, development corporations, the health and safety executive.

Reference: *Municipal Year Book* (includes development corporations).

*Councils, Committees and Boards* (CBD Research). Despite its name, this valuable book does not cover elected councils. It does, however, list a wide range of official and unofficial agencies, many of them involved in local government.

*Report on the Census* (gives facts town by town).

**Department of Environment Local Government Desks**, 2 Marsham Street, London SW1P 3EB.
Tel: 0171–890–4620/18; fax: 0171–890–4689/29

**Association of Councillors**, c/o Town Hall, Ramsden Street, Huddersfield HD1 2TA.
Tel: 01484–442020; fax: 01484–435073

**Association of County Councils**, 66A Eaton Square, London SW1W 9BH (covers the shire counties).
Tel: 0171–235–1200; fax: 0171–235–8458

**Association of Metropolitan Authorities**, 36 Old Queen Street, London SW1H 9JE. Covers the major conurbations.
Tel: 0171–222–8100; fax: 0171–222–0878

**District Planning Officers Society**, c/o D. Pinney, Torridge DC, Riverbank House, Bideford EX39 2QG.
Tel: 01237–476711; fax: 01237–478849

**Institute of Local Government Studies**, Birmingham University, Edgbaston B15 2TT.
Tel: 0121–414–4986

**Local Government Ombudsmen**, 21 Queen Anne's Gate, London SW1H 9BU.
Tel: 0171–915–3286/3289/3210, press; fax: 0171–233–0396

## DIRECT LABOUR AND CONTRACTED-OUT SERVICES

**Association of Direct Labour Organizations**, 4th Floor, Olympic, Whitworth Street West, Manchester M1 5WG.
Tel: 0161–236–8433

**Business Services Association**.
Tel: 0171–405–4449

**Cleaning and Supply Services Association**.
Tel: 0171–403–2747

## FINANCE

**Audit Commission**, 9 Little College Street, London SW1P 3XS.
Tel: 0171–930–6077, press; fax: 0171–233–0335

**Chartered Institute of Public Finance and Accountancy**, 3 Robert Street, London WC2N 6BH (the council treasurers' body; useful for figures on councils' spending).
Tel: 0171–895–8823

**Institute of Revenues, Rating and Valuation**, 41 Doughty Street, London WC1N 2LF. Services local valuers.
Tel: 0171–831–3505; fax: 0171–831–2048

## MEDIA

Reference: *Benn's Media*. Information on press and broadcasting in three volumes for UK, Europe, world (Riverbank House, Angel Lane, Tonbridge TN9 1SE). See also BROADCASTING AND FILM, pages 201–5 and PRINT, pages 222–4.

*Hollis Press and Public Relations Annual.* Gives news contacts.
*Willing's Press Guide.*
*The Guardian Media Guide.*
*The Twentieth Century Newspaper Press in Britain: An Annotated Bibliography* compiled by David Linton (Mansell).
*European TV Directory* (NTC Publications, Henley RG9 1EJ).
*European Newspaper and Magazine Minibook* (NTC Publications, Henley RG9 1EJ).

**British Library Newspaper Library**, Colindale Avenue, London NW9 5HE. Historical collection of newspapers. Also reference.

**Department of National Heritage Media-Matters Desk**, 2 Cockspur Street, London SW1Y 5DH.
Tel: 0171–211–6272/1; fax: 0171–211–6270

**Campaign for Freedom of Information**, 88 Old Street, London EC1V 9AX. Campaigns for open government.
Tel: 0171–253–2445

**Campaign for Press and Broadcasting Freedom**, 8 Cynthia Street, N1 9JF. Campaigns for public access to media.
Tel: 0171–278–4430

**Federation Against Copyright Theft**, 7 Victory Business Centre, Worton Road, Isleworth TW7 6ER.
Tel: 0181–568–6646; fax: 560–6364

## ADVERTISING

Reference: *European Advertising and Media Yearbook* (NTC Publications, Henley RG9 1EJ).

**Advertising Association**, 15 Wilton Road, London SW1V 1NJ.
Tel: 0171–828–2771; fax: 0171–931–0376

**Advertising Standards Authority**, 2 Torrington Place, London WC1E 7HW. Enforces code for non-broadcast advertisements.
Tel: 0171–580–5555; fax: 0171–631–3051

**Broadcast Advertising Clearance Centre**, 200 Gray's Inn Road, London WC1X 8HF. Oversees broadcast commercials.
Tel: 0171–843–8265; fax: 0171–843–8154

**Institute of Practitioners in Advertising**, 44 Belgrave Square, London SW1X 8QS. Represents advertising agencies.
Tel: 0171–235–7020; fax: 0171–245–9904

## JOURNALISTS

**Association of British Editors**, 49 Frederick Road, Birmingham B15 1HN. Active on journalists' freedom.
Tel: 0121–455–7949

**British Association of Industrial Editors**, 3 Locks Yard, High Street, Sevenoaks TN13 1LT. Editors of company in-house journals.
Tel: 01732–459331

**British Association of Journalists**, 99 Fleet Street, London EC4Y 1DE. Set up by former NUJ general secretary.
Tel: 0171–353–3003; fax: 0171–353–2310

**Bureau of Freelance Photographers**, 497 Green Lane, London N13 4BP.
Tel: 0181–882–3315

**Chartered Institute of Journalists**, 2 Dock Offices, Surrey Quays Road, London SE16 2XU.
Tel: 0171–252–1187; fax: 232–2302

**Commonwealth Journalists Association**, 17 Nottingham Street, London W1M 3RD.
Tel: 0171–486–3844; fax: 0171–486–3822

**Guild of Newspaper Editors**, Great Russell Street, London WC1B 3DA.
Tel: 0171–636–7014

**International Federation of Journalists**, Boulevard Charlemagne Bte 5, B1041 Brussels.
Tel: 00–322–238–0951; fax: 00–322–230–3633

**National Union of Journalists**, 314 Gray's Inn Road, London WC1X 8DP.
Tel: 0171–278–7916; fax: 0171–837–8143

**Society of Women Writers and Journalists**, 110 Whitehall Road, London E4 6DW.
Tel: 0181–529–0886

### *Freedom of journalists*

**ARTICLE 19**, 33 Islington High Street, N1 9LH.
Tel: 0171–278–9292

**Index on Censorship magazine**, 33 Islington High Street, London N1 9LH.
Tel: 0171–278–2313; fax: 0171–278–1878; e-mail: index on censo@gn.apc.org

**Reporters Sans Frontieres**, 13 Rue du Mail, 75002 Paris, France.
Tel: 00–331–49–26–01–88; fax: 00–331–26–00–83 and
17 Rue Abbe de l'Epee, 34000 Montpellier.
Tel: 00–33–67–79–81–82; fax: 00–33–67–79–60–80

## *Training*

**National Council for Training of Broadcast Journalists**, 188 Lichfield
Court, Sheen Road, Richmond TW9 1BB.
Tel: 0181–940–0694

**National Council for Training of Journalists**, Latton Bush Centre,
Southern Way, Harlow CM18 7BL.
Tel: 01279–430009

**Newspaper Qualifications Council.** This is formed by the Newspaper
Society (see below under PRINT), Guild of Editors and Scottish
newspapers.

**Periodicals Training Council**, Imperial House, Kingsway, London WC2B
6UN.
Tel: 0171–836–8798; fax: 0171–379–5661

**Thomson Foundation**, Bute Buildings, Edward VII Avenue, Cathays
Park, Cardiff CF1 3NB. Trains overseas journalists.
Tel: 01222–874873/664902; fax: 01222–225194

## MEDIA STUDIES

**Centre for Media and Public Communication**, Liverpool University, L69
3BX.
Tel: 0151–794–2000

**Communication Research Centre**, Loughborough University, LE11 3TU.
Tel: 01509–263171

**European Institute for the Media**, Dusseldorf.
Tel: 00–49–211–901040

**Institute of Communication Studies**, Leeds University, LS2 9JT.
Tel: 0113–233–5805

**International Institute of Communications**, Tavistock House South,
WC1H 9LF (publishes *Intermedia*).
Tel: 0171–388–0671

**John Logie Baird Centre for Film and TV Studies**, Strathclyde University, Glasgow G1 1XH.
Tel: 0141–552–4400

**Centre for Communication and Information Studies**, Westminster University, 235 High Holborn, WC1V 7DN.
Tel: 0171–911–5000

**Centre for Mass Communication Research**, 104 Regent Road, Leicester LE1 7LT.
Tel: 0116–252–3863

**Department of Film and Media Studies**, Stirling University, FK9 4LA.
Tel: 01786–467520

# PRINT

## ELECTRONIC PUBLISHING

**International Electronic Publishing Research Centre**, Pira House, Randalls Road, Leatherhead KT22 7RU.
Tel: 01372–802000; fax: 802244

**Learned Information**, Woodside, Hinksey Hill, Oxford OX1 5BE. Runs On-Line Exhibition.
Tel: 01865–730275; fax: 01865–736354; e-mail: learned@learned.co.uk

## MAGAZINES

**Periodical Publishers Association**, Imperial House, Kingsway, London WC2B 6UN.
Tel: 0171–379–6268; fax: 0171–379–5661

## NEWS AND PICTURE AGENCIES

**Associated Press**, 12 Norwich Street, EC4A 1AP.
Tel: 0171–1515/583–0196

**Camera Press**, 21 Queen Elizabeth Street, SE1 2LP. Specializes in portraits of leaders etc. worldwide.
Tel: 0171–378–1300

**Council of Photographic News Agencies**, 29 Saffron Hill, London EC1N 8FH.
Tel: 0171–421–6000

**Gemini News Service**, 9 White Lion Street, London N1 9PD (international features service).
Tel: 0171–833–4141; e-mail: gemini@gn.apc.org

**Press Association**, 292 Vauxhall Bridge Road, London SW1V 1AE. Has library of 14 million cuttings from 1926 which can be consulted for a fee.
Tel: 0171–963–7000

**Reuter**, 85 Fleet Street, London EC4P 4AJ.
Tel: 0171–250–1122

**Universal Pictorial Press**, 29 Saffron Hill, London EC1N 8FH.
Tel: 0171–421–6000

## NEWSPAPERS

**Audit Bureau of Circulations**, Black Prince Yard, 207 High Street, Berkhamsted HP4 1AD.
Tel: 01442–870800

**Commonwealth Press Union**, Studio House, Hen and Chickens Court, 184 Fleet Street, EC4A 2DU.
Tel: 0171–242–1056; fax: 831–4923

**Newspaper Society**, 74 Great Russell Street, London WC1B 3DA
Provincial and London suburban papers.
Tel: 0171–636–7014

**Newspaper Publishers Association**, 34 Southwark Bridge Road, London SE1 9EU. Trade association of the national papers.
Tel: 0171–928–9628; fax: 0171–928–2067

**Press Complaints Commission**, 1 Salisbury Square, London EC4Y 8AE.
Tel: 0171–353–1248; fax: 0171–353–8355

## NEWSPRINT

**British Newsprint Manufacturers Association** and **British Paper and Board Industrial Federation**, Rivenhall Road, Westlea, Swindon SN5 7BD.
Tel: 01793–886086; fax: 01793–886182

## PICTURES

**BBC Photograph Library and Archive**, Unit 1, Royal London Trading Estate, 29 North Acton, NW10 6PE.
Tel: 0181–743–8000

**Picture Sources UK** (handbook). Picture libraries and agencies are also listed in the *Writers and Artists Yearbook.*

## PRINTING

**British Printing Industries Federation**, 11 Bedford Row, London WC1R 4DX.
Tel: 0171–242–6904; fax: 0171–405–7784

**PIRA International** (research body), Randalls Road, Leatherhead, KT22 7RU.
Tel: 01372–802000; fax: 01372–802238

## POST

**Post Office**, 148 Old Street, London EC1V 9HQ.
Tel: 0171–250–2468, press

**Post Office Users National Council**, 6 Hercules Road, London SE1 7DN.
Tel: 0171–928–9458; fax: 0171–928–9076

## PROPERTY

**British Property Federation**, 35 Catherine Place, London SW1E 6DY.
Tel: 0171–828–0111

**Crown Estate Commissioners**, Wardour Street, London W1Y 4AB (owns Windsor Great Park, Regent Street freeholds, farmland, foreshore).
Tel: 0171–734–2779

**Healey and Baker** (a leading property agent), 29 St George Street, London W1A 3BG.
Tel: 0171–629–9292

**Land Management and Development Department**, Reading University RG6 2AH.
Tel: 01734–318178/75, Professor Charles Ward

**Land Securities** (biggest quoted property company), 5 The Strand, London WC2N 5AF.
Tel: 0171–413–9000


## ROADS AND ROAD USERS

The **Highways Agency** (for regional offices, see under regions) is responsible for the building and maintenance of motorways and trunk roads. Councils are responsible for streets and lesser roads. The police are concerned with road safety. You may have local groups of road campaigners and protesters, and local offices of the AA or RAC.
Reference: *Motor Industry of Great Britain: World Automotive Statistics.*

**Department of Transport Roads Press Desk**, 76 Marsham Street, London SW1P 4DR.
Tel: 0171–271–5766/64/51; fax: 0171–271–5975/4/2

**British Roads Federation** (road promotion pressure group), Pillar House, Old Kent Road, SE1 5TH.
Tel: 0171–703–9769; fax: 701–0029

**Driver and Vehicle Licensing Agency**, Longview Road, Swansea SA6 7JL.
Tel: 01792–783010/2070, press

**Highways Agency**, St Christopher House, Southwark Street, London SE1 0TE.
Tel: 0171–921–4443; fax: 0171–921–2214

**Transport Research Laboratory**, Old Wokingham Road, Crowthorne RG11 6AU.
Tel: 01344–773131

**Vehicle Inspectorate**, Berkeley House, Croydon Street, Bristol BS5 0DA.
Tel: 0117–954–3200, press


## BUSES AND COACHES

**Bus and Coach Council**, Sardinia House, 52 Lincoln's Inn Fields, London WC2A 3LZ.
Tel: 0171–831–7546

**Stagecoach Holdings**, 20 Charlotte Street, Perth PH1 5LL.
Tel: 01738–442111; fax: 01738–43648

**Leyland** (bus manufacturer).
Tel: 01772–621400

**National Express**, Edgbaston, Birmingham B15 3ES (also owns East Midlands Airport).
Tel: 0121–625–1122

## CARAVANS

**Which Motorcaravan Magazine**, The Maltings, West Street, Bourne PE10 9PH.
Tel: 01778–393313; fax: 01778–394748

**Camping and Caravanning Club**, Greenfields House, Westwood Way, Coventry CV4 8JH.
Tel: 01203–694995; fax: 01203–694886

## CARS

**Automobile Association**, Norfolk House, Priestley Road, Basingstoke RG24 9NY.
Tel: 01256–492927, press; fax: 01256–492599

**BSM** (British School of Motoring), 81 Hartfield Road, London SW19 3TR.
Tel: 0181–540–8262; fax: 0181–543–7905

**BMW** (GB), Bracknell RG12 8TA.
Tel: 01344–426565; fax: 480306

**DRI Europe** (motor industry facts), Wimbledon Bridge House, Hartfield Road, London SW19 3RU.
Tel: 0181–545–6279

**Euromotor Reports**, 73 Collier Street, N1 9BE.
Tel: 0171–837–1700

**Ford**, Eagle Way, Brentwood CM14 4BY.
Tel: 01277–253000

**Honda**, London W4 5YT.
Tel: 0181–747–1400

**Institute of Advanced Motorists**, 359 Chiswick High Road, London W4 4HS.
Tel: 0181–994–4403

**Jaguar Enthusiasts Club**, Sherborne, Mead Road, Stoke Gifford, Bristol BS12 8PS.
Tel: 0117–969–8186

**Lex Vehicle Leasing**, Globe House, Parkway, Globe Park, Marlow SL7 1LY.
Tel: 01628–898000

**Lotus**, Potash Lane, Norwich NR14 8EZ.
Tel: 01953–608000; fax: 608300

**Motor Industry Research Association**, Watling Street, Nuneaton CV10 0TU.
Tel: 01203–348541; fax: 01203–343772

**Nissan**, Washington Road, Sunderland.
Tel: 0191–415–0000

**Peugeot**, PO Box 227, Aldermoor Lane, Coventry CV3 1LT.
Tel: 01203–884000; fax: 01203–884001

**RAC Motoring Services**, 14 Cockspur Street, London SW1Y 5BL.
Tel: 0171–389–8900; fax: 0171–389–8966

**Renault UK**, Swindon.
Tel: 01793–486001

**Retail Motor Industry Federation**, 201 Great Portland Street, London W1N 6AB. Includes motor-cycle and petrol traders and recovery.
Tel: 0171–580–9122; fax: 0171–580–6376

**Rover**, Bickenhill Lane, Birmingham B37.
Tel: 0121–782–8000

**Society of Motor Auctions**, PO Box 13, Wilmslow, SK9 1LL.
Tel: 01625–536937; fax: 01625–536939

**Society of Motor Manufacturers and Traders**.
Tel: 0171–235–7000; fax: 0171–235–7112

**Toyota Motor Manufacturing UK**, Burnaston, Etwall, Derbyshire.
Tel: 01332–282121

**Vauxhall**, Griffin House, Osborne Road, Luton LU1 3YT.
Tel: 01582–21122; fax: 01582–427400

**Volkswagen/Audi**, Milton Keynes.
Tel: 01908–679121

### University experts

**Professor Kumar Bhattacharyya**, Warwick University, CV4 7AL.
Tel: 01203–523155

**Professor Garel Rhys**, Motor Industry Economics, Cardiff Business School.
Tel: 01222–874281

### Catalytic converters

**IRC in Surface Science**, Liverpool University L69 3BX.
Tel: 0151–794–3543, Professor Neville Richardson

## COMMERCIAL VEHICLES

**Freight Transport Association** (firms carry own goods), 157 St John's Road, Tunbridge Wells TN4 9UZ.
Tel: 01892–526171

**Leyland Daf Vans**, Birmingham.
Tel: 0121–322–2000

**Road Haulage Association** (carries goods for others), 35 Monument Hill, Weybridge KT13 8RN.
Tel: 01932–841515; fax: 01932–852516

## COMPONENTS/ACCESSORIES

**British Gear Association**, Suite 45, IMEX Business Park, Shobnall Road, Burton DE14 2AU.
Tel: 01283–515521; fax: 515841

**British Lubricants Federation**, 6th Floor, 111 Marlowes, Hemel Hempstead HP1 1BB.
Tel: 01442–230589; fax: 01442–259232

**Castrol (UK)**, Burmah-Castrol House, Pipers Way, Swindon SN3 1RE.
Tel: 01793–452034; fax: 01793–453219

**GKN**, PO Box 55, Ipsley Church Lane, Redditch B98 0TL.
Tel: 01527–517715

**Pirelli**, Derby Road, Burton on Trent DE13 0BH.
Tel: 01283–566301; fax: 01283–511196

**T&N**, Bowdon House, Ashburton Road West, Trafford Park, Manchester M17 1RA.
Tel: 0161–872–0155; fax: 0161–877–7657

**Unipart**, Woodstock Road, Oxford OX2 7PB.
Tel: 01865–31944; fax: 01865–512602

## CYCLING

**British Cycling Federation**, National Cycling Centre, 1 Stuart Street, Manchester M11 4DQ.
Tel: 0161–223–2244; fax: 0161–231–0592

**Cyclists Touring Club**, 69 Meadrow, Godalming GU7 3HS.
Tel: 01483–417217; fax: 01483–426994

**Sustrans.** Has £42 million from National Lottery to develop cycleways.
35 King Street, Bristol BS1 4DZ.
Tel: 0117–926–8893

53 Cochrane Street, Glasgow G1 1HL.
Tel: 0141–552–8241

Rockwood House, Barn Hill, Stanley DH9 8AN.
Tel: 01207–281259

## MOTORCYCLES

**British Motorcyclists Federation**, 129 Seaforth Avenue, Motspur Park KT3 6JU.
Tel: 0181–942–7914; fax: 0181–949–6215

**Motorcycling Media Bureau**, 9 Little College Street, London SW1P 3XS.
Tel: 0171–222–0666; fax: 0171–233–0335

**Motorcycle Action Group**, PO Box 750, Birmingham B30 3BA.
Tel: 0121–459–5860; fax: 0121–628–1992

## PEDESTRIANS

**Pedestrians Association**, 126 Aldersgate Street, London EC1A 4JQ.
Tel: 0171–490–0750

## TAXIS

**Taxi Newspaper,** and **Licensed Taxi Drivers Association**, 9 Woodfield
Road, London W9 2BA.
Tel: 0171–286–1046

## TRAMS

**Light Rail Transit Association**, Albany House, Petty France, London
SW1H 9EA.
Tel: 0171–918–3116

## SEA TRANSPORT

**Baltic Exchange**, 24 St Mary Axe, London EC3A 8EP (shipping
market).
Tel: 0171–623–5501

**British Marine Equipment Council**, 32 Leman Street, London E1 8EW.
Tel: 0171–488–0171

**Coastguard Agency**, 105 Commercial Road, Southampton SO1 0ZD.
Tel: 01703–329401, press; fax: 01703–329307

**International Association of Classification Societies**, 5 Old Queen
Street, London SW1H 9JA.
Tel: 0171–976–0660

**International Federation of Shipmasters Associations**, 202 Lambeth
Road, London SE1 7JY.
Tel: 0171–261–0450; fax: 0171–401–2537

**International Maritime Organization**, 4 Albert Embankment, London
SE1 7SR (UN agency).
Tel: 0171–735–7611; fax: 587–3210

**Lloyd's Register**, 71 Fenchurch Street, EC3M 4BS. Provides experts to
ensure ships are safe.
Tel: 0171–709–9166; fax: 488–4796

**Marine Safety Agency**, 105 Commercial Road, Southampton SO1 0ZD.
Tel: 01703–329403, press; fax: 01703–329404

**Marine Technology**, Professor Ray Thompson, Newcastle University
NE1 7RU.
Tel: 0191–222–7960

**Marine Technology Centre**, Glasgow University.
Tel: 0141–339–0969

**Nautical Institute**, 202 Lambeth Road, London SE1 7LQ. International
– promotes safety at sea.
Tel: 0171–928–1351; fax: 0171–401–2537

**Naval Architecture**, Glasgow University, Acre Road, Glasgow G20.
Tel: 0141–946–5213

**P&O Corporate Affairs**, 207 The Chambers, London SW10 0XF.
Tel: 0171–351–5533; fax: 0171–823–3421

**Royal Institute of Naval Architects**, 10 Upper Belgrave Street, London
SW1X 8BQ.
Tel: 0171–235–4622

**Royal National Lifeboat Institution**, West Quay Road, Poole BH15
1HZ.
Tel: 01202–671133; fax: 01202–660306

**Sea Containers Ltd**, 20 Upper Ground, London SE1 9PF.
Tel: 0171–928–6969; fax: 0171–401–3861

**SS & Y Research Services**, 28 St Mary Axe, London EC3A 8DR.
Tel: 0171–283–5200

**Stena Sealink.**
Tel: 01233–647022

**Trinity House Lighthouse Service**, Tower Hill, London EC3N 4DH.
Tel: 0171–480–6601; fax: 0171–480–7662

**Chamber of Shipping**, Carthusian Court, 12 Carthusian Street, London
EC1M 6EB.
Tel: 0171–417–8400

## Channel ferries and safety

**Royal Institute of Naval Architects**, see above.

## Ports

**Associated British Ports** (biggest operator), 150 Holborn, London EC1N
2NH.
Tel: 0171–430–1177

**British Ports Federation**.
Tel: 0171–242–1200; fax: 405–1069

# TELECOMMUNICATIONS

See also SATELLITE AND CABLE, page 204.

**British Telecom**.
Tel: 0171–356–5369, press

**British Telecom Research Laboratories**, Martlesham Heath, Ipswich IP5 7RE.
Tel: 01473–643477

**BT Union Committee**, PP311, Room 304–5, 211 Old Street, London EC1V 9PS.
Tel: 0171–250–5578; fax: 0171–250–5579

**Cellnet**, Slough.
Tel: 01753–504000

**Federation of Communication Services**, 207 Anerley Road, London SE20 8ER. Trade association.
Tel: 0181–778–5656; fax: 0181–778–8402

**GPT**, New Century Park, Coventry CV3 1HJ. Manufacturer.
Tel: 01203–562000; fax: 01203–517700

**Mercury Communications**, Red Lion Square, London WC1R 4HQ.
Tel: 0171–528–2000

**National Communications Union**, 150 Brunswick Road, Ealing, London W5 1AW (largest union in BT).
Tel: 0181–998–2981; fax: 0181–991–1410

**OFTEL** (Office of Telecommunications), 50 Ludgate Hill, London EC4M 7JJ. Telecommunications regulator.
Tel: 0171–634–8751/2, press; fax: 0171–634–8842

**STC Technology Ltd**, London Road, Harlow CM17 9NA.
Tel: 01279–626626

**Vodafone**.
Tel: 01635–33251

# TRANSPORT

Major cities have passenger transport authorities responsible for promoting and subsidizing public transport. There may also be local pressure groups. See also ROADS and SEA.

Reference: *Annual Abstract of Statistics* gives transport statistics and road accident figures.

**Department of Transport**, London SW1P 4DR.
Fax: 0171–271–5975/4/2, press

**Road, Rail, Air and Sea Press Desk**
Tel: 0171–271–5766/64/51

**Urban and London Transport Press Desk**
Tel: 0171–271–5758/44

**Centre for Transport Studies**, Cranfield University, Bedford MK43 0AL.
Tel: 01234–750111

**Chartered Institute of Transport**, 80 Portland Place, London W1N 4DP.
Tel: 0171–636–9952; fax: 0171–637–0511

**Institute of Transport Studies**, Leeds University LS2 9JT.
Tel: 0113–233–5326

**Public Transport Information Unit**, Barclay House, Whitworth Street West, Manchester M1 5HG.
Tel: 0161–236–1970

**Transport 2000**, 10 Melton Street, London NW1 2EJ. Pro-railway pressure group.
Tel: 0171–388–8386

**Transport Research Laboratory**, Old Wokingham Road, Crowthorne RG11 6AU.
Tel: 01344–773131, press

**ESRC Transport Studies Unit**, Dr P.B.Goodwin, Oxford University, 11 Bevington Road, OX2 6NB.
Tel: 01865–274715

# AIR

Reference: *Jane's All the World's Aircraft.*

**Aerospace Engineering Department**, Glasgow University.
Tel: 0141–339–8855

**Air Transport Users Council**, 103 Kingsway, London WC2B 6QX.
Tel: 0171–242–3882; fax: 0171–831–4132

**Air UK**, Stansted House, Stansted Airport CM24 1AE.
Tel: 01279–660400; fax: 01279–660330

**BAA** (British Airports Authority), 130 Wilton Road, London SW1V 1LQ.
Tel: 0171–834–9449

**Boeing Commercial Airplane Group**, PO Box 3707, Seattle, WA
98124–2207, USA.
Tel: 001–206–655–2121; fax: 001–206–237–3491

**British Aerospace**, PO Box 87, Farnborough Aerospace Centre, GU14
6YU.
Tel: 01252–373232, press

**Britannia Airways**, Luton Airport, LU2 9ND (world's largest charter
airline).
Tel: 01582–424155; fax: 01582–458594

**Civil Aviation Authority**, 45 Kingsway, London WC2B 6TE.
Tel: 0171–832–5328/6312; fax: 0171–379–4784

**Professor Rigas Doganis**, Cranfield University, Cranfield, MK43 0AL.
Tel: 01234–750111

**Guild of Air Pilots**, 291 Grays Inn Road, London WC1X 8QF.
Tel: 0171–837–3323

**KLM**, 190 Great South West Road, Feltham TW14 9RL.
Tel: 0181–750–9200; fax: 0181–750–9037

**Royal Aeronautical Society**, 4 Hamilton Place, London W1V 0BQ.
Tel: 0171–499–3515

**Society of British Aerospace Companies**, 29 King Street, London SW1Y
6RD. Runs Farnborough Air Show.
Tel: 0171–839–3231; fax: 0171–930–3577

**Stansted Airport**, CM24 1QW.
Tel: 01279–662709; fax: 662971

**Virgin Atlantic**, 3rd Floor, Griffin House, High Street, Crawley RH10 1DQ.
Tel: 01293–747373; fax: 01293–538337


## CHANNEL TUNNEL

**European Passenger Services** (runs Eurostar), Waterloo Station,
London SE1 8SE.
Tel: 0171–922–4494

**Eurotunnel**, 1 Canada Square, London E14 5DU.
Tel: 0171–715–6789

**Trans-Manche Link** (builders of tunnel). Try Andrew Wadsted, Taylor Woodrow.
Tel: 0181–575–4192

**Union Railways**, Network Technical Centre, Wellesley Grove, Croydon CR9 1DY. Planners of Channel Tunnel rail link.
Tel: 0181–666–6497, press


# RAIL

**ABB Rail Vehicles**, Derby (manufacturers).
Tel: 01332–266471, PR

**Advanced Railway Research Centre**, Sheffield University.
Tel: 0114–276–8555

**British Railways Board**, Euston House, 24 Eversholt Street, PO Box 100, London NW1 1DZ. For regional companies, see under regional headings.
Tel: 0171–922–6901, press; fax: 922–6525

**British Transport Police**, PO Box 260, 15 Tavistock Place, London WC1H 9SJ.
Tel: 0171–830–8854; fax: 0171–830–8935

**Central Rail Users' Consultative Committee**, 14 Gresham Street, London EC2V 7NL.
Tel: 0171–505–9090; fax: 0171–505–9004

**Modern Railways Magazine**, Terminal House, Shepperton TW17 8AS.
Tel: 01932–228950; fax: 01932–247520

**Office of Passenger Rail Franchising**, 2 Hay's Lane, London Bridge, London SE1 2HB.
Tel: 0171–940–4294, press; fax: 0171–940–4259

**Office of the Rail Regulator**, 1 Waterhouse Square, 138 Holborn, London EC1N 2ST.
Tel: 0171–282–2082/2002, press; fax: 0171–282–2040

**Railway Gazette International**, Quadrant House, Sutton SM2 5AS.
Tel: 0181–652–3500

**Railway Industry Association**, 6 Buckingham Gate, London SW1E 6AE.
Tel: 0171–834–1426

**Railtrack**, 41 Bernard Street, London WC1N 1BY. For Railtrack's zonal PR managers, see IPO directory.
Tel: 0171–344–7461/7292

## British and European railways

**John V.Gough**, Engineering, Leicester University.
Tel: 0116–252–2625

## Freight

**Mainline Freight**, 310 Goswell Road, London EC1V 7LL.
Tel: 0171–713–2426, press

**Railfreight Distribution**, 169 Westbourne Terrace, London W2 6JY.
Tel: 0171–922–4284, press

**Rail Freight Group** (lobbies for rail freight), 26 Squitchey Lane, Oxford OX2 7LD.
Tel: 01865–515067

**Transrail Freight**, 1 Eversholt Street, London NW1 1DZ.
Tel: 0171–214–9076, press

## YOUR TOWN IN THE PAST

Try local planners, conservation societies, civic societies, historical societies, libraries.
Reference: *Buildings of England* series (Viking/Penguin).
*Pimlico County History Guides* (to Bedfordshire, Dorset, Norfolk, Somerset, Suffolk, Sussex: Pimlico/Random House, £10).

**Department of National Heritage**, 2 Cockspur Street, London SW1Y 5DH.
Tel: 0171–211–6269/7; fax: 0171–211–6270

**Archaeology Department**, Reading University RG6 2AA.
Tel: 01734–318132

**Association of Railway Preservation Societies**, 7 Robert Close, Potters Bar EN6 2DH.
Tel: 01707–643568; fax: 01707–643568

**Council for British Archaeology**, 111 Walmgate, York YO1 2UA.
Tel: 01904–671417; fax: 01904–671384

**English Heritage**, 23 Savile Row, London W1X 1AB. Has ancient monuments laboratory.
Tel: 0171–973–3252/51, press

**Georgian Group**, 6 Fitzroy Square, London W1P 6DX.
Tel: 0171–387–1720; fax: 0171–387–1721

**National Heritage Memorial Fund**, 20 King Street, London SW1Y 6QY.
Tel: 0171–747–2030, press

**National Trust**, 36 Queen Anne's Gate, London SW1H 9AS.
Tel: 0171–222–9251, press; fax: 0171–233–3037
Photographic library tel: 0171–222–9251

**Royal Commission on Historical Monuments of England**, 23 Savile Row, London W1X 1AB.
Tel: 0171–973–3500

**Twentieth Century Society**, 70 Cowcross Street, London EC1M 6BP.
Tel: 0171–250–3857

**Victorian Society**, 1 Priory Gardens, London W4 1TT.
Tel: 0181–994–1019

# 7 THE UNITED KINGDOM

## BRITISH ISLANDS

### GUERNSEY

**Guernsey Electricity**, PO Box 4, North Side, Vale, Guernsey GY1 3AD (Channel Islands).
Tel: 01481–46931; fax: 46942

### ISLE OF MAN

**Financial Supervision Commission**, 1 Goldie Terrace, Douglas.
Supervises offshore banking.
Tel: 01624–624487; fax: 01624–629342

**Isle of Man Department of Tourism**, Sea Terminal, Douglas, Isle of Man.
Tel: 01624–666801; fax: 01624–686800

**Manx Electricity Authority**, PO Box 177, Douglas IM99 1PS.
Tel: 01624–687687; fax: 01624–687612

### JERSEY

**Channel TV**, St Helier, Jersey JE2 3ZD (Channel Islands).
Tel: 01534–68999; fax: 01534–59446

**Jersey Electricity**, PO Box 45, Queens Road, St Helier JE4 8NY (Channel Islands).
Tel: 01534–505000; fax: 01534–505011

## DEFENCE, THE SERVICES

Defence press officers are listed below and under regions. Find out also who to speak to at local military camps and establishments.

The **Royal British Legion**, the main ex-service organization, has branches and clubs throughout the country. So has the **RAF Association**. There may be a local branch of the **Campaign for Nuclear Disarmament**.

Reference books: *Jane's Fighting Ships*, *Jane's All the World's Aircraft*, *Navy List* (of officers), *Army List*, *Air Force List*.

**Jane's** (163 Brighton Road, Coulsdon CR5 2NH) also publishes *Jane's Defence Weekly* and other journals including reports on the arms market.

### *National sources*

**Ministry of Defence**, Whitehall, SW1A 2HB.
Fax: 0171–218–6460
**Procurement Press Desk.**
Tel: 0171–218–7950
**Royal Navy Press Desk**.
Tel: 0171–218–3257/8
**Army Press Desk**.
Tel: 0171–218–3255/6
**RAF Press Desk**.
Tel: 0171–218–3253/4

**British Aerospace**, PO Box 87, Farnborough Aerospace Centre, GU14 6YU.
Tel: 01252–373232, press

**British American Security Information Council**, 20 Embankment Place, London WC2N 6NN.
Tel: 0171–925–0862; fax: 0171–925–0861

**Centre for Defence Studies**, King's College, Strand, London WC2R 2LS.
Tel: 0171–873–2338; fax: 0171–873–2748

**Centre for Security Studies**, Hull University HU6 7RX.
Tel: 01482–465749, Professor Colin Gray; 01482–465724, Eric Grove

**GEC**, 1 Stanhope Gate, London W1A 1EH.
Tel: 0171–493–8484

**International Institute for Strategic Studies**, 23 Tavistock Street, London WC2E 7NQ.
Tel: 0171–379–7676

**Logica**, 68 Newman Street, London W1A 4SE.
Tel: 0171–637–9111

**Rolls-Royce**, 65 Buckingham Gate, London SW1E 6AT.
Tel: 0171–222–9020; fax: 0171–233–1733

**Royal United Services Institute**, Whitehall, London SW1A 2ET.
Tel: 0171–930–5854

**Vosper Thorneycroft**, 223 Southampton Road, Paulsgrove, Portsmouth.
Tel: 01705–379481; fax: 01705–201540

**World Disarmament Campaign**, 45 Blythe Street, London E2 6LX.
Tel: 0171–729–2523

## EUROPEAN SECURITY

**Dr Andrew Cottey**, Peace Studies, Bradford University BD7 1DP.
Tel: 01274–385239

**Institute for European Defence and Strategic Studies**, 14 Wells Street, London W1P 3FP.
Tel: 0171–637–2152; fax: 0171–637–2155

## GLOBAL SECURITY, PEACEKEEPING

**Global Security Programme**, Social and Political Science, Free School Lane, Cambridge CB2 3RQ.
Tel: 01223–334509

**Professor Alan James**, International Relations, Keele University, ST5 5BG.
Tel: 01782–583210

**Professor Paul Rogers**, Peace Studies, Bradford University, BD7 1DP.
Tel: 01274–384185/385235

# LANDMINES

**UK Working Group on Landmines**, 601 Holloway Road, London N19 4DJ.
Tel: 01296–632056; fax: 01296–632056

**UN Demining Office**, Department of Peacekeeping, United Nations, New York NY 10017.
Tel: 00–1–212–963–2627; fax: 212–963–3452 or 6460

# NUCLEAR

**Campaign for Nuclear Disarmament**, 162 Holloway Road, London N7 8DQ.
Tel: 0171–700–2393; fax: 0171–700–2357

# PEACE

**National Peace Council**, 88 Islington High Street, London N1 8EG.
Tel: 0171–354–5200

**Richardson Institute for Peace Studies**, Dr Morris Bradley, Lancaster University LA1 4YW.
Tel: 01524–594266

# TRADE IN ARMS

**Campaign against the Arms Trade**, 11 Goodwin Street, London N4 3HQ.
Tel: 0171–281–0297

# WELFARE

**British Limbless Ex-Service Men's Association**, 185 High Road, Chadwell Heath RM6 6NA.
Tel: 0181–590–1124; fax: 0181–599–2932

**Ex-Services Mental Welfare Society**, Broadway House, Broadway, Wimbledon SW19 1RL. Helps people affected mentally by fighting.
Tel: 0181–543–6333; fax: 542–7082

**Japanese Labour Camp Survivors Association**, R.W.Wilkins, Rayleigh.
Tel: 01268–743227

**RAF Association**, 43 Grove Park Road, London W4 3RU.
Tel: 0181–994–8504

**Royal British Legion**, 48 Pall Mall, London SW1Y 5JY. Women's
section has the same address.
Tel: 0171–973–7292, press; fax: 0171–973–7399

**Royal Naval Association**, 82 Chelsea Manor Street, London SW3 5QJ.
Tel: 0171–352–6764

**Tri-Service Resettlement Organization**, Room 526, 14 New Oxford
Street, London WC1A 1EJ.
Tel: 0171–305–3786, press

**War Widows Association of Great Britain**, 52 West Street, Gorseinon,
Swansea SA4 2AF.
Tel: 01792–896219

## EAST MIDLANDS

**Central Office of Information**, Belgrave Centre, Talbot Street,
Nottingham NG1 5GG.
Tel: 0115–971–2780; fax: 0115–971–2791

**Department of Trade and Industry**, Nottingham.
Tel: 0115–959–9177, press; fax: 0115–959–0316

## ARTS

**East Midlands Arts**, Mountfields House, Epinal Way, Loughborough
LE11 3HU.
Tel: 01509–218292; fax: 01509–262214

## COUNTRYSIDE

**Ministry of Agriculture** (press), Block 7, Chalfont Drive, Nottingham
NG8 3SN.
Tel: 0115–929–1191, ext. 376

**National Trust**, Clumber Park Stableyard, Worksop S80 3BE.
Tel: 01909–486411; fax: 01909–486377

**Royal Society for Protection of Birds**, 46 The Green, South Bar, Banbury OX16 9AB.
Tel: 01295–253330

## HEALTH

**Trent Regional Health Authority**, Fulwood House, Old Fulwood Road, Sheffield S10 3TH.
Tel: 0114–263–0300

## INDUSTRY

**Confederation of British Industry**, Nottingham.
Tel: 0115–965–3311

**East Midlands Electricity**, PO Box 4, 398 Coppice Road, Arnold NG5 7HX.
Tel: 0115–926–9711; fax: 0115–920–9789

**Electricity Consumers Committee** (East Midlands), Suite 3c, 40 Friar Lane, Nottingham NG1 6DQ.
Tel: 0115–950–8738

## NOTTINGHAM

**AEEU Union** (electricians), 577 Nuthall Road, Nottingham NG8 6AD.
Tel: 0115–978–4684; fax: 0115–942–0826

**Boots**, 2 Thane Road, Beeston.
Tel: 0115–950–6111

**Nottingham Development Enterprise**, 4 Regent Street.
Tel: 0115–950–2233/952–0448

**Nottingham Fashion Centre.**
Tel: 0115–958–7246

## POLITICS

**Labour Party** (Central Region), 1 Lawrence Street, Long Eaton NG10 1JY.
Tel: 0115–946–2195

## SOCIETY

**Benefits Agency**.
Tel: 0115–929–2968, press

## TRADE UNIONS

**AEEU Union** (engineers), 210 Osmaston Road, Derby DE23 8JX.
Tel: 01332–46617; fax: 01332–384036

**GMB Union**, 542 Woodborough Road, Nottingham NG3 5FJ.
Tel: 0115–960–7171; fax: 0115–962–5428

**UCATT** (construction workers), Derby.
Tel: 01332–203656

**UNISON**, 15 Castle Gate, Nottingham NG1 6BY.
Tel: 0115–941–5040; fax: 0115–948–4866

## TRANSPORT

**Highways Agency**.
Tel: 0115–971–2784, press

**East Midlands Airport**, Castle Donington.
Tel: 01332–852852

**Midland Mainline Rail Service**, Midland House, Nelson Street, Derby DE1 2SA.
Tel: 01332–262010, press

## EASTERN ENGLAND

**Central Office of Information**, 72 Hills Road, Cambridge CB2 1LL.
Tel: 01223–311867; fax: 01223–316121

**Department of Environment**.
Tel: 01223–311867, ext. 20

## ARTS, CULTURE, MEDIA

**Anglia TV**, Anglia House, Norwich NR1 3JG.
Tel: 01603–615151; fax: 01603–631032

**Eastern Arts**, Cherry Hinton Hall, Cherry Hinton Road, Cambridge C1 4DW.
Tel: 01223–215355; fax: 01223–248075

## DEVELOPMENT, INDUSTRY

**Department of Trade and Industry**, Cambridge.
Tel: 01223–311867, press; fax: 01223–316121

**Confederation of British Industry**.
Tel: 01223–65636

**East Anglia Tourist Board**, Toppesfield Hall, Hadleigh (Suffolk) IP7 5DN.
Tel: 01473–822922; fax: 01473–823063

## ENERGY

**Eastern Group**, PO Box 40, Wherstead Park, Wherstead, Ipswich IP9 2AQ.
Tel:  01473–688688; fax: 01473–601036

**Electricity Consumers Committee (Eastern)**, 4th Floor, Waveney House, Handford Road, Ipswich IP1 2BJ.
Tel: 01473–216101

## FARMING, COUNTRYSIDE

**Ministry of Agriculture** (press), Block B, Government Buildings, Brooklands Avenue, Cambridge CB2 2DR.
Tel: 01223–462727, ext. 5947

**National Trust**, Blickling, Norwich NR11 6NF.
Tel: 01263–733471; fax: 01263–734924 and
The Dairy House, Ickworth, Horringer IP29 5QE.
Tel: 01284–735480; fax: 01284–735380

**Royal Society for Protection of Birds**, 65 Thorpe Road, Norwich NR1 1UD.
Tel: 01603–661662

## HEALTH, SOCIETY

**Anglia and Oxford Regional Health Authority**, Union Lane, Chesterton CB4 1RF.
Tel: 01223–375375; fax: 01223–353209

**Scope** (formerly Spastics Society), Huntingdon.
Tel: 01480–434445

## POLITICS

**Conservative Party** (London and Eastern), 32 Smith Square, London SW1P 3HH.
Tel: 0171–222–9000; fax: 0171–222–1135

**Labour Party (South-East)**, 97 Fore Street, Ipswich IP4 1JZ.
Tel: 01473–255668

## TELEPHONES

**British Telecom (Northern Home Counties)**, 22 St Peter's Square, Colchester CO1 1ET.
Tel: 01206–892757

## TRADE UNIONS

For **GMB Union**, **TGWU** and **UCATT** regional offices, see London.

**AEEU** (AEU Section), AEEU House, Primrose Hill, Chelmsford CM1 2RQ.
Tel: 01245–355858; fax: 01245–345315

**UNISON**, Church Lane, Chelmsford CM1 1UW.
Tel: 01245–287524; fax: 01245–492863

## TRANSPORT

**Anglia Railways**, 15 Artillery Lane, London E1 7HA.
Tel: 0171–465–9009, press

**Great Eastern Railway**, Room G06, Hamilton House, 3 Appold Street, London EC2A 2AA.
Tel: 0171–922–4842, press

**Highways Agency**.
Tel: 01223–311867, press

**London Tilbury Southend Rail**, Central House, Clifftown Road,
Southend SS1 1AB.
Tel: 01702–357810, press

**Rail Users Consultative Committee**, 46 Priestgate, Peterborough PE1
1LF.
Tel: 01733–312188; fax: 01733–891286

## WATER AND RIVERS

**Anglian Water**, Ambury Road, Huntingdon PE18 6NZ.
Tel: 01480–443000; fax: 01480–443115

**Environment Agency**, Peterborough, PE2 5ZR.
Tel: 01733–371811; fax: 01733–464222

**OFWAT Eastern Customer Committee**, Carlyle House, Carlyle Road,
Cambridge CB4 3DN.
Tel: 01223–323889

## ECONOMY

Reference: *Blue Book: UK National Accounts.*
*Economic Trends* (periodical).

**Adam Smith Institute** (right-wing think-tank), 23 Great Smith Street,
London SW1P 3BL.
Tel: 0171–222–4995

**Centre for Economic Performance**, LSE, Houghton Street, London
WC2A 2AE.
Tel: 0171–955–7048; fax: 0171–955–6848

**Centre for Economic Policy Research**, 25 Old Burlington Street,
London W1X 1LB.
Tel: 0171–734–9110

**Economic and Social Research Council**, Polaris House, North Star
Avenue, Swindon SN2 1UJ.
Tel: 01793–413000, press; fax: 413001

**Economics Faculty**, Cambridge University, Sidgwick Avenue, CB3 9DE.
Tel: 01223–335200

**Financial Markets Group**, LSE.
Tel: 0171–955–7891

**Goldman Sachs**, 133 Fleet Street, London EC4A 2BH (often comments on TV).
Tel: 0171–774–1000

**Institute of Economic Affairs**, 2 Lord North Street, London SW1P 3LB (free market think-tank).
Tel: 0171–799–3745; fax: 0171–799–2137

**National Institute Economic Review, National Institute of Economic and Social Research**, 2 Dean Trench Street, London SW1P 3HB.
Tel: 0171–222–7665

**London Economics**, Professor John Kay, 10th Floor, 66 Chiltern Street, London W1M 1PR.
Tel: 0171–446–8400; fax: 446–8484

**Organization for Economic Co-operation and Development**, Chateau de la Muette, 2 Rue Andre, Pascal, 75775 Paris.
Tel: 00–331–45–24–8200

**Social Market Foundation**, 20 Queen Anne's Gate, London SW1H 9AA. Interested in how social security is to be paid for
Tel: 0171–222–7060

# HISTORY

**Churchill Archives Centre**, Churchill College, Cambridge. Holds papers of many twentieth century politicians.
Tel: 01223–336000

**Historical Association**, 59a Kennington Park Road, London SE11 4JH.
Tel: 0171–735–3901

**Institute of Historical Research**, Senate House, Malet Street, London WC1E 7HU.
Tel: 0171–636–0272

**Public Record Office**, Ruskin Avenue, Kew TW9 4DU. Holds government papers that are open to view.
Tel: 0181–392–5277; fax: 878–8905

**Royal Historical Society**, UCL, Gower Street, WC1.
Tel: 0171–387–7532

# LONDON

Reference: *London Hostels Directory.*
*London Housing Statistics.*
*Names of Streets in London.*
*Survey of London* (detailed account of history and buildings).

**Greater London Group**, London School of Economics, Houghton Street, London WC2A 2AE.
Tel: 0171–955–7570

**Department of Environment**, London desk.
Tel: 0171–890–4627/15; fax: 0171–890–4689

## ADMINISTRATION

**Association of London Government** (represents boroughs), 36 Old Queen Street, London SW1H 9HP.
Tel: 0171–222–7799

**London Research Centre**, 81 Black Prince Road, SE1 7SZ. Researches London and local government issues for London boroughs.
Tel: 0171–735–4250

**Royal Parks Agency**, Old Police House, W2 2UH.
Tel: 0171–298–2031, press

## ARTS, CULTURE, MEDIA

**Barbican Centre**, Silk Street, London EC2Y 8DS.
Tel: 0171–638–4141; fax: 0171–382–7252

**Carlton TV**, 101 St Martins Lane, London WC2N 4AZ.
Tel: 0171–240–4000; fax: 0171–240–4171

**Covent Garden Opera**, London WC2E 7QA.
Tel: 0171–240–1200

**London Arts**, Elme House, 133 Long Acre, London WC2E 9AF.
Tel: 0171–240–1313; fax: 0171–240–4580

**London International Festival of Theatre** (Lift).
Tel: 0171–490–3964/5
or try via Mark Borkowski PR.
Tel: 0171–482–4000

**London News Network**, London TV Centre, Upper Ground, London SE1 9LT. London news and sport for ITV.
Tel: 0171–827–7700; fax: 0171–827–7720

**London Weekend TV**, Upper Ground, London SE1 9LT.
Tel: 0171–620–1620; fax: 0171–261–1290

**Mission to London**, 10 Sovereign Park, Hemel Hempstead.
Tel: 01442–60906

**Notting Hill Carnival**, 35 West Row, London W10 5AS.
Tel: 0181–964–0544

**Royal Academy**, Burlington House, Piccadilly, London W1V 0DS.
Tel: 0171–439–7438; fax: 0171–434–0837

**Royal National Theatre**, London SE1 9PX.
Tel: 0171–928–2833

**Royal Philharmonic Orchestra**, 16 Clerkenwell Gardens, London EC1R 0DP.
Tel: 0171–608–2381; fax: 0171–608–1226

**Society of London Theatre**, Bedford Chambers, Covent Garden, WC2E 8HQ. Publishes the Theatre List, a monthly account of shows.
Tel: 0171–836–0971; fax: 0171–497–2543

**Theatre Royal**, Stratford East, Gerry Raffles Square, London E15 1BN.
Tel: 0181–534–7374

**Victoria and Albert Museum**, Cromwell Road, London SW7 2RL.
Tel: 0171–938–8500; fax: 0171–938–8341

**Westminster Abbey**, Chapter Office, 20 Dean's Yard, London SW1P 3PA.
Tel: 0171–222–5152, press

## CRIME

**Metropolitan Police Press Bureau**, New Scotland Yard, Broadway, London SW1H 0BG.
Tel: 0171–230–2171; fax: 2818
Pre-recorded press bulletins, tel: 0891–900099. The Met also has area information officers who may be easier to reach than the press bureau.

## DEFENCE

**Army Information Officer**, Horseguards Parade, London SW1 2AX.
Tel: 0171–414–2396

## DEVELOPMENT, COMMERCE, INDUSTRY

**Greater London Enterprise.**
Tel: 0171–403–0300

**London Docklands Development Corporation**, 191 Marsh Wall, London E14 9TJ.
Tel: 0171–512–0444; fax: 0171–512–0222

**London First Centre**. Private-sector agency for promoting investment.
Tel: 0171–272–1445

**London Industrial**, Parmiter Road, E2 9HZ. Bought industrial property of Greater London Council.
Tel: 0181–983–0239

**London Tourist Board**, 26 Grosvenor Gardens, London SW1W 0DU.
Tel: 0171–730–3450; fax: 0171–824–8506

## ENERGY

**Electricity Consumers Committee (London)**, 5th Floor, 11 Belgrave Road, London SW1V 1RB.
Tel: 0171–233–6366

**London Electricity**, 81 High Holborn, London WC1V 6NU.
Tel: 0171–242–9050; fax: 0171–242–2815

## ENVIRONMENT

**London Waste Regulation Authority**, 20 Albert Embankment, London SE1 7TJ.
Tel: 0171–587–3000

## FIRE

**London Fire Brigade**, 8 Albert Embankment SE1 7SP.
Tel: 0171–582–3811

## HEALTH AND SOCIAL SERVICES

**Age Concern**, Greater London, 54 Knatchbull Road, SE5.
Tel: 0171–737–3456; fax: 0171–274–6014

**Alcohol Recovery Project**, 68 Newington Causeway, London SE1 6DF.
Tel: 0171–403–3369; fax: 0171–357–6712

**Emergency Bed Service**, 28 London Bridge Street, London SE1 9SG.
Helps doctors find hospital beds in emergencies.
Tel: 0171–407–7181; fax: 0171–357–6705

**Greater London Association of Community Health Councils**, 356
Holloway Road, N7 6PA.
Tel: 0171–700–0100; fax: 0171–700–8126

**Greater London Association of Disabled (GLAD)**, 336 Brixton Road,
London SW9 7AA.
Tel: 0171–274–0107; fax: 0171–274–7840

**Greater London Fund for Blind**, 12 Whitehorse Mews, 37 Westminster
Bridge Road, SE1 7QD.
Tel: 0171–620–2066

**London Lesbian and Gay Switchboard**.
Tel: 0171–837–7324

**London Voluntary Service Council**, 356 Holloway Road, London N7 6PA.
Tel: 0171–700–8107; fax: 0171–700–8108

## HOMELESSNESS

**Big Issue**.
Tel: 0171–418–0418

**Centrepoint**, Bewlay House, 2 Swallow Place, London W1R 7AA. Finds
shelter for young people.
Tel: 0171–629–2229; fax: 0171–493–2120

**Simon Community**, PO Box 1187, London NW5 4HW.
Tel: 0171–485–6639

**Squash** (Squatters Action for Secure Homes), 68 Bedford Road,
London E17 4PX.
Tel: 0181–523–4547

**Squatters Advisory Service**, 2 St Paul's Road, London N1 2QH.
Tel: 0171–359–8814

## POLITICS

**Conservative Party** (London and Eastern), 32 Smith Square, London
SW1P 3HH.
Tel: 0171–222–9000; fax: 0171–222–1135

**Labour Party** (Greater London), 16 Charles Square, London N1 6HP.
Tel: 0171–490–4904

## SPORT (see SOUTH and SOUTH-EAST)

**British Athletics Federation**, London.
Tel: 0171–247–2963

## TELEPHONES

**British Telecom London**, 1 Drury Lane, London WC2B 5RS.
Tel: 0171–829–0401, press; fax: 0171–240–8555.

## TRADE UNIONS

See also under SOUTH and SOUTH-EAST, page 295.

**UNISON**, Civic House, Blackheath, London SE3 0QY.
Tel: 0181–852–2842; fax: 0181–852–2986

## TRANSPORT

**Department of Transport London-Issues Media Desk**, 5th Floor, 76 Marsham Street, London SW1P 4DR.
Tel: 0171–271–5758/44/41; fax: 0171–271–5975/4

**Docklands Light Railway** (media), PO Box 154, Castor Lane, London E14 0DX.
Tel: 0171–537–7023; fax: 0171–538–3818

**Highways Agency** (London).
Tel: 0171–261–8787, press

**London Transport** (media), 55 Broadway, London SW1H 0BD.
Tel: 0171–918–3271/4/5; fax: 0171–918–3134

**Traffic Director for London**, College House, Great Peter Street, London SW1P 3LN. Responsible for red routes.
Tel: 0171–799–1086, press; fax: 0171–976–8640

# NORTH-EAST AND YORKSHIRE

**Central Office of Information**, North-East, Wellbar House, Gallowgate, NE1 4TB.
Tel: 0191–202–3600; fax: 0191–261–8571/222–0892

**COI**, Yorkshire and Humberside, City House, New Station Street, Leeds LS1 4JG.
Tel: 0113–283–6591; fax: 0113–283–6586

**Department of Environment**, North East Press.
Tel: 0191–202–3610
Yorkshire and Humberside Press.
Tel: 0113–283–6600

## ARTS, CULTURE, MEDIA

**Northern Arts**, 9 Osborne Terrace, Newcastle upon Tyne NE2 1NZ.
Tel: 0191–281–6334; fax: 0191–281–3276

**Northern Sinfonia**, Newcastle.
Tel: 0191–240–1812

**Opera North**, Grand Theatre, 46 New Briggate, Leeds LS1 6NU.
Tel: 0113–243–9999; fax: 0113–244–0418

**Tyne Tees TV**, City Road, Newcastle upon Tyne NE1 2AL.
Tel: 0191–261–0181; fax: 0191–261–2302

**Yorkshire and Humberside Arts**, 21 Bond Street, Dewsbury WF13 1AX.
Tel: 01924–455555; fax: 01924–466522

**Yorkshire Cable Communications**, Mayfair Business Park, Broad Lane, Bradford BD4 8PW.
Tel: 01274–828282

**Yorkshire TV**, Leeds LS3 1JS.
Tel: 0113–243–8283; fax: 0113–244–5107

## DEFENCE

**Army (2 Division) Information**, Imphal Barracks, Fulford Road, York YO1 4AU.
Tel: 01904–662020/662533

# DEVELOPMENT, COMMERCE, INDUSTRY

**Department of Trade and Industry**, Newcastle.
Tel: 0191–202–3603/4 fax: 261–8571

**Department of Trade and Industry**, Leeds.
Tel: 0113–283–6601/6595; fax: 0113–283–6586

**Belasis Hall Science Park**, Billingham.
Tel: 01642–370324, PR

**CBI Northern**, 15 Grey Street, Newcastle NE1 6EE.
Tel: 0191–230–4579

**CBI Northern and Yorks**.
Tel: 0113–264–4242

**Humberside European Business Information Centre**, Sally Hewitt, Hull
University HU6 7RX.
Tel: 01482–465940

**Northern Development Company**, Great North House, Sandyford Road,
Newcastle upon Tyne NE1 8ND.
Tel: 0191–261–0026; fax: 0191–232–9069

**Teesside Development Corporation**, Dunedin House, Riverside Quay,
Stockton TS17 6BJ.
Tel: 01642–677123; fax: 01642–676123

**Tyne and Wear Development Corporation**, Scotswood House,
Newcastle Business Park, NE4 7YL.
Tel: 0191–226–1234; fax: 226–1388

**Wise Speke**, 39 Pilgrim Street, Newcastle. Largest North-East
stockbroker.
Tel: 0191–201–3800

**Wool Textile and Clothing Industry Action Committee**, 7th Floor,
Jacobs Well, Bradford BD1 1HY.
Tel: 01274–753958; fax: 01274–393226

**Yorkshire Enterprise Ltd** (venture capital).
Tel: 0113–237–4774

## *Economy, employment*

**Professor John Goddard**, CURDS, Newcastle University.
Tel: 0191–222–7955

**Alan Townsend, Dr David Sadler**, Geography, Durham University, Science Laboratories, South Road, DH1 3LE.
Tel: 0191–374–2462; fax: 2456

## ENERGY

**Electricity Consumers Committee, North-Eastern**, 1st Floor, 35 Nelson Street, Newcastle NE1 5AN.
Tel: 0191–221–22071
**Yorkshire**, 4th Floor, Fairfax House, Merrion Street, Leeds LS2 8JU.
Tel: 0113–234–1866

**Northern Electric**, Carliol House, Market Street, Newcastle NE1 6NE.
Tel: 0191–210–2000; fax: 0191–210–1001

**Yorkshire Electricity**, Wetherby Road, Scarcroft, Leeds LS14 3HS.
Tel: 0113–289–2123; fax: 0113–289–5611

## FARMING, COUNTRYSIDE, GARDENS

**Ministry of Agriculture**, Government Buildings, Crosby Road, Northallerton DL6 1AD.
Tel: 01609–773751, ext. 2415

**Northern Horticultural Society**, Harlow Carr Gardens, Crag Lane, Harrogate HG3 1QB.
Tel: 01423–565418

**National Trust, Northumbria**, Scots' Gap, Morpeth NE61 4EG.
Tel: 01670–774691; fax: 01670–774317

**Royal Society for Protection of Birds**, 4 Benton Terrace, Sandyford Road, Newcastle NE2 1QU.
Tel: 0191–281–3366

**National Trust, Yorkshire**, 27 Tadcaster Road, Dringhouses, York YO2 2QG.
Tel: 01904–702021; fax: 01904–707982

# HEALTH AND SOCIAL SERVICES

**Benefits Agency.**
**North East Press.**
Tel: 0191–261–5500
**Yorks and Humberside Press.**
Tel: 0113–232–4677

**Northern and Yorks Regional Health Authority**, Queen Building, Park Parade, Harrogate HG1 5AH.
Tel: 01423–500066; fax: 01423 843140

# INTERNATIONAL

**Commonwealth Institute**, Salts Mill, Saltaire BD18 3LB.
Tel: 01274–530251; fax: 01274–530253

# POLITICS

**Conservative Party** (North and Yorks), 53 Great George Street, Leeds LS1 3BL.
Tel: 0113–245–0731

**Labour Party** (North-East and Yorks), Trend House, Northgate, Wakefield WF1 3AS.
Tel: 01924–291221

# SHEFFIELD

**Crucible Theatre**, 55 Norfolk Street, S1 1DA.
Tel: 0114–276–0621

**Cutlers Company**, Cutlers Hall, Church Street, S1.
Tel: 0114–272–8456

**Cutlery Research Association**, Henry Street, S3.
Tel: 0114–276–9736

**Sheffield Chamber of Commerce**, Earl Street, S1.
Tel: 0114–276–6667

**Sheffield Development Corporation**, Don Valley House, Savile St East, S4 7UQ.
Tel: 0114–272–0100; fax: 0114–272–6359

**Urban Theology Unit**, 210 Abbeyfield Road, S4 7AZ.
Tel: 0114–243–5342

## SPORT

**Gateshead International Stadium**, Neilson Road.
Tel: 0191–478–1687

**Northern Council for Sport and Recreation**, Aykley Heads, Durham
DH1 5UU.
Tel: 0191–384–9595; fax: 0191–384–5807

**Yorks and Humber Council for Sport and Recreation**, Coronet House,
Queen Street, Leeds LS1 4PW.
Tel: 0113–243–6443; fax: 0113–242–2189

## TELEPHONES

**British Telecom North-East**, 35 Lisbon Street, Leeds LS1 1BA.
Tel: 0113–246–4618

## TRADE UNIONS

**TUC Northern**, Transport House, John Dobson Street, Newcastle upon
Tyne NE1 8TW.
Tel: 0191–232–3175; fax: 0191–232–3190

**TUC Yorkshire and Humberside**, 30 York Place, Leeds LS1 2ED.
Tel: 0113–242–9696; fax: 0113–244–1161

**GMB Union.**
**Northern**, 77 West Road, Newcastle NE15 6RB.
Tel: 0191–273–2321; fax: 0191–272–0054
**Yorkshire and North Derbyshire**, Concord House, Par Lane, Leeds LS3
1NB.
Tel: 0113–245–0608; 0113–244–1078

**TGWU (North and North-East)**, 22 Blenheim Terrace, Leeds LS2 9HF.
Tel: 0113–245–1587/2373; fax: 0113–242–0637

**UCATT** (construction workers), Leeds.
Tel: 0113–264–0211

**UNISON**, Milburn House, 'A' Dean Street, Newcastle upon Tyne NE1
1LE.
Tel: 0191–232–4900; fax: 0191–222–0257 and
3rd Floor, Commerce House, Wade Lane, Leeds LS2 8UJ.
Tel: 0113–244–9111; fax: 0113–244–8852

# TRANSPORT

**Highways Agency.**
**North East Press.**
Tel: 0191–202–3610
**Yorkshire and Humberside Press.**
Tel: 0113–283–6592

**Leeds/Bradford Airport**, Yeadon.
Tel: 0113–250–9696

**Newcastle Airport**, Woolsington.
Tel: 0191–286–0966

**North East Regional Railways.**
Tel: 01904–522825, press

**InterCity East Coast**, York YO1 1HT.
Tel: 01904–523072

**Rail Users Consultative Committee**, Hilary House, St Saviour's Place,
York YO1 2PL.
Tel: 01904–625615; fax: 01904–625615

**RMT York**, Suite T8, 38 Blossom Street, YO2 2AJ.
Tel: 01904–525643

**South Yorkshire Passenger Transport Executive**, Exchange Street,
Sheffield S2 5SZ.
Tel: 0114–276–7575; fax: 0114–273–1821

**Tyne and Wear PTE**, Cuthbert House, All Saints, Newcastle NE1 2DA.
Tel: 0191–203–3333; fax: 0191–203–3180

**West Yorkshire PTE**, 40 Wellington Street, LS1 2DE.
Tel: 0113–251–7272

## WATER AND RIVERS

**Environment Agency**, Northumbria/Yorks.
Tel: 0113–244–0191; fax: 0113–231–2476

**Northumbrian Water**, Abbey Road, Pity Me DH1 5FJ.
Tel: 0191–383–2222; fax: 0191–384–1920

**Yorkshire Water**, 67 Albion Street, Leeds LS1 5AA.
Tel: 0113–244–8201; fax: 0113–232–4322

**OFWAT Northumbria Customer Service Committee**, 2nd Floor, 35
Nelson Street, Newcastle NE1 5AN.
Tel: 0191–221–0646

**OFWAT Yorkshire CSC**, Symons House, Belgrave Street, Leeds LS2
8DF.
Tel: 0113–234–0874

## NORTH-WEST

**Central Office of Information**, Sunley Tower, Piccadilly Plaza,
Manchester M1 4BD.
Tel (Manchester): 0161–952–4502/9; fax: 0161–236–9443;
tel (Liverpool): 0151–224–6412; fax: 0151–224–6470

**Government Office for North West** (Sunley Tower).
Tel: 0161–952–4000

## ARTS, MEDIA

**Border TV**, Durranhill, Carlisle CA1 3NT.
Tel: 01228–25101; fax: 01228–41384

**Granada TV**, Manchester M60 9EA.
Tel: 0161–832–7211

**North West Arts**, 12 Harter Street, Manchester M1 6HY.
Tel: 0161–228–3062; fax: 0161–236–5361

**Royal Northern College of Music**, 124 Oxford Road, Manchester M13.
Tel: 0161–273–6283

# DEFENCE

**Army (5 Division) Information**, Copthorne Barracks, Shrewsbury SY3 8LZ.
Tel: 01743–262252

# ENERGY

**Electricity Consumers Committee (Merseyside)**, 4th Floor, Hamilton
House, Chester CH1 2BH.
Tel: 01244–320849

**Electricity Consumers Committee (North West)**, 1st Floor, 17 Chorlton
Street, Manchester M1 3HY.
Tel: 0161–236–3484

**Manweb**, Sealand Road, Chester CH1 4LR.
Tel: 0345–112211; fax: 01244–377269

**United Utilities**, Great Sankey, WA5 3LW.
Tel: 01925–233230/233033/233135; fax: 01925–233372

# ENVIRONMENT

**Department of Environment Press**.
Tel: 0161–952–4512/0151–224–6412

**National Trust**, The Hollens, Grasmere LA22 9QZ.
Tel: 015394–35599; fax: 015394–35353

**Royal Society for Protection of Birds**, Westleigh Mews, Wakefield
Road, Denby Dale HD8 8QD.
Tel: 01484–861148

# FARMING

**Ministry of Agriculture**, Eden Bridge House, Lowther Street, Carlisle
CA3 8DX.
Tel: 01228–23400, ext. 484

# HEALTH

**North West Regional Health Authority**, 930 Birchwood Blvd, Millenium
Park, Warrington WA3 7QN.
Tel: 01925–704000

## INDUSTRY

**Department of Trade and Industry**, Manchester.
Tel: 0161–952–4508/9, press; fax: 0161–236–9443

**CBI North West.**
Tel: 0161–707–2190

**Lancashire Enterprises**, 17 Ribblesdale Place, Preston.
Tel: 01772–203020

## THE LAKES

**Windermere Lake Cruises**, Lakeside LA12 8AS.
Tel: 015395–31188; fax: 015395–31947

## MANCHESTER

**AEEU Union** (engineers), Parkgates, Bury New Road, Prestwich M25 8JX.
Tel: 0161–798–8976; fax: 0161–798–9721

**Crisis Manchester** (helps homeless).
Tel: 0161–237–1607

**Greater Manchester Passenger Transport Executive**, PO Box 429, 9 Portland Street, M60 1HX.
Tel: 0161–228–6400; fax: 0161–228–3291

**Halle Concerts Society**, 30 Cross Street, Manchester M2 7BA.
Tel: 0161–834–8363; fax: 0161–832–1669

**Manchester Airport**, M22.
Tel: 0161–489–3000

**Manchester Festival**, Central Library, St Peter's Square, Manchester M2 5PD.
Tel: 0161–234–1944; fax: 0161–234–1963

**Royal Manchester Children's Hospital**.
Tel: 0161–794–4696

## MERSEYSIDE

**AEEU Union** (engineers), 46 Mount Pleasant, Liverpool L3 5SD.
Tel: 0151–709–9561; fax: 0151–709–9101

**Everyman Theatre**, Hope Street, Liverpool L1.
Tel: 0151–708–0338

**GMB Union** (Liverpool and North Wales), 99 Edge Lane, Liverpool L7 2PE.
Tel: 0151–263–8261; fax: 0151–260–6722

**Mersey Docks and Harbour Company**, Maritime Centre, Port of Liverpool.
Tel: 0151–949–6000

**Merseyrail Electrics**, Rail House, Lord Nelson Street, Liverpool L1 1JF.
Tel: 0151–702–2298, press

**Merseyside Churches Ecumenical Assembly**, Friends Meeting House, 65 Paradise Street, Liverpool L1.
Tel: 0151–709–0125

**Merseyside Development Corporation**, 4th Floor, Royal Liver Building, Pierhead, Liverpool L3 1JH.
Tel: 0151–236–6090

**Merseyside Passenger Transport Executive**, 24 Hatton Garden, Liverpool L3 2AN.
Tel: 0151–227–5181

**Royal Liverpool Philharmonic Society**, Hope Street, Liverpool L1 9BP.
Tel: 0151–709–3789/2895; fax: 0151–709–0918

**Women's Educational Training Trust**, Blackburne House Centre, Hope Street, Liverpool L1 9JB.
Tel: 0151 709–4356; fax: 8293

## POLITICS

**Conservative Party** (North-West), 17 St Mary's Place, Bury BL9 0DZ.
Tel: 0161–797–1231

**Labour Party** (North-West), St James's Court, Wilderspool Causeway, Warrington WA4 6PS.
Tel: 01925–574913

## SOCIETY, WELFARE

**Benefits Agency**.
Tel: 0161–877–6979, press

**Disabled Living**, 4 St Chad's Street, Manchester M8 8QA.
Tel: 0161–832–3678;  fax: 0161–835–3591

*Family history*

**Dr Elizabeth Roberts, Lancaster University.**
Tel: 01524–593770

## SPORT

**North West Council for Sport and Recreation**, Astley House, Quay
Street, Manchester M3 4AE.
Tel: 0161–834–0338; fax: 0161–834–3678

## TELEPHONES

**British Telecom North-West**, 91 London Road, Manchester M60 1HQ.
Tel: 0161–600–2181

## TOURISM

**North West Tourist Board**, Swan House, Swan Meadow Road, Wigan
Pier WN3 5BB.
Tel: 01942–821222; fax: 01942–820002

## TRADE UNIONS

**TUC North West**, Transport House, Islington, Liverpool L3 8EQ.
Tel: 0151–298–1225; fax: 0151–298–1240

**UCATT North West** (construction workers).
Tel: 0161–224–3391

**GMB Union (Lancashire)**, 36 Station Road, Cheadle Hulme SK8 7AB.
Tel: 0161–485–8111; fax: 0161–485–8968

**TGWU (North West)**, Transport House, 1 Crescent, Salford M5 4PR.
Tel: 0161–736–1407; fax: 0161–737–5299

## TRANSPORT

**Highways Agency.**
Tel: 0161–952–45067, press

**North West Regional Railways**, Rail House, Store Street, Manchester
M60 9AJ.
Tel: 0161–228–5946, press

**Rail Users Consultative Committee**, Room 112, 17 Chorlton Street,
Manchester M1 3HY.
Tel: 0161–228–6247; fax: 236–1476

**RMT Liverpool**, 47 Paradise Street, Liverpool L1 3EH.
Tel: 0151–709–1786

## WATER AND RIVERS

**Environment Agency.**
Tel: 01925–653999; fax: 01925–634840

**United Utilities**, Dawson House, Great Sankey, Warrington WA5 3LW.
Tel: 01925–233230/233033/233135; fax: 01925–233372

**OFWAT North West Customer Service Committee**, 1st Floor, 17
Chorlton Street, Manchester M1 3HY.
Tel: 0161–236–6112

## NORTHERN IRELAND

**Northern Ireland Information Service**, Stormont Castle, Belfast BT4
3ST.
Tel: 01232–520700; fax: 01232–528473/78/82

**Northern Ireland Office**, Dundonald House, Upper Newtownards Road,
BT4 3SB.
Tel: 01232–520700; fax: 658957, press

**Northern Ireland Office**, London, press, Whitehall, London SW1A 2AZ.
Tel: 0171–210–6470/2/3; fax: 0171–210–6823/3785

**Commissioner for Complaints (Ombudsman)**, Wellington Place, Belfast
BT1 6HN.
Tel: 01232–2338213

**Public Records of Northern Ireland**, 66 Balmoral Avenue, Belfast BT9 6NY.
Tel: 01232–251318

**Queen's University**, Belfast BT7 1NN.
Tel: 01232–245133

**School of Public Policy, Economics and Law**, University of Ulster, Jordanstown.
Tel: 01232–366339

## Political parties

**Alliance Party**, 88 University Street, Belfast BT7.
Tel: 01232–324274; fax: 01232– 333147

**Democratic Unionist Party**, Strandtown Hall, Dundela Avenue, Belfast.
Tel: 01232–471155; fax: 01232–471797

**Sinn Fein Press Office**.
Tel: 01232–230261

**Social Democratic and Labour Party**, 611c Lisburn Road, Belfast BT9.
Tel: 01232–668100

**Ulster Unionist Party**, 3 Glengall Street, Belfast BT12.
Tel: 01232–324601

## BELIEF

**Catholic Media Office** (Dublin).
Tel: 00–353–1–288–5043; fax: 00–353–1–283–4161

**Church of Ireland**, 12 Talbot Street, Belfast BT1.
Tel: 01232–232909, press

**Methodist Church in Ireland**, 1 Fountainville Avenue, Belfast BT9 6AN.
Tel: 01232–324554

**Presbyterian Church**, Fisherwick Place, Belfast.
Tel: 01232–322284

## CRIME AND JUSTICE

**Independent Commission for Police Complaints**, 22 Great Victoria Street, Belfast BT2 7LP.
Tel: 01232–244821; fax: 01232–248563

**Law Society**, 98 Victoria Street, Belfast BT1 3JZ.
Tel: 01232–231614; fax: 01232–232606

**Northern Ireland Court Service**.
Tel: 01232–328594, press

**Royal Ulster Constabulary**, Brooklyn House, Knock Road, Belfast BT5 6LE.
Tel: 01232–700085/6; fax: 01232–700029

## ECONOMY/INDUSTRY

**Department of Economic Development**, Netherleigh, Massey Avenue, Belfast BT4 2JP.
Tel: 01232–529900; fax: 01232–529546

**Harland and Wolff** (shipbuilders), Queens Road, Belfast.
Tel: 01232–458456; fax: 01232–458515

**Industrial Development Board**, 64 Chichester Street, Belfast BT1 4JX.
Tel: 01232–233233; fax: 01232–545100

**CBI Northern Ireland**, Belfast.
Tel: 01232–326658

**Laganside Corporation**, 15 Clarendon Road, Belfast BT1 3BG
Tel: 01232–328507; fax: 01232–332141

**Northern Ireland Economic Council**, 2 Linenhall Street, Belfast BT2 8BA.
Tel: 01232–232125; fax: 01232–331250

**Northern Ireland Economic Research Centre**, 48 University Road, Belfast BT7.
Tel: 01232–325594

**Phoenix West Belfast Development Trust**, Unit 15, Westwood Centre, Belfast BT11.
Tel: 01232–431516

**Short Bros**, Airport Road, Belfast BT3.
Tel: 01232–458444

**Esmond Birnie**, Economics Department, Queen's University of Belfast, BT7 1NN.
Tel: 01232–245133

## EDUCATION/TRAINING/EMPLOYMENT

**Department of Education**, Rathgael House, Balloo Road, Bangor BT19 7PR.
Tel: 01247–279279; fax: 01247–279100

**Training and Employment Agency**, 9 Adelaide Street, Belfast BT2 8DJ.
Tel: 01232–541572/541829, press; fax: 01232–541545

**Northern Ireland Council for Curriculum**, 42 Beechill Road, Belfast BT8 4RS.
Tel: 01232–704666; fax: 01232–799913

**Northern Ireland Council for Integrated Education**, 10 Upper Crescent, Belfast BT7 1NT.
Tel: 01232–236200 fax: 01232–236237

## ENERGY

**Northern Ireland Electricity**, 120 Malone Road, Belfast BT9 5HT.
Tel: 01232–661100; fax: 01232–663579

**Premier Power**, Ballylumford, Islandmagee, Larne BT40 3RS.
Tel: 01960–382351; fax: 01960–382611

## ENVIRONMENT

**Department of Agriculture**, Dundonald House, Upper Newtownards Road, BT4 3SB.
Tel: 01232–524806, press; fax: 01232–525003

**Department of Environment Information Office**, Room 715, 12 Adelaide Street, Belfast BT2 8GB.
Tel: 01232–540540; fax: 540029

**National Trust**, Rowallane House, Saintfield, Ballynahinch BT24 7LH.
Tel: 01238–510721; fax: 01238–511242

**Royal Society for Protection of Birds**, Belvoir Park Forest, Belfast BT8 4QT.
Tel: 01232–491547

## HEALTH AND SOCIETY

**Department of Health and Social Services**, Dundonald House, Upper

Newtownards Road, BT4 3SB.
Tel: 01232–520500; fax: 525565

**Equal Opportunities Commission**, 22 Great Victoria Street, Belfast BT2 7BA.
Tel: 01232–242752; fax: 01232–331047

**General Consumer Council for Northern Ireland**, 116 Holywood Road, Belfast BT4 1NY.
Tel: 01232–672488; fax: 01232–657701

**Health and Health Care Research Unit**, Institute of Clinical Science, Mulhouse Building, Queen's University, Grosvenor Road, Belfast BT12 6BL
Tel: 01232–331463, extension 2687/4266; fax: 320664

**Northern Ireland Community Relations Council**, 6 Murray Street, Belfast BT1 6DN.
Tel: 01232–439953; fax: 01232–235208

**Northern Ireland Association for Mental Health**, 80 University Street, Belfast BT7 1EE.
Tel: 01232–328474; fax: 01232–234940

**Northern Ireland Housing Executive**, 2 Adelaide Street, Belfast BT2 8PB.
Tel: 01232–240588

**Rate Collection Agency**, 49 Chichester Street, Belfast (administers housing benefit).
Tel: 01232–250000

## INTERNATIONAL LINKS

**European Commission**, Windsor House, 9 Bedford Street, Belfast BT2 7EG.
Tel: 01232–240708; fax: 01232–248241

## MEDIA

**BBC Northern Ireland**, Belfast.
Tel: 01232–338000

**Ulster TV**, Havelock House, Ormeau Road, Belfast BT7 1EB.
Tel: 01232–328122; fax: 01232–246695

## SPORT

**Sports Council for Northern Ireland**, House of Sport, Upper Malone Road, BT9 5LA.
Tel: 01232–381222; fax: 01232–682757

## TELEPHONES

**British Telecom Northern Ireland**, Churchill House, 20 Victoria Square, Belfast BT1 4BA
Tel: 01232–438181

## TOURISM

**Northern Ireland Tourist Board**, 59 North Street, Belfast BT1 1NB.
Tel: 01232–231221; fax: 01232–240960

## TRADE UNIONS

**AEEU**, 26 Antrim Road, Belfast BT15 2AA.
Tel: 01232–74371/2, engineers; 01232–740244, electricians

**GMB Union**, 20 Mandeville Street, Portadown BT62 3NZ.
Tel: 01762–336004; fax: 01762–338807

**Northern Ireland Committee, International Confederation of Free Trade Unions**, 3 Wellington Park, BT9 6DJ.
Tel: 01232–681726; fax: 682126

**Transport and General Workers Union**, 102 High Street, Belfast BT1 2DL
Tel: 01232–232381; fax: 01232–240133

**UCATT** (construction workers).
Tel: 01232–322366

**Unison**, Unit 4, Fort William Business Park, Dangan Road, Belfast BT3 9BR.
Tel: 01232–770813; fax: 01232–779772

## TRANSPORT

**Northern Ireland Railways Company**, Central Station, East Bridge Street, Belfast BT1 3PB.
Tel: 01232–899400; fax: 01232–899401

## YOUNG PEOPLE

**Duke of Edinburgh's Award**, 109 Royal Avenue, Belfast BT1 1EW.
Tel: 01232–232253; fax: 01232–232386

# PARLIAMENT AND POLITICS

MPs are listed in *Vachers,* in *Dod's Parliamentary Companion* and in *Whitaker's Almanack.* Their outside jobs and consultancies are listed in the *Register of Members' Interests. Hansard* records debates verbatim.

Parties have local agents, often full time. Elections are overseen by council chief executives.

*Parliament and Government Pocket Book* (NTC Publications, Henley RG9 1EJ) covers Europe as well as the UK.

## *National sources*

**House of Commons**, SW1A 0AA (if seeking to reach an MP whose number you do not know).
Tel: 0171–219–3000
**Inquiries**, tel: 0171–219–4272
**Press gallery**, tel: 0171–219–4700
Most MPs have secretaries who will help you reach them. A complimentary copy of the *House of Commons Weekly Information Bulletin* and information on Commons business can be obtained from tel: 0171–219–4272.

**House of Lords inquiries**, London SW1A 0PW. The Lords has a record office.
Tel: 0171–219–3107; fax: 0171–219–5979

**Parliamentary Boundary Commissions**, 1 Drummond Gate, London SW1V 2QQ.
Tel: 0171–533–5177, press; fax: 0171–533–5176

**British National Party**, 154 Upper Wickham Lane, Welling, DA16 3DX.
Tel: 0181–316–4721

**Communist Party of Great Britain**, 1 Ardleigh Road, London N1 4HS.
Tel: 0171–275–8162

**Conservative Central Office**, 32 Smith Square, London SW1P 3HH.
Tel: 0171–222–9000; fax: 0171–222–1135

**Fabian Society**, 11 Dartmouth Street, London SW1H 9BN.
Tel: 0171–222–8877

**Green Party**, 10 Station Parade, London SW12 9AZ.
Tel: 0181–673–0045

**Labour Party**, 150 Walworth Road, London SE17 1JL.
Tel: 0171–277–3393, press; fax: 0171–277–3338

**European Parliamentary Labour Party**, 2 Queen Anne's Gate, London SW1H 9AA.
Tel: 0171–222–1719

**Labour Research Department**, 78 Blackfriars Road, London SE1 8HE (independent of Labour Party; researches pressure groups and company political gifts).
Tel: 0171–928–3649

**Liberal Democratic Party**, 4 Cowley Street, London SW1P 3NB.
Tel: 0171–222–7999
**Parliamentary press office**, tel: 0171–219–4773

**Socialist Workers Party**, PO Box 82, E3 3LT.
Tel: 0171–538–5822

**Politics Department**, Reading University, RG6 2AA.
Tel: 01734–318501 and
**Professor Roy Gregory**, tel: 01734–318500

**Political Theory and Government Department**, University of Wales, Swansea SA2 8PP.
Tel: 01792–295308

**Professor Lord Skidelsky**, Warwick University, CV4 7AL. (Keynes, Thatcher, contemporary politics.)
Tel: 01203–523481

### *Elections*

**Professor Colin Mellors** and **Dr Michel Le Lohe**, Politics Department, Bradford University, BD7 1DP.
Tel: 01274–383816, Professor Mellors; 01274–383815, Dr Lohe

## PUBLIC ADMINISTRATION

*Britain: An Official Handbook* is a mine of information. The *Annual Abstract of Statistics* gives figures of population, production, trade, finance, transport, road accidents. A gazetteer tells you where places are. The

**British Library** (see Books, page 153) includes the **Official Publications Library**. The *British Library of Political and Economic Science* is at the LSE, 10 Portugal Street, London WC2A 2HD (tel: 0171–405–7686).

*Keesing's UK Record* (from CIRCA, 13 Sturton Street, Cambridge CB1 2SN) is a monthly contemporary history.

Government press officers in London and the regions are listed in the *IPO Directory* (PO Box 30, Wetherby LS23 7YA: annual subscription £12 in 1995). They are often able to arrange unattributable background briefings from civil servants on issues of local or national importance. Senior civil servants are listed in the *Civil Service Yearbook*.

Governments keep up a continual flow of new initiatives to help the regions, and these and other regional efforts may attract money from the European Community. However, given its division into departments operating in different fields, the government still has difficulty co-ordinating its regional work and services.

## National information sources

**No 10 Downing Street Press Office**, London SW1A 2AA.
Tel: 0171–930–4433; fax: 0171–930–2831

**Central Office of Information**, Press Desk, Hercules Road, London SE1 7DU.
Tel: 0171–261–8426; fax: 0171–928–7652
**Film and video**, tel: 0171–261–8667; fax: 0171–261–8874
**Radio**, tel: 0171–261–8930; fax: 0171–633–0920

**Nolan Committee on Standards in Public Life**, Horse Guards Road, London SW1P 3AL.
Tel: 0171–270–6345; fax: 0171–270–5874; e-mail: nolan@gtnet.gov.uk

**Centre for Corporate Strategy and Change** (public and private sector), Warwick University, Coventry CV4 7AL.
Tel: 01203–523918

**Centre for Policy Studies**, 52 Rochester Row, London SW1P 1JU (think tank).
Tel: 0171–630–5818/828–1176

**Charter 88**, 3 Pine Street, London EC1R 0JH (wants Bill of Rights, freer information).
Tel: 0171–833–1988; fax: 5895

**Democratic Audit**, Essex University, Colchester CO4 3SQ. Critic of quangos and advisory committees.
Tel: 01206–872568

**Professor Peter Hennessy**, Contemporary History, Queen Mary and Westfield College, London. Has written copiously on how British Government works.
Tel: 0171–975–5555

**Institute for Public Policy Research**, 30 Southampton Street, London WC2E 7RA.
Tel: 0171–379–9400

**Institute of Public Administration and Management**, Liverpool University, PO Box 147, L69 3BX.
Tel: 0151–794–2911

**Millenium Commission**, 2 Little Smith Street, London SW1P 3DH.
Tel: 0171–340–2007, press; fax: 0171–340–2019.

**National Audit Office Information Centre**, 157 Buckingham Palace Road, London SW1W 9SP.
Tel: 0171–798–7400, press; fax: 0171–798–7710; e-mail: nao@gtnet.gov.uk

**Ombudsman**, Church House, Great Smith Street, London SW1P 3BW.
Tel: 0171–276–2082; fax: 0171–276–2140

**Policy Studies Institute**, 100 Park Village East, London NW1 7PX (social and economic studies).
Tel: 0171–387–2171

**Public Service Privatisation Research Unit**, 20 Grand Depot Road, London SE18 6SF.
Tel: 0181–854–2244

**Professor David Dilks**, Vice-Chancellor of Hull University, HU6 7RX (was assistant to Eden and Macmillan).
Tel: 01482–465131

## SECURITY SERVICES

*Lobster Magazine*, 214 Westbourne Avenue, Hull HU5 3JB, (tel: 01482–447558) publishes information twice a year on MI5 (counter-subversion agency), MI6 (overseas intelligence), the Special Branch (police counterpart of MI5) and military intelligence. *Statewatch* (tel: 0181–802–1882) is another periodical covering security issues.

Journalists can put questions about MI5 to the **Home Office police desk** (tel: 0171–273–4610) and about MI6 to the **Foreign Office news department** (tel: 0171–270–3100)

University researchers on the Secret Service include **Professor Bernard Porter** (tel: 0191–222–6694) and **Ian Leigh** (tel: 0191–222–8543), both at Newcastle.

## TAXATION AND SPENDING

**Chartered Institute of Taxation**, 12 Upper Belgrave Street, London
SW1X 8BB.
Tel: 0171–235–9381; fax: 0171–235–2562

**Customs and Excise**, 22 Upper Ground, London SE1 9PJ
Tel: 0171–620–1313; fax: 0171–865–5625
Investigations.
Tel: 0171–696–7829; fax: 0171–696–7817

**Inland Revenue** (press), North West Wing, Bush House, Aldwych,
London WC2B 4PP.
Tel: 0171–438–7327, national; 0171–438–7356 regional; fax:
0171–438–7541

**Treasury Public Spending and Direct Taxes Desk**, Parliament Street,
London SW1P 3AG.
Tel: 0171–270–5245; fax: 0171–270–5244
**Indirect Taxes Desk**.
Tel: 0171–270–5185; fax: 0171–270–5244

**Institute for Fiscal Studies**, 7 Ridgemount Street, London WC1E 7AE.
Tel: 0171–636–3784

**Public Expenditure Review Group** (Maurice Mullard), Hull University
HU6 7RX.
Tel: 01482–466083

**Professor Arthur Midwinter**, Government Department, Strathclyde
University, Glasgow G1 1XQ.
Tel: 0141–552–4400, ext. 2920

**Professor Ian Walker**, Economics, Keele University, ST5 5BG.
Tel: 01782–583111

**Inland Revenue Staff Federation**, 231 Vauxhall Bridge Road, London
SW1V 1EH.
Tel: 0171–834–8254; fax: 630–6258

## TRADE UNIONS

**Council of Civil Service Unions**, 58 Rochester Row, London SW1P 1JU.
Tel: 0171–834–8393; fax: 0171–828–4152

**Association of First Division Civil Servants**, 2 Caxton Street, London
SW1H 0QH.
Tel: 0171–222–6242; fax: 0171–222–5926

**Civil and Public Service Association**, 160 Falcon Road, London SW11 2LN.
Tel: 0171–924–2727; fax: 0171–924–1847

**National Union of Civil and Public Servants**, 5 Great Suffolk Street,
London SE1 0NS.
Tel: 0171–928–9671; fax: 0171–401–2693

## ROYALTY AND THE PEERAGE

Reference: *Burke's Peerage.*
*Debrett.*
*Kelly's Handbook to the Titled, Landed and Official Classes.*

**Buckingham Palace Press Office**, London SW1A 1AA.
Tel: 0171–930–4832; fax: 0171–321–0380;
Prince Charles's press fax: 0171–925–0795

**Duchy of Cornwall.**
Tel: 0171–834–7346, press; fax: 0171–925–0795

**Clarence House Press Office**, London SW1A 1BA.
Tel: 0171–930–3141; fax: 0171–930–9491

The Buckingham Palace Press Office produces a regularly updated diary
of the official engagements of the Queen and members of the Royal
family, except the Gloucesters, the Kents and the Queen Mother (who has
her own press officer). This is distributed to media organizations who
subscribe to the **Central Office of Information's NDS electronic service**.
It also goes to other organizations (for example, the Newspaper
Publishers Association, the Newspaper Society, the Council of
Photographic News Agencies and the Independent Photographers
Association) who take part in the rota system for covering Royal events.

## SCOTLAND

**British Council**, Scotland, 3 Bruntsfield Crescent, Edinburgh EH10
4HD.
Tel: 0131–447–4716; fax: 0131–452–8487

**Royal Society of Edinburgh**, 22 George Street, EH2 2PQ.
Tel: 0131–225–6057; fax: 0131–220–6889

**Scottish Office Information Directorate**, St Andrew's House, Edinburgh
EH1 3TG.
Tel: 0131–244–1111; fax: 0131–244–2918

**Scottish Office London**, Dover House, Whitehall, London SW1A 2AU.
Tel: 0171–270–6760/6745, press; fax: 0171–270–6730

# ANIMALS

See also page 178.

**Scottish Kennel Club**, 3 Brunswick Place, Edinburgh EH7 5HP.
Tel: 0131–557–2877

**Scottish Society for Prevention of Cruelty to Animals**, 603 Queensferry
Road, Edinburgh EH4 6EA.
Tel: 0131–339–0222

# ARTS

**Edinburgh Festival Society**, 21 Market Street, Edinburgh EH1 1BW.
Tel: 0131–226–4001

**Edinburgh Festival Fringe**, 180 High Street, EH1 1QS.
Tel: 0131–226–5257; fax: 0131–220–4205; e-mail:
admin@edfringe.demon.co.uk

**Royal Scottish Academy of Music and Drama**, 100 Renfrew Street,
Glasgow G2.
Tel: 0141–332–4101; fax: 0141–332–8901

**SALVO** (Scottish Arts Lobby), Royal Lyceum Theatre, 30 Grindley
Street, Edinburgh EH3.
Tel: 0131–228–3885

**Scottish Arts Council**, 12 Manor Place, Edinburgh EH3 7DD.
Tel: 0131–226–6051; fax: 0131–225–9833

**Scottish Music Information Centre**, 1 Bowmont Gardens, Glasgow G12
9LR.
Tel: 0141–334–6393; fax: 0141–337–1161

**Scottish Opera**, 39 Elmbank Crescent, Glasgow G2.
Tel: 0141–248–4567; fax: 0141–221–8812

## BOOKS

**Book Trust Scotland**, Scottish Book Centre, 137 Dundee Street, Edinburgh EH11 1BG.
Tel: 0131–229–3663; fax: 0131–228–4293

**Scottish Library Association**, Business Centre, Coursington Road, Motherwell ML1 1PW.
Tel: 01698–252526; fax: 01698–252057

## COUNCILS

**Scottish Office**, Local Government, St Andrew's House, Edinburgh EH1 3TG.
Tel: 0131–244–2542/96/2530, press; fax: 0131–244–2918/2971

**Chartered Institute for Public Finance and Accountancy**, 8 North West Circus Place, EH3 6ST.
Tel: 0131–220–4316; fax: 0131–220–4305

**Commission for Accounts in Scotland**, 18 George Street, Edinburgh EH2 2QU. Local government audit service.
Tel: 0131–226–7346

**Convention of Scottish Local Authorities**, 9 Haymarket Terrace, Edinburgh EH12 5XZ.
Tel: 0131–346–1222

**Local Government Ombudsman**, 23 Walker Street, Edinburgh EH3 7JX.
Tel: 0131–225–5300; fax: 0131–225–9495

**Scottish Local Authorities Management Centre**, Strathclyde University, Glasgow G1 1XQ.
Tel: 0141–552–4400

**UNISON**, 8 Aberdeen Terrace, Glasgow G2 6RX. Health and local government union.
Tel: 0141–332–0006; fax 0141–331–1203

## COUNTRYSIDE

**National Trust for Scotland**, 5 Charlotte Square, Edinburgh EH2.
Tel: 0131–226–5922; fax: 0131–243–9501

**Royal Society for Protection of Birds**, 17 Regent Terrace, Edinburgh EH7 5BN.
Tel: 0131–557–3136
10 Albyn Terrace, Aberdeen AB1 1YP.
Tel: 01224–624824
Etive House, Beechwood Park, Inverness IV2 3BW.
Tel: 01463–715000
Unit 3.1, Science Park, Glasgow G20 0SP.
Tel: 0141–945–5224

**Scottish Natural Heritage**, 12 Hope Terrace, Edinburgh EH9 2AS.
Tel: 0131–447–4784; fax: 0131–446–2279
9 Culduthel Road, Inverness IV2 4AG.
Tel: 01463–239431; fax: 01463–710713
17 Rubislaw Terrace, Aberdeen AB1 1XE.
Tel: 01224–642863; fax: 01224–643347
Battelby, Redgorton, Perth PH1 3EW.
Tel: 01738–444177; fax: 01738–444180
Caspian House, Clydebank Business Park, Clydebank G81 2NR.
Tel: 0141–951–4488; fax: 0141–951–4510

**Scottish Wildlife Trust**, Cramond House, Cramond Glebe Road, Edinburgh EH4 6NS.
Tel: 0131–312–7765; fax: 0131–312–8705

## DEVELOPMENT

**Irvine Development Corporation**, Perceton House, Irvine KA11 2AL.
Tel: 01294–214100; fax: 01294–211467

**Lothian and Edinburgh Enterprise**, 99 Haymarket Terrace, Edinburgh.
Tel: 0131–313–4000; fax: 0131–313–4231

**Scottish Enterprise**, 120 Bothwell Street, Glasgow G2 7JP. Promotes development and training.
Tel: 0141–248–2700; fax: 0141–221–3217

**Centre for Enterprise and Management Development**, Stirling University.
Tel: 01786–467348

## ECONOMY

**Fraser of Allander Institute** (does forecasts), Strathclyde University, G1 1XQ.
Tel: 0141–552–4400

**Dr Ron Weir**, Economics, York University, Y01 5DD.
Tel: 01904–432029, PR


## EDUCATION

**Scottish Office**, Education, St Andrew's House, Edinburgh EH1 3TG.
Tel: 0131–244–2960/7/9, press; fax: 0131–244–2918/2971

**Association of University Teachers** (Scotland), 6 Castle Street,
Edinburgh EH2 3AT.
Tel: 0131–226–6694

**Headteachers Association of Scotland**, Strathclyde University, Southbrae
Drive, Glasgow G13 1PP.
Tel: 0141–950–3298; fax: 950–3268

**Scottish Council for Research in Education**, 15 St John Street,
Edinburgh EH8 8JR.
Tel: 0131–557–2944; fax: 0131–556–9454

**Educational Institute of Scotland** (trade union), also **Scottish
Educational Journal**, 46 Moray Place, Edinburgh EH3 6BH.
Tel: 0131–225–6244; fax: 0131–220–3151

**Scottish Pre-School Play Association**, 14 Elliot Place, Glasgow G3 8EP.
Tel: 0141–221–4148; fax: 0141–221–6043

**Scottish Secondary Teachers Association**, 15 Dundas Street, Edinburgh
EH3 6QG.
Tel: 0131–556–0605/5919; fax: 0131–556–1419


## ENERGY

**Electricity Consumers Committee**, 70 West Regent Street, Glasgow G2
2QZ.
Tel: 0141–331–2678

**Energy Action Scotland**, 21 West Nile Street, Glasgow G1 2PJ.
Tel: 0141–226–3064

**Hydro-Electric**, Perth PH1 5WA.
Tel: 01738–455040; fax: 01738–455045

**OFFER** (Office of Electricity Regulation), New St Andrews House,
EH1 3TG.
Tel: 0131–244–5194/5106, press; fax: 0131–244–2918/2971

**Scottish Nuclear** (press), 3 Redwood Crescent, Peel Park, East Kilbride G74 5PR.
Tel: 01355–262144, press; fax: 01355–262149

**Scottish Power**, 1 Atlantic Quay, Glasgow G2 8SP.
Tel: 0141–248–8200, press; fax: 0141–248–8300

**Total Oil Marine**, Crawpeel Road, Altens, Aberdeen AB9 2AG.
Tel: 01224–858000; fax: 01224–858019

**UKAEA Dounreay**,
Tel: 01847–802233, press

## ENVIRONMENT

**Scottish Office**: Agriculture, Environment, St Andrew's House, Edinburgh EH1 3TG.
Tel: 0131–244–2910/2663, press; fax: 0131–244–2918/2971

**Friends of the Earth Scotland**, 72 Newhaven Road, Edinburgh EH6 5QG.
Tel: 0131–554–9977; fax: 0131–554–8656

## FARMING

**Scottish Office**, see environment above.

**Crofters Commission**, 4 Castle Wynd, Inverness IV2 3EQ.
Tel: 01463–663450; fax: 01463–711820

**Royal Highland and Agricultural Society of Scotland**, Ingliston, Edinburgh EH28 8NF.
Tel: 0131–333–2444; fax: 0131–333–5236

**Scottish Agricultural College**, West Mains Road, Edinburgh EH9 3JG.
Tel: 0131–662–1303; fax: 0131–662–1323

**Scottish Agricultural Science Agency**, East Craigs, Edinburgh EH12 8NJ.
Tel: 0131–244–8843

**Scottish Crofters Union**, The Old Mill, Broadford, Isle of Skye IV49 9AQ.
Tel: 01471–822529; fax: 01471–822799

**Scottish Crop Research Institute**, Invergowrie, Dundee DD2 5DA.
Tel: 01382–562731; fax: 01382–562426

## FINANCE

**Associated Scottish Life Offices**, 40 Thistle Street, Edinburgh EH2 1EN.
Tel: 0131–220–4555; fax: 0131–220–2280

**Banking Insurance and Finance Union**, 146 Argyle Street, Glasgow G2 8BL.
Tel: 0141–221–6475

**Bank of Scotland**, The Mound, Edinburgh EH2.
Tel: 0131–442–7777

**Clydesdale Bank**, 30 St Vincent Place, Glasgow G1 2HL.
Tel: 0141–248–7070; fax: 0141–204–0828

**Royal Bank of Scotland**, 42 St Andrew Square, EH2.
Tel: 0131–556–8555

## FISH

**Scottish Office**.
Tel: 0131–244–2960/7/9

**Scottish Fisheries Protection Agency**, Pentland House, Robb Loan,
Edinburgh EH14 1TW.
Tel: 0131–244–6059

**Scottish Salmon Growers Association**, Drummond House, Scott Street,
Perth PH1 5EJ.
Tel: 01738–635420

## FOOD AND DRINK

**Scottish Licensed Trade Association**, 10 Walker Street, Edinburgh EH3
7LA.
Tel: 0131–225–5169

**William Low Supermarkets**, contact through Tesco.
Tel: 01992–632222

### *Whisky industry*

**Dr Ron Weir**, Economics, York University YO1 5DD.
Tel: 01904–432029, PR

## GAELIC

**Boyd Robertson** and **Chrissie Bannerman**, Gaelic Studies, Strathclyde University, Glasgow G1 1XQ.
Tel: 0141–950–3445

## GLASGOW

**Glasgow Development Agency**, 50 Waterloo Street, Glasgow G2.
Tel: 0141–204–1111

**Glasgow Regeneration Fund**, 7 West George Street, Glasgow G2.
Tel: 0141–221–5454

**Weir Group**, Cathcart, Glasgow G44 4EX.
Tel: 0141–637–7141

## HEALTH

**Scottish Office, Health**, St Andrew's House, Edinburgh EH1 3TG.
Tel: 0131–244–2656/2954/2951, press; fax: 0131–244–2918/2971

**Chest, Heart and Stroke, Scotland**, 65 North Castle Street, Edinburgh EH2 3LT.
Tel: 0131–225–6963; fax: 0131–220–6313

**Health Education Board for Scotland**, Woodburn House, Canaan Lane, Edinburgh EH10 4SG.
Tel: 0131–447–8044; fax: 452–8140

**Health Service Ombudsman**, 1 Atholl Place, Edinburgh.
Tel: 0131–225–7465

**Multiple Sclerosis Society, Scotland**, 2A North Charlotte Street, Edinburgh EH2 4HR.
Tel: 0131–225–3600

**National Board for Nursing**, 22 Queen Street, Edinburgh EH2 1NT.
Tel: 0131–226–7371; fax: 0131–225–9970

**Royal Aberdeen Children's Hospital**.
Tel: 01224–681818

**Royal College of Nursing Scottish Board**, 42 South Oswald Road, Edinburgh EH9 2HH.
Tel: 0131–662–1010; fax: 0131–662–1032

**Royal College of Physicians and Surgeons**, 232 St Vincent Street, Glasgow G2 5RJ.
Tel: 0141–221–6072; fax: 0141–221–1804

**Scottish AIDS Monitor**, 26 Anderson Place, Edinburgh EH6.
Tel: 0131–555–4850

**Scottish Association of Health Councils**, 5 Leamington Terrace, Edinburgh EH10 4JW.
Tel: 0131–229–2344; fax: 0131–228–8250

**Scottish Association for Mental Health**, 38 Gardner's Crescent, Edinburgh EH3 8DQ.
Tel: 0131–229–9687; fax: 0131–229–3558

**Scottish Health Visitors Association**, 94 Constitution Street, Edinburgh EH6 6AW.
Tel: 0131–553–4061; fax: 0131–553–4061

**Scottish National Blood Transfusion Service**, Ellen's Glen Road, Edinburgh EH17 7QT.
Tel: 0131–664–2317; fax: 0131–658–1639

**Scottish Pharmaceutical General Council**, 42 Queen Street, Edinburgh EH2 3NH.
Tel: 0131–467–7766

**UNISON**, 8 Aberdeen Terrace, Glasgow, Glasgow G2 6RX. Health and local government union.
Tel: 0141–332–0006; fax 0141–331–1203

## HISTORY

**Historic Scotland**, Longmore House, Salisbury Place, Edinburgh EH9 1SH.
Tel: 0131–668–8700/8734, press; fax: 0131–668–8741

**Society of Antiquaries of Scotland**, Royal Museum of Scotland, Queen Street, Edinburgh EH2 1JD.
Tel: 0131–225–7534

**Scottish Record Office**, General Register House, Edinburgh EH1 3YY.
Tel: 0131–556–6585

## HIGHLANDS AND ISLANDS

**Scottish Office, Highlands/Islands**, St Andrew's House, Edinburgh EH1 3TG.
Tel: 0131–244–2797/2542/96/30, PR; fax: 0131–244–2918/2971

**Gaelic Television Committee**, 4 Harbour View, Cromwell Street Quay, Stornoway PA87 2DR.
Tel: 01851–705550; fax: 01851–706432

**Highlands and Islands Enterprise** (government agency), 20 Bridge Street, Inverness IV1 1QR.
Tel: 01463–234171; fax: 01463–244469

## *Orkney*

**Orkney Enterprise**, 14 Queen Street, Kirkwall.
Tel: 01865–874638; fax: 01856–872915

## *Shetland*

**Shetland Chamber of Commerce**, 122 Commercial Street, Lerwick ZE1 0HX.
Tel: 01595–4739

**Shetland Enterprise**, Toll Clock Shopping Centre, North Road, Lerwick.
Tel: 01595–3177; fax: 01595–3208

**Shetland Fish Producers Organization**, 14 Alexander Buildings, Lerwick.
Tel: 01595–3197

# HOUSING

**Scottish Office**, Housing PR, St Andrew's House, Edinburgh EH1 3TG.
Tel: 0131–244–2960/7/9; fax: 0131–244–2918/2971

**Scottish Federation of Housing Associations**, 38 York Place, Edinburgh EH1 3HU.
Tel: 0131–556–5777; fax: 0131–557–6028
5 Park Terrace, Glasgow G3 6BY.
Tel: 0141–332–8113; fax: 0141–332–9684
118 Strathearn Road, Broughty Ferry, Dundee DD5 1JN
Tel: 01382–480337; fax: 01382–480151

**Scottish Homes**, 91 Haymarket Terrace, Edinburgh EH12 5HE.
National housing agency for Scotland.
Tel: 0131–313–0044; fax: 0131–479–5177

**Shelter**, 8 Hamton Terrace, Edinburgh EH12 5JD.
Tel: 0131–313–1550; fax: 0131–313–1544

**Sheltered Housing Owners Confederation**, 107 Comely Bank Road, Edinburgh EH4 1DH.
Tel: 0131–343–6100

## INDUSTRY

**Scottish Office, Industry**, St Andrew's House, Edinburgh EH1 3TG.
Tel: 0131–244–2797/2542/96/30, press; fax: 0131–244–2918/2971

**Scottish Office**, Employment Agencies and Health and Safety Executive, St Andrew's House, Edinburgh EH1 3TG.
Tel: 0131–244–2702/2056/2661, press; fax: 0131–244–2918/2971

**CBI Scotland**.
Tel: 0141–332–8661

**Central Region Industry and Business Park**, John Player Building, Stirling FK7 7RP.
Tel: 01786–463416; fax: 01786–479611

**Compaq** (computer manufacturer), Erskine Ferry Road, Bishopton.
Tel: 0141–814–8000

**IBM**, Greenock (IBM's biggest personal computer plant).
Tel: 0171–202–3744, press

**METCOM** (metal trades confederation.), Savoy Tower, 77 Renfrew Street, Glasgow G2 3BZ.
Tel: 0141–332–0826; fax: 0141–332–5788

**Scottish and Northern Ireland Plumbing Employers Federation**, 2 Walker Street, Edinburgh EH3 7LB.
Tel: 0131–225–2255; fax: 0131–226–7638

### *Silicon Glen*

**Dr Ivan Turok**, Centre for Planning, Strathclyde University, Glasgow G1 1XQ.
Tel: 0141–552–4400

## INTERNATIONAL LINKS

**Commonwealth Institute**, 8 Rutland Square, Edinburgh EH1 2AS.
Tel: 0131–229–6894/6668

**European Commission**, 9 Alva Street, Edinburgh EH2 4PH.
Tel: 0131–225–2058; fax: 0131–226–4105

**Scottish Catholic International Aid Fund**, 5 Oswald Street, Glasgow G1
4QR.
Tel: 0141–221–4447; fax: 0141–221–2373

**Sead**, 23 Castle Street, Edinburgh EH2 3DN. Scottish development
education agency.
Tel: 0131–225–6550; fax 0131–226–6384

## JUSTICE

**Scottish Office, Home Affairs**, St Andrew's House, Edinburgh EH1
3TG.
Tel: 0131–244–2952/2939; fax: 0131–244–2918/2971

**Crown Office**, 25 Chambers Street, Edinburgh EH1.
Tel: 0131–226–2626; fax: 0131–226–6564

**Faculty of Advocates**, Advocates Library, Parliament House, Edinburgh
EH1 1RF.
Tel: 0131–226–5071; fax: 0131–225–5341

**Law Society of Scotland**, 26 Drumsheugh Gardens, Edinburgh EH3 7YR.
Tel: 0131–226–7411; fax: 0131–220–6293

**Scottish Council for Civil Liberties**, 146 Holland Street, Glasgow G2
4NG.
Tel: 0141–332–5960; fax: 0141–332–5209

## MEDIA

**BBC Scotland**, Glasgow.
Tel: 0141–338–2240, press

**Celtic Film and Television Association**, Library, Farraline Park,
Inverness IV1 1LS.
Tel: 01463–226189; fax: 01463–237001

**Grampian TV**, Queens Cross, Aberdeen AB9 2XJ.
Tel: 01224–646464; fax: 01224–635127

**Independent Television Commission**, 123 Blythswood Street, Glasgow
G2 4AN.
Tel: 0141–226–4436; fax: 0141–226–4682

**Scottish Daily Newspapers Society**, 30 George Square, Glasgow G2 1EG.
Tel: 0141–248–2375; fax: 0141–248–2362

**Scottish Newspaper Publishers Association**, 48 Palmerston Place, Edinburgh EH12 5DE. Weekly papers.
Tel: 0131–220–4353; fax: 0131–220–4344

**Scottish TV**, Cowcaddens, Glasgow G2 3PR.
Tel: 0141–332–9999; fax: 0141–332–4868

## POLITICS

**Conservative Party**, Suite 1#1, 14 Links Place, Leith EH6 7EZ.
Tel: 0131–555–2900

**Labour Party**, Keir Hardie House, Lynedoch Place, Glasgow G3 6AB.
Tel: 0141–332–8946

**Liberal Democrats**, 4 Clifton Terrace, Edinburgh EH12.
Tel: 0131–337–2314

**Scottish National Party**, 6 North Charlotte Street, Edinburgh EH2.
Tel: 0131–226–3661; fax: 0131–225–9597

## RELIGION

**Action of Churches Together in Scotland** (Acts), Scottish Churches House, Dunblane FK15 0AJ.
Tel: 01786–823588; fax: 825844

**Catholic Press Office**, 5 St Vincent Place, Glasgow G1.
Tel: 0141–221–1168

**Church of Scotland**, 121 George Street, Edinburgh EH2 4YN.
Tel: 0131–225–5722; fax: 0131–225–6475

**Scottish Episcopal Church**, 21 Grosvenor Crescent, Edinburgh EH12 5EE.
Tel: 0131–225–6357; fax: 0131–346–7247

## RIVERS

**Purification boards.**
    **Clyde**, Rivers House, Murray Road, East Kilbride G75 0LA.
    Tel: 01355–238181; fax: 01355–264323

**Forth**, Clearwater House, Heriot-Watt Research Park, Avenue North, Riccarton EH14 4AP.
Tel: 0131–449–7296
**Highland**, Groesser House, Fodderty Way, Dingwall IV15 9XB.
Tel: 01349–862021; fax: 01349–863987
**North-East**, Greyhope House, Greyhope Road, Aberdeen AB1 3RD.
Tel: 01224–248338; fax: 01224–248591
**Solway**, Irongray Road, Dumfries DG2 0JE.
Tel: 01387–720502; fax: 01387–721154
**Tay**, 1 South Street, Perth PH2 8NJ.
Tel: 01738–627989; fax: 01738–630997
**Tweed**, Burnbrae, Mossilee Road, Galashiels TD1 1NF.
Tel: 01896–752425; fax: 01896–754412

## SCIENCE

**Royal Botanic Garden**, Edinburgh EH3 5LR.
Tel: 0131–552–7171

**Scottish Crop Research Institute**, Invergowrie, Dundee DD2 5DA.
Tel: 01382–562731; fax: 01382–562426

## SOCIETY AND WELFARE

**Scottish Office, Social Work**, St Andrew's House, Edinburgh EH1 3TG.
Tel: 0131–244–2656/2954/2951; fax: 0131–244–2918/2971

**Age Concern Scotland**, 113 Rose Street, Edinburgh EH2 3DT.
Tel: 0131–220–3345

**Children in Scotland**, 5 Shandwick Place, Edinburgh EH2 4RG.
Tel: 0131–228–8484; fax: 0131–228–8585

**Crossroads Care Attendant Schemes**, 24 George Square, Glasgow G2 1EG (help for carers).
Tel: 0141–226–3793

**DSS Benefits Agency**, Argyle House, 3 Lady Lawson Street, Edinburgh EH3 9SH.
Tel: 0131–222–5228; fax: 0131–222–5251

**Equal Opportunities Commission**, 7 Nelson Mandela Place, Glasgow G2.
Tel: 0141–248–5833; fax: 0141–248–5834

**Marriage Counselling Scotland**, 105 Hanover Street, Edinburgh EH2 1DJ.
Tel: 0131–225–5006; fax: 0131–220–0639

**Royal Scottish Society for Prevention of Cruelty to Children**, 41
Polwarth Terrace, Edinburgh EH11 1NU.
Tel: 0131–337–8539; fax: 346–8284

**Scottish Council for Voluntary Organizations**, 18 Claremont Crescent,
Edinburgh EH7 4QD.
Tel: 0131–556–3882

**Scottish National Federation for Welfare of Blind**, PO Box 500,
Gillespie Crescent, Edinburgh EH10 4HZ.
Tel: 0131–229–1456; fax: 0131–229–4060

## *Young people*

**Boys Brigade**, Carronvale House, Carronvale Road, Larbert FK5 3LH.
Tel: 01324–562008; fax: 01324–552323

## SPORT

**Scottish Football Association**, 6 Park Gardens, Glasgow G3 7YF.
Tel: 0141–332–6372; fax: 0141–332–7559

**Scottish Sports Council**, Caledonia House, South Gyle, Edinburgh EH12
9DQ.
Tel: 0131–317–7200; fax: 0131–339–7150; e-mail: ssclis@easynet.co.uk

## TELEPHONES

**British Telecom Scotland**, 11 Hope Street, Glasgow G2 6AB
0141–220–5337

## TOURISM

**Orkney Tourist Board**, 6 Broad Street, Kirkwall KW15 1NX.
Tel: 01865–872856; fax: 01856–875056

**Scottish Borders Tourist Board**, 70 High Street, Selkirk TD7 4DD.
Tel: 01750–20555; fax: 01750–21886

**Scottish Tourism Research Unit**, Tony Seaton, Strathclyde University,
Glasgow G1 1XQ.
Tel: 0141–552–4400, ext. 3949;

**Scottish Tourist Board**, 23 Ravelston Terrace, Edinburgh EH4 3EU.
Tel: 0131–332–2433; fax: 0131–315–2906

## TRADE UNIONS

**GMB Union**, 1–3 Woodside Crescent, Charing Cross, Glasgow G3 7UJ.
Includes the **Scottish Professional Footballers Association**.
Tel: 0141–332–8641; fax: 0141–332–4491

**Scottish TUC**, 16 Woodlands Terrace, Glasgow G3 6DF.
Tel: 0141–332–4946; fax: 0141–332–4649

**TGWU**, 290 Bath Street, Glasgow G2 4LD.
Tel: 0141–332–7321; fax: 0141–332–6157

**UCATT** (construction workers).
Tel: 0141–221–4893

**Unison**, 8 Aberdeen Terrace, G2 6RX.
Tel: 0141–332–0006 fax: 331–1203

## TRANSPORT

**Scottish Office**, Roads and Transport, St Andrew's House, Edinburgh
EH1 3TG.
Tel: 0131–244–2952/2939; fax: 0131–244–2918/2971

**Northern Lighthouse Board**, 84 George Street, Edinburgh EH2 3DA.
Tel: 0131–226–7051; fax: 0131–220–2093

**RMT Glasgow**, 180 Hope Street, Glasgow G2 2UE.
Tel: 0141–332–1117

**RMT Aberdeen**, 3 Commerce Street, AB2 1UB.
Tel: 01224–582688

**Scotrail** (press), 87 Union Street, Glasgow G1 2JE.
Tel: 0141–335–4788

**Scottish Citylink** (bus operator), Killermont Street, Glasgow G2 3NP.
Tel: 0141–332–9644

**Scottish Road Safety Campaign**, Saughton House, Broomhouse Drive,
Edinburgh EH11.
Tel: 0131–444–2230

**Strathclyde Buses**, 197 Victoria Road, Glasgow G42.
Tel: 0141–423–6600; fax: 0141–636–3223

**Strathclyde Passenger Transport Executive**, 12 West George Street,
Glasgow G2 1HN.
Tel: 0141–332–6811; fax: 0141–332–3076

## WATER

**East of Scotland Water Authority**.
Tel: 0131–225–7979

**North of Scotland Water Authority**.
Tel: 0131–244–2930

**West of Scotland Water Authority**, Glasgow.
Tel: 0141–355–5177

## SOUTH AND SOUTH-EAST

**COI** (Kent to Oxon), Hercules Road, London SE1 7DU.
Tel: 0171–261–8795; fax: 0171–928–6974

**Department of Environment** (South-East).
Tel: 0171–261–8803, press

## ARTS, MEDIA

**Bournemouth Orchestra**, 2 Seldown Lane, Poole BH15 1UF.
Tel: 01202–670611

**Meridian TV**, Southampton SO14 0PZ.
Tel: 01703–222555; fax: 01703–335050

**South East Arts**, 10 Mount Ephraim, Tunbridge Wells TN4 8AS.
Tel: 01892–515210; fax: 01892–549383

**Southern Arts**, 13 St Clement Street, Winchester SO23 9DQ.
Tel: 01962–855099; fax: 01962–861186

## COUNTRYSIDE

**Ministry of Agriculture** (press), Block A, Government Offices, Coley
Park, Reading RG1 6DT.
Tel: 01734–581222, ext. 3268

*National Trust*

**Kent and East Sussex**, Scotney Castle, Lamberhurst TN3 8JN.
Tel: 01892–890651; fax: 01892–890110
**Southern**, Polesden Lacey, Dorking RH5 6BD.
Tel: 01372–453401; fax: 01372–452023
**Thames and Chilterns**, Hughenden Manor, High Wycombe HP14 4LA.
Tel: 01494–528051; fax: 01494–463310

**Royal Society for Protection of Birds**, 8 Church Street, Shoreham-by-Sea BN43 5DQ.
Tel: 01273–463642

# CRIME

**South-East Regional Crime Squad.**
Tel: 0171–238–8487, press

# DEFENCE

**Army (4 Division) Information**, Steeles Road, Aldershot GU11 2DP.
Tel: 01252–347011/347012

# ENERGY

**Electricity Consumers Committee**
**South Eastern**, 1 Lambert's Yard, Tonbridge TN9 1ER.
Tel: 01732–351356
**Southern**, 30 Friar Street, Reading RG1 1DX.
Tel: 01734–560211

**Seeboard**, Forest Gate, Brighton Road, Crawley RH11 9BH.
Tel: 01293–565888; fax: 01293–657327

**Southern Electric**, Westacott Way, Littlewick Green, Maidenhead SL6 3QB.
Tel: 01628–822166; fax: 01628–584400

# HEALTH

**Anglia and Oxford Regional Health Authority**, Old Road, Headington, Oxford OX3 7LF
Tel: 01865–742277; fax: 01865–226911

**North and South Thames Regional Health Authorities**, 40 Eastbourne Terrace, London W2 3QR.
Tel: 0171–725–2500; fax: 0171–258–3908

## INDUSTRY

**Department Trade and Industry**, South East.
Tel: 0171–261–8666/8813, press;  fax: 0171–928–6974

**CBI South Eastern and South**.
Tel: 01732–454040

**EEF South** (engineering employers), Station Road, Hook RG27 9TL.
Tel: 01256–763969; fax: 01256–768530

## POLITICS

**Conservative Party** (South), 1a High Street, Cobham KT11 3DH.
Tel: 01932–866477

**Labour Party**.
**South-East**, 97 Fore Street, Ipswich IP4 1JZ.
Tel: 01473–255668
**South**, 149 London Road, Chippenham SN15 3AN.
Tel: 01249–460011

## SOCIETY AND WELFARE

**Benefits Agency** (South-East).
Tel: 0181–652–9911, press

**Girl Guides Association**, 3 Jaggard Way, London SW12 8SG.
Tel: 0181–675–7572

**Royal Association in Aid of Deaf People**, 27 Old Oak Road, London W3 7HN.
Tel: 0181–7343–6187; fax: 0181–740–6551

**Royal National Institute for Deaf People**, 39 Store Street, London WC1E 7DB.
Tel: 0171–916–4144; fax: 0171–916–4546

**Scope** (formerly Spastics Society).
Tel: 01293–522655

# SPORT

**South-East Council for Sport and Recreation**, PO Box 480, Crystal Palace National Sports Centre, London SE19 2BQ.
Tel: 0181–778–8600; fax: 676–9812

**Southern Council for Sport and Recreation**, 51a Church Street, Caversham RG4 8AX.
Tel: 01734–483311; fax: 01734–475935

# TELEPHONES

**British Telecom Southern Home Counties**, Telephone House, Rheims Way, Canterbury CT1 3BA.
Tel: 01227–474022

# TOURISM

**South-East England Tourist Board**, 1 Warwick Park, Tunbridge Wells TN2 5TU.
Tel: 01892–540766; fax: 01892–511008

**Southern Tourist Board**, 40 Chamberlayne Road, Eastleigh SO50 5JH.
Tel: 01703–620006; fax: 01703–620010

# TRADE UNIONS

**GMB Union**.
**London Region**, 152 Brent Street, London NW4 2DP.
Tel: 0181–202–3272; fax: 0181–202–2893
**Southern Region**, 205 Hook Road, Chessington KT9 1EA.
Tel: 0181–397–8881; fax: 0181–397–1588

**Transport and General Workers** (South-East and Anglia), 218 Green Lanes, London N4 2HB.
Tel: 0181–800–4281; fax: 0181–809–6501

**UCATT** (construction workers), 177 Abbeville Road, London SW4 9RL.
Tel: 0171–622–2362

**UNISON**.
**South**, 8 Church Street, Reading RG1 2SB.
Tel: 01734–596466; fax: 01734–597860
**South-East**, High Street, Banstead, SM7 2LH.
Tel: 01737–733300; fax: 01737–733328

## TRANSPORT

**Highways Agency** (South-East).
Tel: 0171–261–8787, press

**Rail Users Consultative Committee (South)**, 35 Old Queen Street,
London SW1H 9JA.
Tel: 0171–222–0391; fax: 0171–222–0392

**Chiltern Railways**, Great Central House, Marylebone Station, London
NW1 6JJ.
Tel: 0171–922–9534

**Gatwick Express**, 52 Grosvenor Gardens, London SW1W 0AU.
Tel: 0171–973–5035, press

**Island Line**, Station Offices, Sandown, Isle of Wight.
Tel: 01983–408585

**Network Southcentral**, 2 Cherry Orchard Road, Croydon CR9 6JB.
Tel: 0181–667–2952, press

**North London Railways**, 6th Floor, 65 Clarendon Road, Watford WD1
1DP.
Tel: 01923–207778

**South Eastern Railways**, 41 Blackfriars Road, London SE1 8NZ.
Tel: 0171–620–5080

**Thameslink**, 41 Blackfriars Road, London SE1 8NZ.
Tel: 0171–620–5282

**South West Trains** (out of Waterloo), 41 Blackfriars Road, London SE1
8NZ.
Tel: 0171–620–5229, press

**Thames Trains**, 37 Blagrave Street, Reading RG1 1RY.
Tel: 01734–579731, press

**West Anglia Great Northern Railways**, 1st Floor, 1 Cranwood Street,
London EC1V 9GT.
Tel: 0171–713–2121, press

## WATER AND RIVERS

**Environment Agency**, Southern.
Tel: 01903–820692; fax: 01903–214298
Thames.
Tel: 01734–535000; fax: 01734–592160

**OFWAT Southern and Thames Customer Service Committees**, 15
Ridgmount Road, London WC1E 7AH.
Tel: 0171–636–3656

**Southern Water**, Yeoman Road, Worthing BN13 3NX.
Tel: 01903–264444; fax: 01903–262100

**Thames Water**, Nugent House, Vastern Road, Reading RG1 8DB.
Tel: 01734–591159; fax: 01734–593203

### SOUTH-WEST

**Central Office of Information**, The Pithay, Bristol BS1 2NF.
Tel (Bristol): 0117–927–3767; fax: 0117–929–8612;
tel (Plymouth): 01752–635000

**Department of Environment** (press).
Tel: 0117–927–3767, ext. 6871

**South West Regional Planning Conference**, Room A105, County Hall,
Taunton TA1 4DY.
Tel: 01823–255017; fax: 01823–255258

## ARTS, MEDIA

**BBC South** (press).
Tel: 0117–974–2382

**HTV**, Bath Road, Bristol BS4 3HG.
Tel: 0117–977–8366, fax: 972–2400

**South-West Arts**, Bradninch Place, Gandy Street, Exeter EX4 3LS.
Tel: 01392–218188; fax: 01392–413554

**Westcountry TV**, Western Wood Way, Langage Science Park, Plymouth
PL7 5BG.
Tel: 01752–333333; fax: 01752–333030

## BRISTOL AND AVON

**AEEU Union** (engineers), 8 St Paul's Road, Bristol BS8 1LU
Tel: 0117–973–9321;  fax: 0117–974–5310

**AEEU Union** (electricians), 11 Belgrave Road, Clifton BS8 2AA.
Tel: 0117–973–4039; fax: 0117–946–6069

**Bristol Children's Hospital**.
Tel: 0117–921–5411

**Bristol and West Building Society**, New Road, Stoke Gifford.
Tel: 0117–979–2222

**Bristol and Western Engineering Manufacturers Association**, 4 Broad
Plain, Bristol BS2 0NB.
Tel: 0117–926–5930; fax: 923–0036

**GMB Union**, 4 Hide Market, Waterloo Street, Bristol BS2 0PH.
Tel: 0117–955–4470; fax: 0117–955–4409

**Royal West of England Academy**, Queens Road, Clifton, Bristol BS8 1PX.
Tel: 0117–973–5129; fax: 0117–923–7874

## COUNTRYSIDE

**Ministry of Agriculture**, Government Buildings, Alphington Road,
Exeter EX2 8NQ.
Tel: 01392–77951, ext. 8737 and
Burghill Road, Westbury BS10 6NJ.
Tel: 0117–959–1000, ext. 587

**National Trust.**
**Cornwall**, Lanhydrock, Bodmin PL30 4DE.
Tel: 01208–74281; fax: 01208–77887
**Devon**, Killerton House, Broadclyst EX5 3LE.
Tel: 01392–881691; fax: 01392–881954
**Wessex**, Eastleigh Court, Bishopstrow BA12 9HW.
Tel: 01985–843600; fax: 01985–843624

**Royal Society for Protection of Birds**, 10 Richmond Road, Exeter EX4
4JA.
Tel: 01392–432691

**Send a Cow**, Unit 4, Priston Mill, Bath BA2 9EQ (farmers help Uganda).
Tel: 01225–447041; fax: 01225–317627

# DEFENCE

**Army** (3 Division) Information SP4 9NY.
Tel: 01980–673329/672946

# ENERGY

**Electricity Consumers Committee** (South Western), Unit 1, Hide Market, West Street, Bristol BS2 0BH.
Tel: 0117–954–0934

**South Western Electricity**, 800 Park Avenue, Aztec West, Almondsbury, Bristol BS12 4SE.
Tel: 01454–201101; fax: 616369

# HEALTH

**South and West Regional Health Authority**, 26 King Square, Bristol BS2 8EF.
Tel: 0117–942–3271; fax: 0117–942–5398

# INDUSTRY, DEVELOPMENT

**Department of Trade and Industry** (press), Bristol.
Tel: 0117–945–6868/65; fax: 0117–945–8612

**CBI South West**.
Tel: 0117–973–7065

**Plymouth Development Corporation**, 1 Royal William Yard.
Tel: 01752–256132

**Western Development Partnership**, PO Box 606, 120 Redcliffe Street, Bristol BS99 5RE.
Tel: 0117–929–8884; fax: 0117–929–9166

# POLITICS

**Conservative Party (West)**, 3 Marlborough Court, Manaton Close, Matford Business Park, Exeter EX2 8PF.
Tel: 01392–58231

**Labour Party (South and South-West)**, 149 London Road, Chippenham
SN15 3AN.
Tel: 01249–460011

## SOCIETY AND WELFARE

**Benefits Agency** (press).
Tel: 0171–724–3489

**Scope** (formerly Spastics Society).
Tel: 0117–941–4424

## SPORT

**South Western Council for Sport and Recreation**, Ashlands House,
Crewkerne TA18 7LQ.
Tel: 01460–73491; fax: 01460–77263

## TELEPHONES

**British Telecom South-West**, Telephone House, Queen Charlotte Street,
Bristol BS1 1BA.
Tel: 0117–920–5264

## TOURISM

**Cornwall Tourist Board**, 59 Lemon Street, Truro TR1 2SY.
Tel: 01872–74057; fax: 01872–40423

**Somerset Tourism**, County Hall, Taunton TA1 4DY.
Tel: 01823–255255; fax: 01823–255572

**West Somerset Tourism**, 20 Fore Street, Williton, Taunton TA4 4QA.
Tel: 01984–632291; fax: 01984–633022

## TRADE UNIONS

**TUC South-West**, 1 Henbury Road, Westbury BS9 3HH.
Tel: 0117–950–6425

**Transport and General Workers (South and South-West)**, Transport House, Victoria Street, Bristol BS1 6AY.
Tel: 0117–923–0555; fax: 923–0560

**UCATT** (construction workers).
Tel: 0117–966–7649

**UNISON**, 853 Fishponds Road, BS16 2LG.
Tel: 0117–965–6081 fax: 9044

## TRANSPORT

**Highways Agency** (press).
Tel: 0117–945–6867

**Rail Users Consultative Committee (West)**, 13th Floor, Tower House, Fairfax Street, BS1 3BN.
Tel: 0117–926–5703; fax: 929–4140

**Great Western Trains**, 1 Milford Street, Swindon SN1 1DW.
Tel: 01793–499499, press

## WATER AND RIVERS

**Environment Agency** (press).
Tel: 01392–444000; fax: 01392–442026

**OFWAT South West Customer Service Committee**, 1st Floor, Broadwalk House, Southernhay West, Exeter EX1 1TS.
Tel: 01392–428028

**OFWAT Wessex CSC**, Unit 2, The Hide Market, West Street, St Philips, Bristol BS2 0BH.
Tel: 0117–955–7001

**South West Water**, Peninsula House, Rydon Lane, Exeter EX2 7HR.
Tel: 01392–219666; fax: 01392–434966

**Wessex Water**, Passage Street, Bristol BS2 0JQ.
Tel: 0117–929–0611; fax: 0117–929–3137

## WALES

**Central Office of Information**, 4th Floor, Companies House, Cardiff CF4 3UW. See also COI in South-West section.
Tel: 01222–388085; fax: 01222–380847

**Welsh Office (London)**, Gwydyr House, Whitehall, London SW1A 2ER. For Cardiff office numbers, see under headings below.
Tel: 0171–270–0565/6, press

**European Commission**, 4 Cathedral Road, Cardiff CF1 9SG.
Tel: 01222–371631; fax: 01222–395489

## ARTS, CULTURE, MEDIA

Reference: *Buildings of Wales* series (Viking/Penguin). Glamorgan published November 1995, £30.

**Arts Council of Wales**, 9 Museum Place, Cardiff CF1 3NX.
Tel: 01222–394711; fax: 01222–221447

**BBC Wales** (press), Cardiff.
Tel: 01222–572115

**CADW: Welsh Historic Monuments**, 2 Fitzalan Road, Cardiff CF2 1UY.
Tel: 01222–500235; fax: 01222–500300

**HTV Wales**, Culverhouse Cross, Cardiff CF5 6XJ.
Tel: 01222–590590; fax: 01222–592134

**North Wales Arts Association**, 10 Wellfield House, Bangor LL57 1ER.
Tel: 01248–353248; fax: 01248–351077

**Royal National Eisteddfod of Wales**, 40 Parc Ty Glas, Llanishen CF4 5WU.
Tel: 01222–763777; fax: 01222–763737

**S4C** (Welsh TV service), Parc Busnes Ty Glas, Llanishen, Cardiff CF4 5DU.
Tel: 01222–741444; fax: 01222–741417

**Welsh National Opera**, John Street, Cardiff.
Tel: 01222–464666; fax: 01222–483050

## CARDIFF

**Cardiff Bay Development Corporation.**
Tel: 01222–585858

## COUNCILS

**Welsh Office Local Government Press Desk**, Cathays Park, Cardiff CF1 3NQ.
Tel: 01222–825647/5/4; fax: 01222–823807

**Local Government Ombudsman**, Derwent House, Court Road, Bridgend CF31 1BN.
Tel: 01656–661325; fax: 01656–658317


# DEFENCE

**Army (5 Division) Information**, Copthorne Barracks, Shrewsbury SY3 8LZ.
Tel: 01743–262252


# EDUCATION

**Welsh Office Education Press Desk**, Cathays Park, Cardiff CF1 3NQ.
Tel: 01222–825646/3/2; fax: 01222–823807


# ENERGY

**Electricity Consumers Committee (Mersey and North Wales)**, 4th Floor, Hamilton House, Chester CH1 2BH.
Tel: 01244–320849

**Electricity Consumers Committee (South Wales)**, 5th Floor West Wing, St David's House, Cardiff CF1 1ES.
Tel: 01222–228388

**SWALEC**, Newport Road, St Mellons, Cardiff CF3 0XW.
Tel: 01222–792111; fax: 01222–777759


# ENVIRONMENT

**Welsh Office Environment Press Desk**, Cathays Park, Cardiff CF1 3NQ.
Tel: 01222–825647/5/4; fax: 01222–823807

**Campaign for Protection of Rural Wales**, 31 High Street, Welshpool.
Tel: 01938–552525; fax: 01938–552741

**Countryside Council for Wales (Cyngor Cefn Gwlad Cymru)**, Plas Penrhos, Bangor LL57 2LQ.
Tel: 01248–370444; fax: 355782

**National Trust.**
**North Wales**, Trinity Square, Llandudno LL30 2DE.
Tel: 01492–860123; fax: 01492–860233
**South Wales**, King's Head, Bridge Street, Llandeilo SA19 6BB.
Tel: 01558–822800; fax: 01558–822872

**Environment Agency** (press).
Tel: 01222–770088; fax: 01222–770551

**Royal Society for Protection of Birds**, Bryn Aderyn, The Bank,
Newtown SY16 2AB.
Tel: 01686–626678

# FARMING

**Welsh Office Farming Press Desk**, Cathays Park, Cardiff CF1 3NQ.
Tel: 01222–825646/3/2; fax: 01222–823807

**Welsh Lamb Enterprise** (farmers co-operative), Brynawe, Great
Darkgate Street, Aberystwyth.
Tel: 01970–624011

# HEALTH, HOUSING, SOCIETY

**Welsh Office Health, Housing, Social Services**, Cathays Park, Cardiff
CF1 3NQ. This is the Welsh HQ for the NHS.
Tel: 01222–825647/5/4; fax: 01222–823807

**Benefits Agency** (press).
Tel: 01222–665927

**Equal Opportunities Commission**, Caerwys House, Windsor Lane,
Cardiff CF1 1LB.
Tel: 01222–343552

**Health Promotion Wales** (press), Ty Glas Avenue, Llanishen, Cardiff
CF4 5DZ.
Tel: 01222–681215; fax: 01222–755813

**Health Service Ombudsman**, 4th Floor, Pearl Assurance House,
Greyfriars Road, Cardiff CF1 3AG.
Tel: 01222–394621

**Scope** (formerly Spastics Society).
Tel: 01222–797706

**Wales Youth Agency**, Leslie Court, Lon-y-Llyn, Caerphilly CF8 1BQ.
Tel: 01222–880088; fax: 01222–880824

## INDUSTRY, COMMERCE, DEVELOPMENT

**Welsh Office Industry Press Desk**, Cathays Park, Cardiff CF1 3NQ.
Tel: 01222–825646/3/2; fax: 01222–823807

**Bank of Wales**, The Kingsway, Cardiff.
Tel: 01222–229922

**Cardiff Business School**.
Tel: 01222–874000, ext. 6792

**CBI Wales** (press).
Tel: 01222–232536

**D'Arcy Development**, Britannic Way, Llandarcy. BP-created enterprise
agency near Swansea.
Tel: 01792–321009

**Development Board for Rural Wales**, Ladywell House, Newtown SY16 1JB.
Tel: 01686–626965; fax: 01686–627889/622499

**Land Authority for Wales** (works with developers).
Tel: 01222–223444, Cardiff; 01978–357133, Wrexham

**Professor Kevin Morgan**, European Regional Development, University
of Wales, Cardiff.
Tel: 01222–874851

**Neath Development Partnership**, D'Arcy Business Centre, Llandarcy.
Tel: 01792–817575

**Wales Chamber of Commerce and Industry**, Exchange Building, Mount
Stuart Square, Cardiff.
Tel: 01222–481648

**Welsh Development Agency**, Principality House, The Friary, Cardiff
CF1 4AE.
Tel: 01222–828693/1, press

## LANGUAGE

**Welsh Department**, Cardiff University.
Tel: 01222–874843

## POLITICS

**Conservative Party**, 4 Penlline Road, Whitchurch, Cardiff CF4 2XS.
Tel: 01222–616031

**Labour Party**, Transport House, 1 The Cathedral Road, Cardiff CF1 9HA.
Tel: 01222–398567

**Liberal Democrats**, 57 St Mary Street, Cardiff.
Tel: 01222–382210

**Plaid Cymru**, 51 Cathedral Road, Cardiff.
Tel: 01222–231944

## RAILWAYS

**Rail Users Consultative Committee**, St David's House, Wood Street, Cardiff CF1 1ES.
Tel: 01222–227247; fax: 01222–223992

**South Wales and West/Cardiff Railway**, 1 Holbrook Way, Swindon SN1 1BY.
Tel: 01793–515618, press

## SPORT

**Sports Council for Wales**, Welsh Institute of Sport, Sophia Gardens, Cardiff CF1 9SW.
Tel: 01222–397571

**Welsh Rugby Union**, PO Box 22, Westgate Street, Cardiff CF1 1JL.
Tel: 01222–390111

## TELEPHONES

**British Telecom Wales**, 25 Pendwyallt Road, Coryton, Cardiff CF4 7YR.
Tel: 01222–391279

## TOURISM

**Wales Tourist Board**, Brunel House, 2 Fitzalan Road, Cardiff CF2 1UY.
Tel: 01222–475252, press; fax: 01222–475322

# TRADE UNIONS

**Wales TUC**.
Tel: 01222–372345; fax: 01222–221940

**TGWU** (Wales), 1 Cathedral Road, Cardiff CF1 9SD
Tel: 01222–394521; fax: 01222–390684

**GMB Union** (South Western), 17 Newport Road, Cardiff CF2 1TB.
Tel: 01222–491260; fax: 01222–462056

**UCATT** (construction workers).
Tel: 01222–498664

**UNISON**, 1 Cathedral Road, CF1 9SB.
Tel: 01222–383271; fax: 220398

# WATER

**OFWAT Customer Service Committee (Wales)**, Room 140, Caradog
House, Cardiff CF1 3BE.
Tel: 01222–239852

**Welsh Water**, Plas-y-Ffynnon, Cambrian Way, Brecon LD3 7HP.
Tel: 01874–623181; fax: 01874–624167

# WEST MIDLANDS AND WEST OF ENGLAND

**Central Office of Information**, Five Ways House, Islington Row
Middleway, Birmingham B15 1SH.
Tel: 0121–626–2036/33/22/40; fax: 2041

**Department of Environment**, Midlands (press).
Tel: 0121–626–2036

**Government Office for West Midlands**.
Tel: 0121–212–5151; fax: 5084

# ARTS, CULTURE, MEDIA

**BBC Midlands and East**, Pebble Mill Road, Birmingham B5 7SD.
Tel: 0121–414–8435, press

**Central TV**, Broad Street, Birmingham B1 2JP.
Tel: 0121–643–9898; fax: 0121–634–4766

**City of Birmingham Symphony Orchestra**, Paradise Place, Birmingham B3.
Tel: 0121–236–1555

**Shakespeare Birthplace Trust**, Shakespeare Centre, Henley Street, Stratford upon Avon CV37 6QW.
Tel: 01789–204016; fax: 296083

**West Midlands Arts**, 82 Granville Street, Birmingham B1 2LH.
Tel: 0121–631–3121; fax: 0121–643–7239

## DEVELOPMENT, ECONOMY, INDUSTRY

**Birmingham Economic Development Department**, PO Box 2470, Baskerville House, Broad Street, B1 2NF.
Tel: 0121–235–4874, PR

**Department of Trade and Industry**, Birmingham.
Tel: 0121–626–2024/22, press; fax: 0121–626–2041

**Black Country Development Corporation**, Rounds Green Road, Oldbury.
Tel: 0121–511–2000

**CBI West Midlands**.
Tel: 0121–454–7991; fax: 456–1634

**Engineering Employers**, West Midlands.
Tel: 0121–456–2222; fax: 0121–454–6745

**National Exhibition Centre**, Birmingham B40 1PA.
Tel: 0121–780–2721; fax: 0121–782–9302

**West Midlands Enterprise Board**, Wellington House, Waterloo Street, Birmingham B3.
Tel: 0121–236–8855

## ENERGY

**Electricity Consumers Committee (Midlands)**, 11th Floor, 83 Hagley Road, Birmingham B16 8QG.
Tel: 0121–456–4424

**Midlands Electricity**, Mucklow Hill, Halesowen B62 8BP.
Tel: 0121–423–2345; fax: 0121–422–3311

# FARMING, COUNTRYSIDE

**Ministry of Agriculture** (press),
Berkeley Towers, Nantwich Road, Crewe CW2 6PT.
Tel: 01270–69211, ext.350 and
Whittington Road, Worcester WR5 2LQ.
Tel: 01905–763355, ext. 8267

**National Trust**
**Mercia**, Attingham Park, Shrewsbury SY4 4TP.
Tel: 01743–709343; fax: 01743–709352
**Severn**, Mythe End House, Tewkesbury GL20 6EB.
Tel: 01684–850051; fax: 01684–850090

# HEALTH, SOCIETY

**Birmingham Voluntary Service Council**, 138 Digbeth, B5 6DR.
Tel: 0121–643–4343

**West Midlands Health Research Unit**, Room 133, 168 Corporation
Street, Birmingham B4 6TF.
Tel: 0121–236–0483

**West Midlands Regional Health Authority**, 146 Hagley Road,
Birmingham B16 9DP
Tel: 0121–456–1444; fax: 0121–454–4406

# POLITICS

**Conservative Party** (Midlands), Cedar Lawns, Church Street, Burbage,
Hinckley LE10 2DE.
Tel: 01455–239556

**Labour Party** (West Midlands), 323 High Street, West Bromwich B70 8LU.
Tel: 0121–553–6601

# SPORT

**West Midlands Council for Sport and Recreation**, 1 Hagley Road, Five
Ways, Birmingham B16 8TT.
Tel: 0121–456–3444; fax: 456–1583

# 8 THE WORLD

## GLOBAL AFFAIRS

*The Statesman's Yearbook* (Macmillan) covers international developments. The **Economist Intelligence Unit** publishes regular, detailed reports on countries throughout the world. These are available in major libraries such as the City Business Library, London; the British Library; the Central Reference Library, London WC2; the London Business School Library; Birmingham Central Libraries; Leeds City Library; Institute of Development Studies, Sussex University.

Banks often have country profiles. The **British Council** (tel: 0171–389–4878, press) has offices all over the world.

Embassies and high commissions, in the **Diplomatic Service List** or the **London business phone book**, can usually provide something about their countries, often with pictures. The American (tel: 0171–499–9000) and German (tel: 0171–235–5033) embassies have large libraries.

*Keesing's Record of World Events* is a monthly-updated account of what has just happened. It is compiled and published by CIRCA (13 Sturton Street, Cambridge CB1 2SN, tel: 01223–568017; fax: 01223–354643).

Reuter and the Associated Press are major international news agencies operating in Britain. Many Gemini News Service articles are written by people of the countries concerned.

Travel agents to try for cheap travel overseas include: **Austravel** (tel: 0171–734–7755), **Quest Worldwide** (tel: 0181–547–3322), **Supersonic** (tel: 0171–839–6856), **Trailfinders** (tel: 0171–938–3366) and **Travel Bag** (tel: 0171–497–0515).

Journalists group: **Association of Foreign Affairs Journalists**, Administrative Secretary, tel: 01277–821997

Reference: *Economist Pocket World in Figures* (Hamish Hamilton: £9.99).
*Monthly Bulletin of Statistics* (published by UN).
*Telephone books* (in libraries).
*World Bibliographical Series* – lists books written about all the countries in the world.

**Foreign and Commonwealth Office News Department**, Downing Street (West), London SW1A 2AL.
Tel: 0171–270–3100; fax: 0171–270–3094/3734

**British Consultants Bureau**, 1 Westminster Palace Gardens, 1 Artillery Row, London SW1P 1RJ. British consulting firms are very active overseas.
Tel: 0171–222–3651; fax: 0171–222–3664

**Chatham House** (Royal Institute of International Affairs), 10 St James's Square, London SW1Y 4LE.
Tel: 0171–957–5700; fax: 0171–957–5710

**English Speaking Union**, 37 Charles Street, London W1X 8AB.
Tel: 0171–493–3328

**International Monetary Fund**, 700 19th St NW, Washington DC 20431.
Tel: 00–1–202–623–7000; fax: 00–1–202–623–4661

**International Relations Department**, LSE, Houghton Street, London WC2A 2AE.
Tel: 0171–955–7404

**International Relations Department**, St Andrews University, KY16 9AJ.
Tel: 01334–476161

**International Relations and Politics Department**, Staffordshire University, Stoke ST4 2DE.
Tel: 01782–294000

**Organization for Economic Co-operation and Development**, 2 rue Andre Pascal, 75775 Paris.
Tel: 00–331–45–24–8200

**Politics and International Relations Department**, Edward Wright Building, University, Old Aberdeen AB9 2TY.
Tel: 01224–272714

**Royal Geographical Society (with the Institute of British Geographers)**, 1 Kensington Gore, London SW7.
Tel: 0171–589–5466

# ARCHAEOLOGY

**Institute of Archaeology**, UCL, Professor David Harris, 31 Gordon Square, London WC1H 0PY.
Tel: 0171–380–7495; fax: 383–2572

## *Archaeological science*

**Radiocarbon Accelerator Laboratory**, Dr Robert Hedges, 6 Keble Road, Oxford OX1 3QJ.
Tel: 01865–273930

**Research Laboratory for Archaeology and History of Art**, Professor Michael Tite, 6 Keble Road, Oxford OX1 3QJ.
Tel: 01865–515211

# BOUNDARIES

**Geopolitics and International Boundaries Research Centre**, School of Oriental and African Studies, Thornhaugh Street, Russell Square WC1H 0XG.
Tel: 0171–323–6308

**International Boundaries Research Unit**, Durham University, South Road, DH1 3LT.
Tel: 0191–374–2486; fax: 0191–374–2456

# CITIES

**City and Regional Planning**, University of Wales, PO Box 906, Cardiff CF1 3YN.
Tel: 01222–874308

**Development Administration Group**, Birmingham University, Edgbaston, B15 2TT.
Tel: 0121–414–4987

**Town and Regional Planning**, Sheffield University S10 2TN.
Tel: 0114–282–6180

# COMMONWEALTH

**Centre of Commonwealth Studies**, Stirling University, FK9 4LA.
Tel: 01786–473171

**Commonwealth Development Corporation**, 1 Bessborough Gardens, London SW1V 2JQ. Invests in private firms overseas.
Tel: 0171–963–3864, press; fax: 0171–828–6505

**Commonwealth Foundation**, Marlborough House, Pall Mall, London SW1Y 5HY. Helps Commonwealth voluntary organizations.
Tel: 0171–930–3783; fax: 0171–839–8157

**Commonwealth Institute**, Kensington High Street, W8 6NQ. Centre for Commonwealth culture.
Tel: 0171–603–4535

**Commonwealth Secretariat**, Marlborough House, Pall Mall, London SW1Y 5HX.
Tel: 0171–839–3411; fax: 0171–839–9081, press

**Institute of Commonwealth Studies**, 28 Russell Square, London WC1B 5DS.
Tel: 0171–580–5876

**Professor David Dilks**, Vice-Chancellor, Hull University.
Tel: 01482–465131

### *Literature*

**Professor John Thieme**, English, Hull University HU6 7RX.
Tel: 01482–465666

**Dr A. N. N. Niven**, Arts Council, 14 Great Peter Street, London SW1P 3NQ.
Tel: 0171–333–0100

## ECONOMIES, FINANCE

**Institute of Economics and Statistics**, St Cross Building, Manor Road, Oxford OX1 3UL.
Tel: 01865–271073; fax: 01865–271094

**Professor Susan Strange**, Politics, Warwick University.
Tel: 01203–523302

## EDUCATION

**Mrs Jackie Brunner**, Education, Reading University.
Tel: 01734–318858

**International Education Department**, Institute of Education, 20 Bedford Way, London WC1H 0AL.
Tel: 0171–580–1122

## *Universities*

**Association of Commonwealth Universities**, 36 Gordon Square, London WC1H 0PF.
Tel: 0171–387–8572

**World University Service**, 20 Compton Terrace, London N1 2UN.
Tel: 0171–226–6747

## LAW AND JUSTICE

**International Bar Association**, 2 Harwood Place, 271 Regent Street, London W1R 7PA.
Tel: 0171–629–1206; fax: 0171–409–0456

**International Court of Justice**, Peace Palace, 2517 KJ The Hague, Netherlands.
Tel: 00–31–70–392–4441; fax: 364 9928

**Research Centre for International Law**, 5 Cranmer Road, Cambridge CB3 9BL.
Tel: 01223–332352/338300/335358

## LOCAL GOVERNMENT

**Local Government International Bureau**, 35 Great Smith Street, London SW1P 3BJ.
Tel: 0171–222–1636; fax: 0171–233–2179

## MEDIA

Reference: *Benn's Media* has European and international sections. The *World's News Media* (Longman, 1992) covers major publications and broadcasters worldwide.

For difficulties faced by journalists see *Reporters Sans Frontieres's* annual reports on media freedom throughout the world (published by Libbey). **Commonwealth Broadcasting Association**, **Commonwealth Press Union** and **Commonwealth Journalists Association** journals report developments in the Commonwealth.

*Media Moguls* by Jeremy Tunstall and Michael Palmer (Routledge 1991) is international in scope.

# MUSIC

**National Sound Archive** (international music section), 29 Exhibition Road, London SW7 2AS.
Tel: 0171–412–7440

# NATURE CONSERVATION

**World Conservation Monitoring Centre**, 219 Huntingdon Road, Cambridge CB3 0DL.
Tel: 01223–277314

# TERRORISM

**Research Institute for Study of Conflict and Terrorism**, 136 Baker Street, London W1M 1FH.
Tel: 0171–224–2659

**Centre for Study of Terrorism**, and **Professor Paul Wilkinson**, St Andrews University, KY16 9AJ.
Tel: 01334–476161

# AFRICA

**Africa Centre**, 38 King Street, London WC2H 8JT.
Tel: 0171–836–1973

**African Studies Centre**, Free School Lane, Cambridge University, CB2 3RQ.
Tel: 01223–334396

**Centre of African Studies**, Adam Ferguson Building, George Square, Edinburgh EH8 9LL.
Tel: 0131–650–3878

**Institute for African Alternatives**, 23 Bevenden Street, London N1 6BH.
Tel: 0171–251–1503

**School of African and Asian Studies**, Sussex University, Brighton BN1 9QN.
Tel: 01273–606755, ext. 2262

**School of Oriental and African Studies Briefing Service**, Graham Thomas.
Tel: 0171–323–6378; fax: 436–3844; e-mail: gt@soas.ac.uk

## *Books*

**African Books Collective**, 27 Park End Street, Oxford OX1 1HU.
Tel: 01865–726686; fax: 01865–793298

## *Non-fiction*

**James Currey, Publisher**, 73 Botley Road, Oxford OX2 0BS.
Tel: 01865–244111; fax: 01865–246454

## *Fiction*

**Heinemann African Writers Series**, Halley Court, Jordan Hill, Oxford OX2 8EJ.
Tel: 01865–314153

## *Economy*

**Centre for Study of African Economies**, Professor Paul Collier, St Cross Building, Manor Road, Oxford OX1 3UR.
Tel: 01865–271084

## *Human rights*

**African Rights**, 11 Marshalsea Road, London SE1 1EP.
Tel: 0171–717–1224; fax: 0171–717–1240; e-mail: afrights@gn.apc.org

**Africa Watch**, 33 Islington High Street, London N1 9LH.
Tel: 0171–713–1995

## *Music*

**Stern African Record Centre**, 74 Warren Street, London W1P 5PA.
Tel: 0171–387–5550

## *Rural change*

**Gavin Williams**, St Peter's, Oxford OX1 2DL
Tel: 01865–278851

## EAST AFRICA

**Dr Michael Twaddle**, Institute of Commonwealth Studies, 28 Russell Square, London WC1B 5DS.
Tel: 0171–580–5876

## *Eritrea*

**Dr Gary Littlejohn**, Bradford University.
Tel: 01274–384771

## *Ethiopia*

**John Cameron**, School of Development Studies, East Anglia University,
NR4 7TJ.
Tel: 01603–456161

**Professor C. S.Clapham**, Politics and International Relations, Lancaster
University.
Tel: 01524–594264

## *Mauritius*

**Mauritius Sugar**, 35 Grosvenor Gardens, SW1W 0BS.
Tel: 0171–834–3381

## *Somalia*

**African Rights**, 11 Marshalsea Road, London SE1 1EP.
Tel: 0171–717–1224; fax: 0171–717–1240

**Professor Ioan Lewis, Dr E. A. Brett**, London School of Economics.
Tel: 0171–955–7056 (Lewis); 0171–955–7406 (Brett)

## *Tanzania*

**Ellen Wratten**, Social Policy, LSE, WC2A 2AE.
Tel: 0171–955–7355

## *Uganda*

**Professor Deryke Belshaw**, School of Development Studies, East Anglia
University, Norwich NR4 7TJ.
Tel: 01603–456161

## FRANCOPHONE AFRICA

**Adrian Hewitt**, Overseas Development Institute, Portland House, Stag
Place, London SW1E 5DP.
Tel: 0171–393–1600; fax: 0171–393–1699

**Politics Department**, School of Oriental and African Studies, Professor Donal Cruise O'Brien, (ask Graham Thomas, School of Oriental and African Studies Briefing Service).
Tel: 0171–323–6378

## NORTH AFRICA

See also MIDDLE EAST. Many Middle East specialists also cover North Africa.

**Dr G.H.Blake**, Collingwood College, Durham University DH1 3LT.
Tel: 0191–374–2479

### Algeria

**Dr N.Kessous**, French Studies, Lancaster University.
Tel: 01524–592662

### Egypt

**Egyptian-British Chamber of Commerce**, Kent House, Market Place, London W1A 4EG.
Tel: 0171–323–2856

**Dr Peter Woodward**, Politics Department, Reading University RG6 2AA.
Tel: 01734–318503

### Archaeology

**Egypt Exploration Society**, 3 Doughty Mews, London WC1N 2PG.
Tel: 0171–242–1880

### Sudan

**Dr Peter Woodward**, Reading, see above.

**Sudan Update**, Hebden Bridge.
Tel and fax: 01422–845827

## PORTUGUESE-SPEAKING AFRICA

**Portuguese Department**, Kings College, The Strand, London WC2R 2LS.
Tel: 0171–873–2507

**Mozambique Institute**, 31 Bedford Square, London WC1B 3SG.
Tel: 0171–323–2722; fax: 0171–631–4659

## SOUTHERN AFRICA

**ACTSA**, Action for Southern Africa, 28 Penton Street, N1 9SA (successor to Anti-Apartheid Movement).
Tel: 0171–833–3133

**Dr Colin Stoneman**, Southern Africa Studies, York University YO1 5DD.
Tel: 01904–432029, PR

**FT Southern Africa Business Intelligence**, 149 Tottenham Court Road, London W1P 9LL.
Tel: 0171–896–2222; fax: 0171–896–2333

**Media Institute of Southern Africa**, Private Bag 13386, Windhoek, Namibia.
Tel: 00–264–61–232975; fax: 00–264–61–248016; e-mail:
postmaster@misa.alt.na

### *Botswana, Bushmen*

**Dr Alan Barnard**, Social Anthropology Department, Adam Ferguson Building, George Square, Edinburgh EH8 9LL.
Tel: 0131–650–3938

### *Namibia*

**Dr David Simon**, Centre for Developing Areas Research, Royal Holloway and Bedford, Egham TW20 0EX.
Tel: 01784–443651

### *South Africa*

**Jesmond Blumenfeld**, Economics Department, Brunel University, Uxbridge UB8 3PH.
Tel: 01895–274000; fax: 01895–203384; e-mail:
jesmond.blumenfeld@brunel.ac.uk

**Centre for Economics and Finance in South Africa**, LSE, Houghton Street, London WC2A 2AE.
Tel: 0171–955–7280; fax: 0171–430–1769

**James Hamill**, Politics, Leicester University.
Tel: 0116–252–2710

**Professor Jack Spence**, Chatham House, 10 St James's Square, London SW1.
Tel: 0171–957–5700

**RESA**, Research into Education in South Africa, Institute of Education, London WC1.
Tel: 0171–580–1122

## *Zimbabwe*

**Professor George Kay**, Geography, Staffordshire University, Leek Road, Stoke ST4 2DF.
Tel: 01782–294000

**Politics Department**, Leeds University, LS2 9JT.
Tel: 0113–233–4382

**Professor Richard Hodder-Williams**, Politics, 12 Priory Road, Bristol BS8 1TU.
Tel: 0117–928–7898

**Professor Terence Ranger**, St Antony's, Oxford.
Tel: 01865–284700

## WEST AFRICA

**Centre for West African Studies**, Birmingham University B15 2TT.
Tel: 0121–414–5128

## *Nigeria*

**Gavin Williams**, St Peter's, Oxford OX1 2DL.
Tel: 01865–278851

**Dr John Wiseman**, Politics Department, Newcastle upon Tyne University, NE1 7RU.
Tel: 0191–222–7527

## *Sahel region*, south of Sahara

**SOS Sahel**, 1 Tolpuddle Street, London N1 0XT.
Tel: 0171–837–9129; fax: 0171–837–0856

# ARCTIC AND ANTARCTIC

**British Antarctic Survey**, High Cross, Madingley Road, Cambridge CB3
0ET.
Tel: 01223–251400; PR fax: 01223–302093

**Centre for Arctic Biology**, Williamson Building, Manchester University,
Oxford Road, Manchester M13 9PL.
Tel: 0161–275–2112/4, PR

**Dr Peter Wadhams**, Scott Polar Research Institute, Cambridge
University.
Tel: 01223–336542/40

## *Military and environmental co-operation*

**David Scrivener**, International Relations, Keele University.
Tel: 01782–583212

# ASIA

**Asian Review of Business and Technology**, 27 Wilfred Street, London
SW1E 6PR.
Tel: 0171–834–7676; fax: 0171–973–0076

**Centre of Asian Studies**, School of Oriental and African Studies, ask
Graham Thomas, Briefing Service.
Tel: 0171–323–6378

**Oriental Studies**, Cambridge CB3 9DA.
Tel: 01223–335106

**Oriental Institute**, Pusey Lane, Oxford OX1 2LE.
Tel: 01865–278200

**Royal Society for Asian Affairs**, 2 Belgrave Square, London SW1X
8PJ.
Tel: 0171–235–5122

**School of Asian and African Studies**, Sussex University, Brighton BN1
9QN.
Tel: 01273–606755, ext. 2262

**School of Oriental and African Studies Briefing Service**, Graham
Thomas.
Tel: 0171–323–6378, fax: 436–3844; e-mail: gt@soas.ac.uk

## CENTRAL ASIA

**Central Asian Studies Department**, School of Oriental and African Studies, Thornhaugh Street, Russell Square, London WC1H 0XG.
Tel: 0171–323–6300

**Mongolia and Inner Asia Studies Department**, Sidgwick Avenue, Cambridge CB3 9DA.
Tel: 01223–335102

### *Business, economy*

**Dr John Henley**, Edinburgh University Management School, 50 George Square, EH6 9JY.
Tel: 0131–650–3814

## FAR EAST/ASIA PACIFIC

**Asia and Pacific Business and Development Research Unit** (Hafiz Mirza), Bradford University, BD7 1DP.
Tel: 01274–384389

**Centre for Japanese and East Asian Studies**, 56 Britton Street, London EC1M 5NA.
Tel: 0171–608–2279; fax: 0171–608–2291

**Centre for South-East Asian Studies**, Hull University HU6 7RX.
Tel: 01482–465758, Professor Terry King; tel: 01482–465760, Dr Michael Parnwell; e-mail: m.j.parnwell@seas.hull.ac.uk.

**East Asian Studies**, Leeds University LS2 9JT.
Tel: 0113–233–3462

**East Asian Studies**, Sheffield University S10 2TN. Has Chinese, Japanese and Korean sections.
Tel: 0114–282–4854

**Institute of Pacific Asia Studies**, Dr Mike Hitchcock, Hull University HU6 7RX.
Tel: 01482–466398

### *East Asia and the United States*

**Dr Rosemary Foot**, St Antony's, Oxford OX2 6JF.
Tel: 01865–284700

## Cambodia

**Cambodia Trust**, PO Box 14, Woodstock OX20 1JF.
Tel: 01993–813542

**Dr Peter Carey**, Trinity College, Oxford OX1 3BH.
Tel: 01865–279900

## China

**China-Britain Trade Group**, 15 Wilton Road, London SW1V 1LT.
Tel: 0171–828–5176

**Great Britain-China Centre**, 15 Belgrave Square, London SW1X 8PS.
Tel: 0171–235–6696

**Institute for Chinese Studies**, Oxford OX1 2HG.
Tel: 01865–280387

**Percival David Foundation of Chinese Art**, 53 Gordon Square, London WC1H 0PD.
Tel: 0171–387–3909; fax: 0171–383–5163

**Dr Michael Dillon**, East Asian Studies, Durham University, Elvet Hill, DH1 3TH.
Tel: 0191–374–3231; fax: 0191–374–3242

**Michael Yahuda**, International Relations, LSE.
Tel: 0171–955–7399; e-mail: m.b.yahuda@lse.ac.uk

**China Economic Review.**
Tel: 0171–834–7676; fax: 0171–973–0076

**China Practice Group**, Clifford Chance, 200 Aldersgate Street, London EC1A 4JJ. Legal issues, copyright.
Tel: 0171–282–7000; fax: 0171–600–5555

**Anti-Slavery International** (human rights), The Stableyard, Broomgrove Road, London SW9 9TL.
Tel: 0171–924–9555; fax: 738–4110

## Hong Kong, Taiwan

**Dr Steve Tsang**, Chinese Studies, Oxford.
Tel: 01865–280384

**Hong Kong Government**, 6 Grafton Street, London W1X 3LB.
Tel: 0171–499–9821

## *Tibet*

**Tibet Information Network**, 7 Beck Road, London E8 4RE.
Tel: 0181–533–5458

**Tibet Support Group UK**, 9 Islington Gardens, London N1 2XH.
Tel: 0171–359–7573; fax: 0171–354–1026

## *East Timor*

**Catholic Institute for International Relations.**
Tel: 0171–354–0883

## *Indonesia*

**Dr Peter Carey**, Trinity College, Oxford OX1 3BH.
Tel: 01865–279900

## *Japan*

**Nissan Institute**, Oxford University, 1 Church Walk, OX2 6LY.
Tel: 01865–274570

**Japan Centre**, Manchester University M13 9PL.
Tel: 0161–275–2112/4, PR

**Ms Hitomi Tobe**, Languages, Keele University ST5 5BG.
Tel: 01782–583278

**Dr Peter Clarke**, Theology and Religious Studies, King's College, The Strand, London WC2R 2LS. Japanese religion.
Tel: 0171–836–5454

## *Korea*

**Centre for Korean Studies**, School of Oriental and African Studies, Thornhaugh Street, Russell Square, London WC1H 0XG. Ask for Graham Thomas.
Tel: 0171–323–6378

**Korea Business Services**, 317 Glossop Road, Sheffield S10 2HP.
Tel: 0114–268–2800; fax: 0114–266–6063

**East Asian Studies**, Sheffield University, S10 2TN.
Tel: 0114–282–4854

**Politics Department**, Newcastle upon Tyne University, NE1 7RU.
Tel: 0191–222–7742, Barry Gills; 0191–222–7554, Dr Roland Wein

## Malaysia

**Bank Negara Malaysia**, Berkeley Square House, Berkeley Square, London W1X 5LA.
Tel: 0171–495–0222

**Malaysian Industrial Development Authority**, 17 Curzon Street, London W1Y 4BE.
Tel: 0171–493–0616; fax: 0171–493–8804

## Philippines

**Dr James Putzel**, Government Department, LSE.
Tel: 0171–955–6743/7425

**Professor R.H.Taylor**, Politics Department, School of Oriental and African Studies, Thornhaugh Street, Russell Square, London WC1H 0XG.
Tel: 0171–637–2388

## INDIAN SUB-CONTINENT

**Centre of South Asian Studies**, Laundress Lane, Cambridge CB2 1SD.
Tel: 01223–338094

**John Cameron**, School of Development Studies, East Anglia University, Norwich NR4 7TJ.
Tel: 01603–456161

## Bangladesh

**Development Studies Centre**, Bath University, Claverton Down BA2 7AX.
Tel: 01225–826826; fax: 01225–826391

## Burma-Myanmar

**Dr Peter Carey**, Trinity College, Oxford OX1 3BH.
Tel: 01865–279900

**Professor R. H.Taylor**, School of Oriental and African Studies, Thornhaugh Street, Russell Square, London WC1H 0XG.
Tel: 0171–637–2388

**Human Rights Watch**, 33 Islington High Street, London N1.
Tel: 0171–713–1995

## *India*

**Centre for Indian Studies**, Professor Bhikhu Parekh, Hull University HU6 7RX.
Tel: 01482–465798

**Politics Department**, Dr David Taylor, School of Oriental and African Studies, ask Graham Thomas, Briefing Service.
Tel: 0171–323–6378

**India Business Intelligence**, FT Newsletters, 149 Tottenham Court Road, London.
Tel: 0171–896–2222

**Institute of Indian Art and Culture**, 4A Castletown Road, London W14 9HQ.
Tel: 0171–381–3086

**World Kashmir Freedom Movement**, 41 Monsell Road, London N4 2EF.
Tel: 0171–354–5305; fax: 0171–354–0840

**Dr Joyce Pettigrew**, Social Anthropology, Queens University, Belfast BT7 1NN. Punjab.
Tel: 01232–245133, ext. 3702

## *Pakistan*

**Professor D. George Boyce**, Politics Department, University of Wales, Swansea SA2 8PP.
Tel: 01792–295302

# AUSTRALASIA

## AUSTRALIA

**Professor Lyn Innes, Dr Sean Glynn**, Kent University, Canterbury CT2 7NZ.
Tel: 01227–451805, press

## *Aborigines*

**Dr David McKnight**, Anthroplogy, LSE.
Tel: 0171–955–7215

# NEW ZEALAND

**NZ UK Chamber of Commerce**, London W1R 5AB.
Tel: 0171–636–4525

# CARIBBEAN

**Centre for Caribbean Studies**, North London University, Holloway Road, London N7 8DB.
Tel: 0171–607–2789

**Dr David Dabydeen**, Warwick University, Coventry CV4 7AL.
Tel: 01203–523523

**Dr Paul Sutton**, Politics, Hull University.
Tel: 01482–465750

## CUBA

**Cuba Business** (magazine), 254 Goswell Road, London EC1V 7EB.
Tel: 0171–490–1997; fax: 0171–253–7358

## JAMAICA

**Gleaner Publications UK Ltd**, Unit 220–223 Elephant and Castle Shopping Centre, London SW1 6TE.
Tel: 0171–277–1714

# COMMODITIES

See also METALS and MINERALS, page 133 and FOOD, page 48.

**Commodities Department**, Kleinwort Benson, 20 Fenchurch Street, London EC3P 3DB.
Tel: 0171–623–8000

**CRU International**, 31 Mount Pleasant, London WC1X 0AD.
Tel: 0171–278–0414

**E. D. and F. Man**, Sugar Quay, Lower Thames Street, London EC3R 6DU.
Tel: 0171–285–3000

**Liverpool Cotton Exchange.**
Tel: 0151–236–6041

**LMC** (Landell Mills Commodities), 14 George Street, Oxford OX1 2AF.
Tel: 01865–791737

**London Commodity Exchange**, 1 Commodity Quay, St Katharine's Dock, E1 9AX.
Tel: 0171–481–2080; fax: 702–9923


## COCOA

**Biscuit, Cocoa, Chocolate and Confectionery Alliance**, London.
Tel: 0171–404–9111

**International Cocoa Organization**, 22 Berners Street, London W1P 4DD.
Tel: 0171–637–3211


## COFFEE

**International Coffee Organization**, 22 Berners Street, London W1P 4DD.
Tel: 0171–580–8591

**GNI Coffee Experts**, 25 Dowgate Hill, London EC4R 2GN.
Tel: 0171–337–3500

**Merrill Lynch**, 25 Ropemaker Street, EC2Y 9AS.
Tel: 0171–628–1000


## EUROPE

**Journalists' Group**: Association of Foreign Affairs Journalists, Administrative, Secretary.
Tel: 01277–821997

**FT European Handbook**. Reviews companies in Europe.

**Foreign and Commonwealth Office News Department**, London SW1A 2AL.
Tel: 0171–270–3100; fax: 0171–270–3094/3734

**Council of Europe**, Avenue d'Europe, BP 431/R6, 67006 Strasbourg, Cedex, France. Wider than EU: parent of European Court of Human Rights.
Tel: 00–33–88–61–49–61

**European Commission on Human Rights** (puts cases to the Court).
Tel: 00–33–88–41–2000

**Centre for European Politics, Economics and Society**, George Street, Oxford OX1 2RL.
Tel: 01865–278718

**European Institute**, London School of Economics, Houghton Street, London WC2A 2AE.
Tel: 0171–955–6780/6839; e-mail: m.clarke@lse.ac.uk

**European Studies**, University College, Stockton on Tees, TS17 6BH.
Tel: 01642–335334; fax: 01642–618345

**School of European Studies**, Cardiff University.
Tel: 01222–874248

**Sussex Europe Institute**, Sussex University, Brighton BN1 9QN.
Tel: 01273–678560

# ARCHAEOLOGY

**Institute of Archaeology**, Professor Barry Cunliffe, Oxford University, 34 Beaumont Street, OX1 2PG.
Tel: 01865–278240

# DEFENCE

See page 240.

# HEALTH

**European Health Policy Research Network**, c/o LSE, Houghton Street, London WC2A 2AE.
Tel: 0171–955–7540/6840; fax: 0171–955–6803

## SOCIETY

### *Policies on ageing*

**Dr Thomas Scharf**, Modern languages, Keele University.
Tel: 01782–584079

## EUROPEAN UNION

*FT European Handbook*. Reviews companies in Europe.
Reference: *Encyclopaedia of European Community Law* (fills a library shelf).
*European Public Affairs Directory*. This is a guide to the Brussels Mafia, including academics and think-tanks.
*Panorama of EU Industry*, issued by Directorate.
General III (figures not broken down by countries).

**Foreign and Commonwealth Office News Department**, London SW1A 2AL.
Tel: 0171–270–3100; fax: 0171–270–3094/3734

**Sir Leon Brittan's spokesman**, Brussels.
Tel: 00–322–295–8562

**Neil Kinnock's spokesman.**
Tel: 00–322–296–8562

**EU spokesmen's fax:** 00–322–295–0143

**Eurobarometer** (EU's public-opinion survey team).
Tel: 00–322–299–1111

**European Commission**, London, 8 Storeys Gate, SW1P 3AT.
Tel: 0171–973–1971, press; fax: 0171–973–1900

**European Monetary Institute**, Frankfurt.
Tel: 00–49–69–272–270

**Eurostat** (statistics), Jean Monnet Building, rue Alcide de Gasperi, L-2920 Luxembourg.
Tel: 00–352–4301–34567; fax: 00 352 436404

**Centre for European Union Studies**, Professor Juliet Lodge, Hull University HU6 7RX.
Tel: 01482–465844

**European Movement**, 11 Tufton Street, London SW1P 3QB.
Tel: 0171–233–1422

**European Policy Forum**, 20 Queen Anne's Gate, London SW1H 9AA. Think-tank critical of Euro regulations.
Tel: 0171–222–0733

**Research Group in European Monetary Union**, Professor Kenneth Dyson, Bradford University BD7 1DP.
Tel: 01274–383805

# AGRICULTURE AND CAP

**Ministry of Agriculture CAP Press Desk**, 3 Whitehall Place, London SW1A 2HH.
Tel: 0171–270–8025; fax: 0171–270–8447

**Agra Europe** (research group), 25 Frant Road, Tunbridge Wells TN2 5JT.
Tel: 01892–533813

**Agriculture, Economics and Food Marketing**, Newcastle University, NE1 7RU.
Tel: 0191–222–6872, Professor David Harvey; tel: 0191–222–6909, Professor Chris Ritson

# ANTI-DUMPING POLICY

**Dr Brian Hindley**, London School of Economics.
Tel: 0171–955–7497

# EUROPEAN PARLIAMENT

**European Parliament**, 2 Queen Anne's Gate, London SW1H 9AA.
Tel: 0171–222–4300; fax: 0171–222–4302

**Conservatives in the European Parliament**, 32 Smith Square, London SW1P 3HH.
Tel: 0171–222–1720

**European Parliamentary Labour Party**, 2 Queen Anne's Gate, London SW1H 9AA.
Tel: 0171–222–1719

## INDUSTRY

**UNICE** (Union des Confederations de l'Industrie et des Employeurs d'Europe).
Tel: 00–322–237–6511; fax: 00–322–231–1445

**European Trade Union Confederation**, Bd Emile Jacqmain 155, 1210 Brussels.
Tel: 00–322–224–0411; fax: 00–322–224–0454/5

## INVESTMENT

**European Investment Bank**, Luxembourg.
Tel: 00–352–43791 and
68 Pall Mall, London SW1Y 5ES.
Tel: 0171–839–3351

## LAW

**Damian Chalmers**, European Law, LSE, Houghton Street, London WC2A 2AE.
Tel: 0171–405–7686

**European Law Institute**, Durham University, 50 North Bailey, DH1 3ET.
Tel: 0191–374–2030; fax: 0191–374–2068

**Institute of European Public Law**, Hull University HU6 7RX.
Tel: 01482–466342, Christopher Bovis

### *Policing*

**Mike King**, Centre for Study of Public Order, Leicester University LE1 7RH.
Tel: 0116–252–3948

## REGIONS

**Mediterranean Desertification and Land Use (Medalus)**, 20a High Street, Thatcham RG19 3JD.
Tel/fax: 01635–876015

**Professor Kevin Morgan**, European Regional Development, University of Wales, Cardiff.
Tel: 01222–874851

# EUROPEAN UNION COUNTRIES

## AUSTRIA

**Dr Frank Fields**, History, Keele University ST5 5BG.
Tel: 01782–583200

## BELGIUM

**Andrew MacMullen**, Politics, Durham University, 48 Old Elvet, DH1 3LZ.
Tel: 0191–374–2810; fax: 0191–374–2680

## FINLAND

**Stewart Arnold**, Management Systems, Hull University HU6 7RX.
Tel: 01482–466319; e-mail: s.d.arnold@uk.ac.hull.msd

**Dr Christopher Hall**, German Department, Leicester University.
Tel: 0116–252–2667

## FRANCE

**Dr Roger Duchaud-Williams**, Politics, Warwick University.
Tel: 01203–523106

**Professor Martin Harrison**, Politics, Keele University.
Tel: 01782–583354

**Dr Ella Ritchie**, Politics, Newcastle University.
Tel: 0191–222–7548

**French Studies**, Reading University.
Tel: 01734–318121

### *Feminism*

**Dr Diana Holmes**, Languages, Keele University.
Tel: 01782–584077

### *Right-wing politics*

**Dr Jim Shields**, French Department, Warwick University.
Tel: 01782–523334/523013

## GERMANY

**Peter Graves**, German, Leicester University LE1 7RH.
Tel: 0116–252–2665

**A. J. Nicholls**, Director European Studies Centre, St Antony's College, Oxford OX2 6JF.
Tel: 01865–284700

**Professor John Sandford**, German, Reading.
Tel: 01734–318332/218330

**Professor Gordon Smith**, Government, LSE.
Tel: 0171–955–7198

### *Green politics*

**Dr Thomas Scharf**, Languages, Keele University.
Tel: 01782–584079

### *Women in Germany*

**Professor Eva Kolinsky**, Languages, Keele University.
Tel: 01782–583283

## GREECE

**George Cataphores**, Economics, UCL.
Tel: 0171–387–7050, ext. 2301

**Dr Harry Papapanagos**, Economics, Kent University.
Tel: 01227–451805, PR

### *Relations with Turkey*

**Dr Peter Loizos**, Anthropology, LSE, WC2A 2AE.
Tel: 0171–955–7212

## IRELAND

**Professor Roy Foster**, Hertford College, Oxford OX1 3BW.
Tel: 01865–279400

**Stephen Hopkins**, Politics, Leicester University, LE1 7RH.
Tel: 0116–270–7172/252–2709

**Dan Keohane**, International Relations, Keele University.
Tel: 01782–583214

**Dr Brendan O'Leary**, Government, LSE. Has written books on
Northern Ireland conflict.
Tel: 9171–955–7748

**Dr Ron Weir**, Economics, York University.
Tel: PR: 01904–432029

## ITALY

**Italian Studies**, Reading University.
Tel: 01734–318402

**Dr Luciano Cheles**, Italian, Lancaster University.
Tel: 01524–593002

**Mrs Paola Keyse**, Italian, Leicester University.
Tel: 0116–252–2569

## NETHERLANDS

**Dutch Department** (Professor Reinier Salverda), UCL, Gower Street,
London WC1E 6BT.
Tel: 0171–419–3113; fax: 0171–916–6985

## SPAIN, PORTUGAL

**Centre for Iberian Studies**, Dr John Naylon, Keele University ST5 5BG.
Tel: 01782–621111, ext. 7558

**Dr Jose Magone**, Politics, Hull University HU6 7RX.
Tel: 01482–465808; e-mail: j.m.magone@poldpt.hull.ac.uk

**Professor Paul Preston**, International History, LSE, Houghton Street,
London WC2A 2AE.
Tel: 0171–955–7107

**Portuguese Department**, King's College, The Strand, London WC2R 2LS.
Tel: 0171–873–2507

**Spanish and Portuguese Departments**, Leeds University LS2 9JT.
Tel: 0113–233–3523

## SWEDEN, DENMARK

**Scandinavian Studies**, Professor Michael Barnes, UCL, Gower Street,
London WC1E 6BT.
Tel: 0171–380–7177/6; fax: 0171–380–7750

**John Madeley**, Government, LSE, WC2A 2AE.
Tel: 0171–955–7186

## EUROPE OUTSIDE EUROPEAN UNION

## AZERBAIJAN

**Dr John Henley**, University Management School, 50 George Square,
Edinburgh EH8 9JY.
Tel: 0131–650–3814

## BALKANS

**Dr Spyros Economides**, International Relations, London School of
Economics, WC2A 2AE.
Tel: 0171–955–7384

## BALTIC STATES

**Baltic Research Unit**, Bradford University BD7 1DP.
Tel: 01274–383809, Professor John Haden; tel: 01274–383814, Thomas Lane

**Stewart Arnold**, Management Systems, Hull University HU6 7RX.
Tel: 01482–466319; e-mail: s.d.arnold@uk.ac.hull.msd

**Dr Graham Smith**, Geography, Cambridge University.
Tel: 01223–333356

## BULGARIA

**Professor Michael Waller**, European Studies, Keele University ST5 5BG.
Tel: 01782–583481

## CYPRUS

**Association for Cyprus, Greek and Turkish Affairs**, 17 Scott Hall Square, Leeds LS7 3JN.
Tel: 0113–293–0747; e-mail: 101371.2006@compuserve.com

**Haravgi** (newspaper), 534A Holloway Road, London N7 6JP.
Tel: 0171–272–6777

## CZECH REPUBLIC, SLOVAKIA

**Dr Alex Pravda**, St Antony's, Oxford OX2 6JF.
Tel: 01865–284700

## EASTERN EUROPE

**European Bank for Reconstruction and Development**, 1 Exchange Square, London EC2A 2EH.
Tel: 0171–338–6372; fax: 0171–338–6690

**East European Centre**, Manchester University.
Tel: 0161–275–2112/4, PR

**Finance East Europe**, FT Newsletters, 149 Tottenham Court Road, London.
Tel: 0171–896–2222

**Terry McNeill**, Politics, Hull University HU6 7RX.
Tel: 01482–465756; e-mail: t.p.mcneil@poldept.hull.ac.uk

**Dr Larry Ray**, Sociology, Lancaster University.
Tel: 01524–594180

**Dr Terry Cox, Professor Richard Rose**, Strathclyde University, Glasgow G1 1XQ.
Tel: 0141–552–4400, ext. 2699 Dr Cox; ext. 3217, Professor Rose

**Dr L. Rychetnik**, Sociology, Reading University.
Tel: 01734–875123, ext. 7513

**Slavonic Studies Department**, Cambridge University.
Tel: 01223–335007

### *East European economies*

**Professor Wojciech W. Charemza**, Economics, Leicester University LE1 7RH.
Tel: 0116–252–2899

**John S. Flemming**, Wadham College, Oxford.
Tel: 01865–277403

**Peter R.Lawrence**, Economics, Keele University, ST5 5BG.
Tel: 01782–583110

*Gypsies*

**Dr Michael Stewart**, Anthropology, LSE, London WC2A.
Tel: 0171–955–7056

# HUNGARY

**George Gomori**, Languages, Cambridge University.
Tel: 01223–335023/335000

# MALTA

**Dr Douglas Lockhart**, Geography, Keele University.
Tel: 01782–583165

# POLAND

**George Gomori**, Languages, Cambridge University.
Tel: 01223–335023/335000

**Dr Stanislaw Gomulka**, Economics, LSE, London WC2A.
Tel: 0171–955–7510

**Dr Anita J. Prazmowska**, International  History, LSE (foreign investment, reorganizing state enterprises).
Tel: 0171–955–7601

**Dr John Henley**, University Management School, 50 George Square,
Edinburgh EH8 9JY.
Tel: 0131–650–3814

# ROMANIA

**Romanian Child Action**, Witnesham IP6 9HL.
Tel: 01473–785206

# RUSSIA

**Professor Archie Brown**, St Antony's College, Oxford OX2 6JF.
Tel: 01865–284748/284700

**Dr John Barber**, Social and Political Science, Cambridge University.
Tel: 01223–334521/331256

**Dr Elaine Holobaff**, War Studies, King's College, London WC2R 2LS.
Tel: 0171–873–2831

**Dr James Hughes**, Politics, Keele ST5 5BG.
Tel: 01782–583350

**Professor Dominic Lieven**, LSE, London WC2A 2AE.
Tel: 0171–955–7184

## *Siberia*

**Dr James Hughes**, see above and **Dr Alan Wood**, History, Lancaster University.
Tel: 01524–592604

# SCANDINAVIA, ICELAND

**Scandinavian Studies**, Professor Michael Barnes, UCL, Gower Street, London WC1E 6BT.
Tel: 0171–380–7177/6; fax: 0171–380–7750

**John T. S. Madeley**, Government, LSE, London WC2A 2AE.
Tel: 0171–955 7186

# SLOVAKIA

See CZECH REPUBLIC above.

# SOVIET UNION'S SUCCESSORS

**Mark Galeotti**, History, Keele ST5 5BG
Tel: 01782–584041

**Terry McNeill**, Politics, Hull University HU6 7RX.
Tel: 01482–465756; e-mail: t.p.mcneil@poldept.hull.ac.uk

**Dr Alan Wood**, History, Lancaster University.
Tel: 01524–592604

## SWITZERLAND

**Dr Andy Williams**, International Relations, Kent University, Canterbury CT2 7NZ.
Tel: 01227–451805, PR

## UKRAINE

**Alan Rose**, Economics, Warwick University, CV4 7AL.
Tel: 01203–523326

## YUGOSLAVIA'S SUCCESSORS

**International Criminal Tribunal for the former Yugoslavia**, Churchillplein 1, PO Box 13888, 2501 EW The Hague.
Tel: 00–31–70–344–5343; fax: 00–31–70–344–5355

**Serbian Information Centre**, 89 Lancaster Road, London W11 1QQ.
Tel: 0171–792–9711; fax: 0171–221–2224

**Dr Peter Ferdinand**, Politics, Warwick University.
Tel: 01203–523419/523302

**Glenn Bowman**, Kent University CT2 7NZ.
Tel: 01227–451805, PR

## HEALTH OVERSEAS

**Centre for International Health Studies**, Queen Margaret College, Clerwood Terrace, Edinburgh EH12 8TS.
Tel: 0131–317–3491; fax: 0131–317–3494

**Liverpool School of Tropical Medicine**, Pembroke Place, Liverpool L3 5QA.
Tel: 0151–708–9393

**London School of Hygiene and Tropical Medicine**, Keppel Street, London WC1E 7HT.
Tel: 0171–636–8636

**LSE Health** (research centre), Houghton Street, London WC2A 2AE.
Tel: 0171–955–7540/6840; fax: 0171–955–7546

**International Division**, Nuffield Institute of Health Service Studies,
Leeds LS2 9PL.
Tel: 0113–233–6633; fax: 0113–246–0899

## AIDS

**Panos Institute**, 9 White Lion Street, London N1 9PD.
Tel: 0171–278–1111

## CHILD HEALTH

**International Child Health Department**, Institute of Child Health, 30
Guilford Street, WC1.
Tel: 0171–242–9789; fax: 831–0488

### *Child deaths*

**Centre for Population Studies**, London School of Hygiene, 99 Gower
Street, London WC1E 6AZ.
Tel: 0171–388–3071

## EARS

**Commonwealth Society for the Deaf**, Dilke House, Malet Street,
London WC1E 7JA.
Tel: 0171–631–5311

## DISEASES

**Hospital for Tropical Diseases**, 4 St Pancas Way, London NW1.
Tel: 0171–387–4411

**Tropical Medicine Department**, Liverpool School of Tropical Medicine,
L3 5QA.
Tel: 0151–708–9393

## EYES

**British Council for Prevention of Blindness**, 12 Harcourt Street, London
W1H 1DS.
Tel: 0171–724–3716

**International Centre for Eye Health**, Bath Street, London EC1V 9EL.
Tel: 0171–608–6909/7; fax: 0171–250–3207

**Sight Savers**, Grosvenor Hall, Bolnore Road, Haywards Heath RH16 4BX.
Tel: 01444–412424; fax: 01444–415866

**Vision Aid Overseas**, 56 Highlands Road, Leatherhead KT22 8NR.
Opticians charity supplying training and secondhand glasses.
Tel: 01372–360822; fax: 01372–360823

## FOLK MEDICINE

**Anthropology Department**, Goldsmiths College, New Cross, London
SE14 6NW.
Tel: 0181–692–7171

**Centre for Complementary Health Studies**, Exeter University.
Tel: 01392–264494/6

## INSECTS AND DISEASE

### *Malaria, river blindness etc.*

**Medical Entomology Department**, Liverpool School of Tropical
Medicine, L3 5QA.
Tel: 0151–708–9393

**Tsetse Research Laboratory**, Langford House, Langford, Bristol BS18 7DU.
Tel: 0117–928–9495

**Vector Biology Unit, and Medical Parasitology**, London School of
Hygiene, Keppel Street, WC1E 7HT.
Tel: 0171–636–8636

**Professor Peter Ham**, Biological sciences, Keele University.
Tel: 01782–583028

**Biomolecular Sciences**, Professor Frank Cox, King's College, Campden
Hill Road, London W8 7AH.
Tel: 0171–836–5454, ext. 3202, PR

## LEPROSY

**Lepra**, Fairfax House, Causton Road, Colchester CO1 1PU.
Tel: 01206–562286; fax: 01206–762151

**Leprosy Mission**, Goldhay Way, Orton Goldhay, Peterborough PE2 0GZ.
Tel: 01733–370505

## MALNUTRITION

**Nutrition Department**, London School of Hygiene, Keppel Street, London WC1H 7HT.
Tel: 0171–636–8636

**Tropical Paediatrics Department**, Liverpool School of Tropical Medicine, Pembroke Place, L3 5QA.
Tel: 0151–708–9393

## PARASITES

**CAB International Institute of Parasitology**, 395a Hatfield Road, St Albans AL4 0XU.
Tel: 01727–833151

**Parasitology Department**, Liverpool School of Tropical Medicine, Pembroke Place, L3 5QA.
Tel: 0151–708–9393

## PUBLIC/COMMUNITY HEALTH

**International Community Health Department**, Liverpool School of Tropical Medicine, L3 5QA.
Tel: 0151–708–9393

**Public Health and Public Policy Department**, London School of Hygiene, London WC1E 7HT.
Tel: 0171–636–8636

## WOMEN

**Maternal and Child Epidemiology Unit**, London School of Hygiene, Keppel Street, WC1H 7HT.
Tel: 0171–636–8636

# HUMAN RIGHTS

**Amnesty International**, British Section,　99 Rosebery Avenue, London EC1R 4RE.
Tel: 0171–814–6200; fax: 0171–833–1510

**Anti-Slavery International**, Broomgrove Road, London SW9 9TL.
Tel: 0171–924–9555; fax: 0171–738–4110

**Human Rights Centre**, Professor Kevin Boyle, Essex University, Colchester CO4 3SQ.
Tel: 01206–872568; fax: 01206–873428

**Human Rights Watch**, 33 Islington High Street, London N1 9LH.
Tel: 0171–713–1995

**Minority Rights Group**, 379 Brixton Road, London SW9 7DE.
Tel: 0171–978–9498

## *Britons abroad*

**Prisoners Abroad**, 82 Rosebery Avenue, London EC1R 4RR. Welfare charity for Britons held overseas.
Tel: 0171–833–3467; fax: 0171–833–3460

## *Persecuted Christians*

**Keston Research**, PO Box 276, Oxford OX2 6BF.
Tel: 01865–311022; fax: 01865–311280

**Jubilee**, St Johns, Cranleigh Road, Wonersh, Guildford GU5 0QX.
Tel: 01483–894787; fax: 01483–894797

## *Trade unions*

**International Centre for Trade Union Rights**, 177 Abbeville Road, London SW4 9RL.
Tel: 0171–498–4700

# LATIN AND SOUTH AMERICA

**Catholic Institute for International Relations**, Unit 3, 190a New North Road, London N1 7BJ.
Tel: 0171–354–0883; fax: 0171–359–0017

**Central America Human Rights Committee**, 83 Margaret Street, London W1.
Tel: 0171–631–4200

**Centre for Latin American Studies**, 86 Bedford Street South, PO Box 147, Liverpool L69 3BX.
Tel: 0151–794–3079

**Centre of Latin American Studies**, West Road, Cambridge.
Tel: 01223–334520

**Economics Department**, Lloyds Bank, 71 Lombard Street, London EC3. Lloyds includes the former Bank of London and South America.
Tel: 0171–626–1500

**Institute of Latin American Studies**, 31 Tavistock Square, London WC1H 9HA.
Tel: 0171–387–5671

**Latin America Bureau**, 1 Amwell Street, London EC1R 1UL.
Tel: 0171–278–2829

**Latin America Centre**, St Antony's College, Woodstock Road, Oxford OX2 6JF.
Tel: 01865–284700

**Roberto Espindola**, Bradford University BD7 1DP.
Tel: 01274–383823

## *Indians*

**Dr John Hemming**, Royal Geographical Society.
Tel: 0171–589–5466

## *Literature*

**Hispanic Studies**, Professor Peter Beardsell, Hull University HU6 7RX.
Tel: 01482–465840

**Hispanic and Latin American Studies**, Nottingham University NG7 2RD.
Tel: 0115–951–5800

**Latin American Literature**, Manchester University M13 9PL.
Tel: 0161–275–2112/4, press

## *Rainforests*

**Royal Botanic Garden**, Edinburgh EH3 5LR.
Tel: 0131–552–7171

**Royal Botanic Gardens**, Kew TW9 3AB.
Tel: 0181–332–5000; fax: 0181–948–1197

**Royal Geographical Society**, 1 Kensington Gore, London SW7 2AR.
Tel: 0171–589–5466

## ARGENTINA

**Professor Peter Calvert**, Southampton University.
Tel: 01703–592577

## BRAZIL

**Professor Peter Flynn**, Institute of Latin American Studies, Glasgow
University G12 8QH.
Tel: 0141–339–8855

**Dr David Treece**, King's College, London WC2R 2LS
Tel: 0171–836–5454, ext. 3534

## CHILE

**Ruth Aedo-Richmond**, Hispanic Studies, Hull University.
Tel: 01482–465854

## COLOMBIA

**Malcolm Deas**, St Antony's, Oxford OX2 6JF.
Tel: 01865–284700

## FALKLAND ISLANDS

**Dr Peter J.Beck**, International History, Kingston University, Penrhyn
Road, KT1 2EE.
Tel: 0181–549–1366; fax: 0181–547–1341

**Victor Bulmer-Thomas**, Institute of Latin American Studies, London
WC1H 9HA.
Tel: 0171–387–5671

**Falkland Islands Government**, 14 Broadway, London SW1H 0BH.
Tel: 0171–222–2542

## MEXICO

**Professor Peter Calvert**, Southampton University.
Tel: 01703–592577

**Dr Guy Thomson**, History, Warwick University, Coventry CV4 7AL.
Tel: 01203–523457; e-mail: GThom@CSV.warwick.ac.uk

## URUGUAY

**British Uruguayan Society**, Shreelane, Brooklands Road, Weybridge
KT13 0RG.
Tel: 01932–847455

## MIDDLE EAST

**Centre for Middle East and Islamic Studies**, South End House, South
Road, Durham DH1 3TG.
Tel: 0191–374–2822; fax: 2830

**Islamic and Middle East Studies**, Edinburgh University, 7 Buccleuch
Place, EH8 9LW.
Tel: 0131–650–4180

**Middle East Association**, 33 Bury Street, London SW1Y 6AX.
Tel: 0171–839–2137

**Middle East Centre**, St Antony's College, Woodstock Road, Oxford
OX2 6JF.
Tel: 01865–284700

**Middle East Programme**, Chatham House, 10 St James's Square,
London SW1Y 4LE.
Tel: 0171–957–5700

**Middle East Studies**, Manchester University.
Tel: 0161–275–2112/4, PR

**School of Oriental and African Studies Briefing Service**, Graham Thomas.
Tel: 0171–323–6378; fax: 0171–436–3844; e-mail: gt@soas.ac.uk

**Professor J.A.Allan**, Geography Department, School of Oriental and African Studies, Thornhaugh Street, Russell Square, London WC1H 0XG.
Tel: 0171–637–2388

**Professor Michael Gilsenan**, Magdalen College, Oxford University, OX1 4AU.
Tel: 01865–276015

## ARABS, ARABIC

**Anglo-Arab Association**, 21 Collingham Road, London SW5 0NU.
Tel: 0171–373–8414

**Arab-British Chamber of Commerce**, 6 Belgrave Square, London SW1 8PH.
Tel: 0171–235–4363; fax: 0171–235–1748

**Arab League**, 52 Green Street, London W1 3RH.
Tel: 0171–629–0732

**Arabic and Islamic Studies Department**, Old Library, Prince of Wales Road, Exeter EX4 4JZ.
Tel: 01392–264026

**Arabic and Islamic Studies Department**, University of Glasgow G12 8QQ.
Tel: 0141–339–8855

## BAHRAIN

**Bahrain-British Foundation**, 1 Battersea Bridge Road, London SW11 3BG.
Tel: 0171–223–3431

**Bahrain Society**, Secretary.
Tel: 0171–831–6292

## GULF

**Birks, Sinclair and Associates**, Mountjoy Research Centre, Durham DH1 3UR.
Tel: 0191–386–4484

**Centre for Arab Gulf Studies**, Old Library, Prince of Wales Road, Exeter EX4 4QH.
Tel: 01392–264025

**Gulf Centre for Strategic Studies**, 3rd and 4th Floors, 5 Charterhouse Buildings, Goswell Road, EC1M 7AN.
Tel: 0171–253–3805

# IRAQ

**Iraqi Community Association**, 241 King Street, London W6 9LP.
Tel: 0181–741–5491

# ISRAEL JORDAN, AND PALESTINIANS

**Glenn Bowman**, Communications Department, Rutherford College, Kent University, Canterbury CT2 7NX.
Tel: 01227–451805, PR

**Jordan Information Services.**
Tel: 0171–400–3333

**Dr Moshe Maor**, European Institute, LSE, Houghton Street, London WC2A 2AE.
Tel: 0171–955–7539

**Dr Eugene Rogan**, St Antony's, Oxford OX2 6JF.
Tel: 01865–284700

**Palestine Liberation Organization**, 4 Clareville Grove, London SW7.
Tel: 0171–370–3244

# LEBANON

**Centre for Lebanese Studies**, 59 Observatory Street, Oxford OX2 6EP.
Tel: 01865–58465

**Dr Rogan**, see above.

# SAUDI ARABIA

**Saudi-British Society**, 21 Collingham Road, SW5 0NU.
Tel: 0171–373–8414

**Saudi Information Office**, 18 Cavendish Square, London W1.
Tel: 0171–629–8803

## TURKEY

**Dr Cigdem Balim**, Middle East Department, Manchester University
M13 9PL.
Tel: 0161–275–3069

**Dr Celia Kerslake**, Oriental Institute, Oxford.
Tel: 01865–278213/278200

**Turkish British Chamber of Commerce**, 6th Floor, 360 Oxford Street,
London W1N 9HA.
Tel: 0171–499–4265

## NORTH AMERICA

## UNITED STATES

The **US Information Service** has a reference library at the US Embassy,
24 Grosvenor Square, London W1, tel: 0171–499–9000.

**Centre for Research on the USA**, Dr Michael Hodges, LSE, Houghton
Street, London WC2A 2AE.
Tel: 0171–955–7325

**American Studies**, Manchester University.
Tel: 0161–275–2112/4, PR

**Peter Fearon**, Economic and Social History, Leicester University, LE1
7RH.
Tel: 0116–252–2583

**Dr Robert Garson**, American studies, Keele University.
Tel: 01782–583015

**Dr David Mervin**, Politics, Warwick University.
Tel: 01203–523302

**Professor Richard Rose**, Strathclyde University.
Tel: 0141–552–4400, ext. 3217

**Dr Michael Sewell**, Cambridge University.
Tel: 01223–335883

**Professor Byron E. Shafer**, American Government, Oxford University, Nuffield College, OX1 1NF.
Tel: 01865–278509

*African-Americans*

**John Runcie**, History, Leicester University.
Tel: 0116–252–2815

**Dr William Dusinberre**, History, Warwick University.
Tel: 01203–523315

## CANADA

**Dr Michael Burgess**, Politics, Hull University.
Tel: 01482–465754

**Dr Didi Herman**, Law, Keele University ST5 5BG.
Tel: 01782–523225

*Eskimos*

**Professor Susan Pearce**, Museum Studies, Leicester.
Tel: 0116–252–3964

## PACIFIC

**Professor Alan Rew**, Centre for Development Studies, University, Swansea SA2 8PP.
Tel: 01792–295332; fax: 01792–295682

**John Cameron**, School of Development Studies, East Anglia University, Norwich NR4 7TJ.
Tel: 01603–456161

## THIRD WORLD

The **School of Oriental and African Studies** in London now offers a briefing service. Contact Graham Thomas, tel: 0171–323–6378; fax: 0171–436–3844: e-mail: gt@soas.ac.uk.

Also worth consulting is **John Cameron**, School of Development Studies, East Anglia University, tel: 01603–456161.

See also DEVELOPMENT STUDIES centres below.

## AID

**International Fund for Agricultural Development**, Via del Serafico 107, 00142 Rome.
Tel: 00–39–6–54591; fax: 00 39 6 504 3463

**Overseas Development Administration**, 94 Victoria Street, London SW1E 5JL.
Tel: 0171–917–0950/0821, PR; fax: 0171–917–0523
Emergency Aid.
Tel: 0171–917–0533, press

**World Bank**, New Zealand House, London SW1Y 4TE.
Tel: 0171–930–8511

### *Research into aid and its use*

**Institute of Development Studies**, Sussex University, Brighton BN1 9RE.
Tel: 01273–606261

**Overseas Development Institute**, Portland House, London SW1E 5DP.
Tel: 0171–393–1600; fax: 0171–393–1699; e-mail: odi@odi.org.uk

**Queen Elizabeth House**, Oxford OX1 3LA.
Tel: 01865–273600

### *Voluntary agencies*

**ActionAid**, Hamlyn House, Macdonald Road, London N19 5PG.
Tel: 0171–281–4101; fax: 0171–281–5146

**Aga Khan Foundation**, PO Box 6179, Geneva, Switzerland.
Tel: 00–41–22–736–0344; fax: 00–41–22–736–0948

**British Red Cross Society**, 9 Grosvenor Crescent, London SW1X 7EJ.
Tel: 0171–235–5454

**Cafod**, 2 Garden Close, Stockwell, London SW9 9TY. Catholic Fund for Overseas Development.
Tel: 0171–733–7900; fax: 0171–737–6877

**Care**, 36 Southampton Street, London WC2E 7EE. Agency working mainly with public money.
Tel: 0171–379–5247; fax: 0171–379–0543

**Christian Aid**, PO Box 100, London SE1 7RT.
Tel: 0171–620–4444; fax: 0171–620–0719

**Christmas Cracker**, c/o Oasis, 5 Ethel Street, Birmingham B2 4BG. Gets youngsters throughout the country to raise funds.
Tel: 0121–633–0873; fax: 0121–633–0875; e-mail: 100620.11@compuserve.com

**Comic Relief**, c/o Charity Projects.
Tel: 0171–436–1122

**Oxfam**, 274 Banbury Road, Oxford OX2 7DZ.
Tel: 01865–312498, press; fax: 01865–312580

**Tear Fund**, 100 Church Road, Teddington TW11 8QE.
Tel: 0181–977–9144

**UK Jewish Aid and International Development**, 30 Gordon Street, London WC1H 0AN.
Tel: 0171–387–3281

**WaterAid**, 1 Queen Anne's Gate, London SW1H 9BT. Water industry's charity.
Tel: 0171–233–4800; fax: 0171–233–3161

**World Vision UK**, 599 Avebury Boulevard, Milton Keynes MK9 3PG.
Tel: 01908–841020; fax: 01908–841021

## *Volunteers*

**British Executive Service Overseas**, 164 Vauxhall Bridge Road, London SW1V 2RB.
Tel: 0171–630–0644

**Earthwatch**, Oxford. Sends paying volunteers on ecological work.
Tel: 01865–516366

**International Co-operation for Development**, Unit 3, 190a New North Road, London N1 7BJ.
Tel: 0171–354–0883; fax: 359–0017

**Skillshare Africa**, 3 Belvoir Street, Leicester LE1 6SL.
Tel: 0116–254–1862

**UNA International Service**, Suite 3A, 57 Goodramgate, York.
Tel: 01904–647799

**Voluntary Service Overseas**, 37 Putney Bridge Road, London SW15 2PN.
Tel: 0181–780–2266

## CAMPAIGNING

**Catholic Institute for International Relations**, Unit 3, 190a New North Road, London N1 7BJ.
Tel: 0171–354–0883

**World Development Movement**, 25 Beehive Place, London SW9 7QR.
Tel: 0171–737–6215

## CHILDREN

**Save the Children Fund**, 17 Grove Lane, London SE3 8RD.
Tel: 0171–703–5400

**UN Children's Fund (UNICEF)**, 55 Lincolns Inn Fields, London WC2A 3NB.
Tel: 0171–405–5592

### *Child labour*

**Anti-Slavery International**, The Stableyard, Broomgrove Road, London SW9 9TL.
Tel: 0171–924–9555; fax: 0171–738–4110

### *Street children, child abuse*

**Jubilee**, St Johns, Cranleigh Road, Wonersh, Guildford GU5 0QX.
Tel: 01483–894787; fax: 01483–894787

## CITIES

**City and Regional Planning Department**, PO Box 906, University of Wales, Cardiff CF1 3YN.
Tel: 01222–874308

**Development Administration Group**, University of Birmingham, Edgbaston B15 2TT.
Tel: 0121–414–4987

**Town and Regional Planning Department**, Sheffield University, S10 2TN.
Tel: 0114–282–6180

## COASTS, REEFS

**Centre for Tropical Coastal Management**, Dr Barbara Brown, Ridley Building, Newcastle University, NE1 7RU.
Tel: 0191–222–6653

**Hunting Aquatic Resources**, Innovation Centre, York Science Park, University Road, YO1 5DG.
Tel: 01904–435165; fax: 01904–416611; e-mail: 101361.1010@compuserve.com

## CRAFTS AND TRADING

**Oxfam Trading**, Murdoch Road, Bicester OX6 7RF.
Tel: 01869–245011

**Traidcraft**, Kingsway, Gateshead NE11 0NE.
Tel: 0191–491–0591

**Twin Trading**, 5 Worship Street, London EC2A 2BH.
Tel: 0171–628–6878; fax: 0171–628–1859

### *Latin American*

**Tumi**, 8 New Bond Street Place, Bath BA1 1BH.
Tel: 01225–462367

## DEBT, ECONOMICS

**Institute of Development Studies**, Sussex University, Brighton BN1 9RE.
Tel: 01273–606261

**Institute of Economics and Statistics**, St Cross Building, Manor Road, Oxford OX1 3UL.
Tel: 01865–271073

**Overseas Development Institute**, Stag Place, London SW1E 5DP.
Tel: 0171–393–1600; fax: 0171–393–1699; e-mail: oda@odi.org.uk

**Oxfam**, 274 Banbury Road, Oxford OX2 7DZ.
Tel: 01865–312498

**Professor Andrew Hughes Hallett**, Economics, Strathclyde University, Glasgow G1 1XQ.
Tel: 0141–552–4400, ext. 3581

*Debt trading*

**Dillon Read**, Devonshire House, Mayfair Place, London W1X 5PH.
Tel: 0171–493–1239

## DEVELOPMENT STUDIES

Apart from centres mentioned earlier.

**Centre for Developing Areas Research**, Royal Holloway and Bedford
New College, Egham TW20 0EX.
Tel: 01784–434455

**Centre for Development Studies**, University of Wales, Swansea SA2
8PP.
Tel: 01792–205678

**Developing Countries Research**, Strathclyde University, Glasgow G1
1XQ.
Tel: 0141–552–4400, ext.  3580/3848/3863

**Development and Project Planning Centre**, Bradford University, BD7
1DP.
Tel: 01274–733466

**Development Education Association**, 29 Cowper Street, London EC2A
4AP. Central body for development centres round Britain.
Tel: 0171–490–8108; fax: 0171–490–8123

**Institute for Development Policy and Management**, Manchester
University M13 9QS.
Tel: 0161–275–2800

**School of Development Studies**, East Anglia University, Norwich NR4
7TJ.
Tel: 01603–456161

## DISASTERS

**Cranfield Disaster Preparedness Centre**, Shrivenham SN6 8LA.
Tel: 01793–785287; fax: 01793–782179

**International Red Cross**, Case postale 372, CH-1211 Geneve 19,
Switzerland.
Tel: 00–41–22–730–42–22; fax: 00–41–22–733–03–95

**International Rescue Corps**, 8 King's Road, Grangemouth FK3 9BB.
Tel: 01324–665011; fax: 01324–666130

**Overseas Development Institute**, Dr Ed Clay, Portland House, Stag
Place, London SW1E 5DP.
Tel: 0171–393–1600; fax: 0171–393–1699; e-mail: odi@odi.org.uk

**Oxford Centre for Disaster Management**, Brookes University, Gipsy
Lane, OX3 0BP.
Tel: 01865–484086

**Register of Engineers for Disaster Relief (REDR)**, 25 Eccleston Square,
London SW1V 1NX.
Tel: 0171–233–3116

## EDUCATION

**Book Aid International**, 39 Coldharbour Lane, London SE5 9NR.
Supplies secondhand books to schools and universities.
Tel: 0171–733–3577; fax: 0171–978–8006

**Centre for International Studies in Education**, 35 Berkeley Square,
Bristol BS8 1JA.
Tel: 0117–928–9000

**Education and Science Department**, British Council, 10 Spring Gardens,
London SW1A 2BN.
Tel: 0171–930–8466; 0171–389–4878, press, fax: 0171–389–4971

**Overseas Education**, School of Education, Leeds LS2 9JT.
Tel: 0113–233–6699, PR

## EMPLOYMENT

**Anti-Slavery International**, Broomgrove Road, London SW9 9TL.
Tel: 0171–924–9555; fax: 0171–738–4110

**International Labour Office**, Vincent House, Vincent Square, London
SW1P 2NB.
Tel: 0171–828–6401

## ENVIRONMENT

See pages 181–7.

## FARMING

**Agricultural Economics Department**, Manchester University, M13 9PL.
Tel: 0161–275–4793

**Agricultural Economics and Management Department**, Reading
University, 4 Earley Gate, PO Box 237, RG6 2AR.
Tel: 01734–318965; fax: 01734–352421

**Agriculture Extension and Rural Development Department**, Reading
University, 3 Earley Gate, RG6 2AL.
Tel: 01734–318119

**Agriculture Department**, Reading University, PO Box 236,
Whiteknights, Reading RG6 2AT.
Tel: 01734–318471

**Wye College**, Ashford, Kent TN25 5AH.
Tel: 01233–812401; fax: 01233–813187

### *Animals*

**Centre for Tropical Veterinary Medicine**, Easter Bush, Roslin EH25 9RG.
Tel: 0131–650–6216

### *Animal parasites*

**Veterinary Parasitology Department**, Liverpool School of Tropical
Medicine, Pembroke Place, L3 5QA.
Tel: 0151–708–9393

### *Farming facts and figures*

**Landell Mills Management Consultants**, Columbus House, Trossachs
Drive, Bath BA2 6RR.
Tel: 01225–462891

### *Fertilizers*

**Soil Science Department**, Reading University, RG1 5AQ.
Tel: 01734–318911

### *Irrigation*

**Institute of Irrigation Studies**, Southampton University, SO9 5NH.
Tel: 01703–593728; fax: 01703–593017

**Silsoe College**, Bedford MK45 4DT
Tel: 01525–863000

## *Oil palms*

**Harrisons and Crosfield**, No 1 Great Tower Street, London EC3R 5AH.
Tel: 0171–711–1400

**Unilever**, Blackfriars, London EC4.
Tel: 0171–822–5252

## *Pest control*

**Centre for Pest Management**, Silwood Park, Sunninghill SL5 7PY.
Tel: 01344–23911 and

**International Institute of Biological Control**, Silwood Park, SL5 7TA.
Tel: 01344–872999; fax: 01344–872901

**Scottish Crop Research Institute**, Invergowrie, Dundee DD2 5DA.
Tel: 01382–562731; fax: 01382–562426

## *Plantations*

**International Centre for Plantation Studies**, Silsoe MK45 4DT.
Tel: 01525–863000; fax: 01525–861527

**Unilever**, see above.

## *Equipment*

**Geest Overseas Mechanisation**, White House Chambers, Spalding PE11 2AL.
Tel: 01775–761111

**Silsoe Research Institute**, Wrest Park, Silsoe MK45 4HS.
Tel: 01525–860000

## *Virus diseases*

**John Innes Centre**, Colney Lane, Norwich NR4 7UH.
Tel: 01603–452571

**Tropical Virus Unit**, Rothamsted.
Tel: 01582–763133

## FISH FARMING

**Institute of Aquaculture**, Stirling University.
Tel: 01786–467878; fax: 472133

## HOUSING

**Centre for Architectural Research and Development Overseas**,
Newcastle upon Tyne NE1 7RU.
Tel: 0191–222–6024

**Development Planning Unit**, 9 Endsleigh Gardens, London WC1H
0ED.
Tel: 0171–388–7581

**Homeless International**, 5 The Butts, Coventry CV1 3GH.
Tel: 01203–632802

**Institute of Advanced Architectural Studies**, Charles Cockburn, Kings
Manor, York YO1 2EP.
Tel: 01904–433964

**Martin Centre**, 6 Chaucer Road, Cambridge CB2 2EB.
Tel: 01223–332981

## INDUSTRIAL DEVELOPMENT

**Patrick Ryan** and **Dr Michael Tribe**, Bradford University, BD7 1DP.
Tel: 01274–383976, Patrick Ryan; 01274–383978, Dr Tribe

**Dr Colin Stoneman**, Southern African Studies, York University YO1
5DD.
Tel: 01904–432029, PR

## INVESTMENT FINANCE

**Global Strategy Unit**, Baring Securities, 1 America Street, London
EC3N 2LT.
Tel: 0171–522–6000

**Genesis Investment Management**, 21 Knightsbridge, London SW1X
7LX.
Tel: 0171–235–5040; fax: 0171–235–8065

# NATIVE PEOPLES

**Alliance for Rights of Indigenous Peoples**, 2 Romero Close, Stockwell Road, London SW9 9TY.
Tel: 0171–924–0490; fax: 274–9630

**Survival International.**
Tel: 0171–242–1441

# NORTH-SOUTH ISSUES

**Dr Caroline Thomas**, Politics, Southampton University.
Tel: 01703–592517

# POPULATION

**Demography Department**, Southampton University, SO9 5NH.
Tel: 01703–595000

**International Planned Parenthood Federation**, Regent's College, London NW1 4NS.
Tel: 0171–486–0741; fax: 0171–487–7950; e-mail: jgizbert@ippf.attmail.com.

**Population Centre**, University of Wales, PO Box 915, Cardiff CF1 3TL.
Tel: 01222–493746; fax: 01222–450538

**Population Concern**, 231 Tottenham Court Road, London W1P 9AE.
Tel: 0171–631–1546; fax: 0171–436–2143

**Population Investigation Committee**, Professor John Hobcraft, LSE, Houghton Street, London WC2A 2AE.
Tel: 0171–955–7666/7659

**Population Studies Institute**, 101 Pennsylvania Road, Exeter EX4 6DT.
Tel: 01392–57936; fax: 01392–263801

# POVERTY

**Ellen Wratten**, Social Policy, LSE, WC2A 2AE.
Tel: 0171–955–7355

## RAINFORESTS

**Edinburgh Centre for Tropical Forests**, Darwin Building, Mayfield Road, Edinburgh EH9 3JU.
Tel: 0131–662–0752

**Royal Botanic Garden**, Inverleith Row, Edinburgh EH3 5LR.
Tel: 0131–552–7171

**Royal Botanic Gardens**, Kew TW9 3AB.
Tel: 0181–332–5000; fax: 0181–948–1197

**World Wide Fund for Nature**, Panda House, Weyside Place, Godalming GU7 1XR.
Tel: 01483–426444

## REFUGEES

**Refugee Studies Programme**, Dr Barbara Harrell-Bond, Queen Elizabeth House, Oxford OX1 3LA.
Tel: 01865–270722

**UN High Commission for Refugees,**
Tel: 0171–828–9191

## RURAL DEVELOPMENT

**Hunting Technical Services**, Thamesfield House, Boundary Way, Hemel Hempstead HP2 7SR.
Tel: 01442–231800

## SCIENCE AND TECHNOLOGY

**Centre for Alternative Technology**, Machynlleth SY20 9AZ.
Tel: 01654–702400

**Commonwealth Science Council**, Marlborough House, Pall Mall, London SW1Y 5HX.
Tel: 0171–839–3411

**Development Policy and Practice Department**, Open University, Walton Hall, Milton Keynes MK7 6AA.
Tel: 01908–652103

**Intermediate Technology Development Group**, Myson House, Railway Terrace, Rugby CV21 3HT.
Tel: 01788–560631; fax: 01788–540270; e-mail itdg@gn.apc.org and 103 Southampton Row, London WC1B 4HH.
Tel: 0171–436–9761; fax: 0171–436–2013

**IT Power**, Bramshill Road, Eversley RG27 0PR.
Tel: 01734–730073

**IT Transport**, Old Power Station, Ardington, Wantage OX12 8QJ.
Tel: 01235–833753

**Natural Resources Institute**, Central Avenue, Chatham Maritime ME4 4TB.
Tel: 0181–331–8092/01634–883129, press; fax: 0181–331–8093

**Science Policy Research Unit**, Sussex University, Brighton BN1 9RF.
Tel: 01273–686758

# WATER

**Binnie, Black and Veatch**, 60 London Road, Redhill RH1 1LQ.
Tel: 01737–774155; fax: 01737–772767

**Institute of Hydrology**, Crowmarsh Gifford, Wallingford OX10 8BB.
Tel: 01491–838800

**Robens Institute**, Surrey University, Guildford GU2 5XH.
Tel: 01483–259209

**WaterAid**, 27 Albert Embankment, London SE1 7UB.
Tel: 0171–793–4505; fax: 0171–793–4545

**Water, Engineering and Development Centre**, Loughborough University LE11 3TU.
Tel: 01509–222885

# TRADE

**Department of Trade and Industry Trade Issues Desk**, 1 Victoria Street, London SW1H 0ET.
Tel: 0171–215–5976/8; fax: 0171–222–4382

**Centre for Research in Economic Development and International Trade**, Nottingham University NG7 2RD.
Tel: 0115–951–5250

**Overseas Development Institute**, Portland House, Stag Place, London SW1E 5DP.
Tel: 0171–393–1600; fax: 0171–393–1699; e-mail: odi@odi.org.uk

**World Trade Organization**, Palais des Nations, CH-1211 Geneva 10.
Tel: 00–41–22–739–5111; fax: 00–41–22–739–5458

**Professor Andrew Hughes Hallett**, Economics Department, Strathclyde University, Glasgow G1 1XQ.
Tel: 0141–552–4400, ext. 3581

## Exports

**British Exporters Association**, 16 Dartmouth Street, London SW1H 9BL.
Tel: 0171–222–5419

**ECGD** (Export Credits Guarantee Department), PO Box 2200, 2 Exchange Tower, London E14 9GS.
Tel: 0171–512–7421, press; fax: 0171–512–7021

**Institute of Export**, 64 Clifton Street, London EC2A 4HB.
Tel: 0171–247–9812; fax: 0171–377–5343

**NCM Credit Insurance**, 63 Queen Victoria Street, London EC4N 4UA.
Provides 80 per cent of short-term export credit cover in UK.
Tel: 0171–248–6121

## Fair trade

**Twin Trading**, 5 Worship Street, London EC2A 2BH.
Tel: 0171–628–6878; fax: 0171–628–1859

**UK Fair Trade Foundation**, 7th Floor, 89 Kingsway, London WC2B 6RH.
Tel: 0171–405–5942

## Law

**Baker and McKenzie**, Solicitors, 100 New Bridge Street, London EC4V 6JA.
Tel: 0171–919–1000; fax: 0171–919–1999

## Piracy

**ICC International Maritime Bureau**, Maritime House, 1 Linton Road, Barking IG11 8HG.
Tel: 0181–591–3000; fax: 594–2833

# UNITED NATIONS

You may have a local branch of the **United Nations Association**, or local university teachers interested in UNO.

## *National sources*

**UN Information Centre**, Millbank Tower, London SW1P 4QH.
Tel: 0171–630–1981; fax: 0171–976–6478

**United Nations Association**, 3 Whitehall Court, London SW1A 2EL.
Tel: 0171–930–2931

**International Finance Corporation**. Private enterprise promotion arm of World Bank.
Tel: 0171–930–8741

**UNCTAD** (UN Conference on Trade and Development), CH-1211 Geneva 10.
Tel: 00–41–22–907–5816/28; fax: 00–41–22–917–0123

**UN Development Programme**, One UN Plaza, New York NY 10017.
Tel: 00–1–212–906–5312; fax: 00–1–212–906–5367

**UN Environment Programme UK**, c/o IIED, 3 Endsleigh Street, London WC1H 0DD.
Tel: 0171–388–2117

**UNESCO**, 7 place de Fontenoy, 75700 Paris. France.
Tel: 00–331–45–68–1000; fax: 00–331–45–67–16–90

**UNIDO** (UN Industrial Development Organization), PO Box 300, A-1400, Vienna.
Tel: 00–43–1–21131–3693; fax: 00–43–1–232156

**UN High Commission for Refugees.**
Tel: 0171–828–9191

**UN International Drug Control Programme**, PO Box 500, A-1400 Vienna.
Tel: 00–43–1–211310; fax: 00–43–1–230–70–02

**World Health Organization**, 20 avenue Appia, 1211 Geneva 27, Switzerland.
Tel: 00–41–22–791–2111; fax: 00–41–22–791–0746

## *Comment on UN*

**Professor Adam Roberts**, International Relations, Oxford University,

Balliol College, OX1 3BJ.
Tel: 01865–277804

**David Travers**, Politics and International Relations, Lancaster
University.
Tel: 01524–594278/261

## INTERNATIONAL MONETARY FUND/ WORLD BANK

**IMF**, 700 19th Street, NW, Washington DC 20431.
Tel: 001–202–623–7000; fax: 001–202–623 4661

**World Bank Group**, New Zealand House, Haymarket, London SW1Y
4TE.
Tel: 0171–930–8511

### *Comment*

**Tony Killick**, Overseas Development Institute, Stag Place, London
SW1E 5DP. Wrote *IMF Programmes in Developing Countries* (1995).
Tel: 0171–393–1600; fax: 0171–393–1699; e-mail: odi@odi.org.uk.

## PEACEKEEPING

**Professor Alan James**, International Relations, Keele University, ST5
5BG.
Tel: 01782–583210

**David Travers**, Politics and International Relations, Lancaster
University.
Tel: 01524–594278/261

# APPENDIX
# THE JOURNALIST AS
# AN INVESTIGATIVE
# REPORTER

A substantial area of reporting could be called investigative journalism in that obviously available facts do not necessarily tell the whole story. The reporter might have to seek out and follow up 'insider' information to get to the bottom of a situation.

A contractor who gave evidence in court in the 1970s, in a case in which Bradford Council officials were alleged to have taken bribes told Ray Fitzwalter of the Bradford's *Telegraph and Argus* that he should look into a company called Open System Building. This set him off on three months of inquiries which led to his writing the first published article about the architectural practice of John Poulson who won work in Yorkshire, the North-East and elsewhere by making gifts to key local councillors and officials.

Fitzwalter did most of the inquiries in his spare time, because he had a full-time day job as deputy news editor. He had never previously heard of Poulson whose business success had escaped much notice. The contractor who gave evidence, however, alleged that a key local councillor was in Poulson's pay. This turned out not to be true: the contractor had confused two councillors. But a search at Companies House showed that Open System Building was based at Poulson's Pontefract office (as an architect he could not be a director of the company).

A search through Bradford, Pontefract and West Yorkshire council minutes showed that Poulson had won one contract after another. And the company search showed that the clerk to the county council was a director of OSB.

Fitzwalter also sought out former Poulson employees. Some hated Poulson and were prepared to tell what they knew.

Because of the danger of a libel action, the *Telegraph and Argus's* article was low key; but it was spotted by Paul Foot who, with Fitzwalter's help, wrote three pages about the 'Slicker of Wakefield' for *Private Eye*. Foot was able to include allegations of corruption in Wandsworth, London, involving Dan Smith, a leading Newcastle politician whose PR companies were a channel for Poulson's bribes.

The rest of the media failed to react either to the Bradford article or *Private Eye*. At his bankruptcy hearing two years later, however, Poulson was questioned about the money he had paid Dan Smith and others. The scandal was then big news.

Fitzwalter meanwhile had moved to Granada TV where he pursued the Poulson story and other investigations for *World in Action*, becoming its editor. He and David Taylor described the Poulson affair in *Web of Corruption* published by Granada in 1983.

Fitzwalter's work on Poulson back in the 1970s has features which other investigative reporters will recognize. It required an insider (the contractor) to tell him where to look; and the looking took much time and patience. Fitzwalter says that opinions are not much good if you want a publishable story about wrongdoing. You need the hardest form of evidence, which is original documents. The next hardest is photocopies. Then comes evidence from witnesses.

In another example of investigative reporting a few years ago, reporter David Hencke was sent to the House of Commons by the then editor of *The Guardian*, Peter Preston. Preston believed, rightly, that the House was a place where clues for investigation would crop up.

Hencke got interested in the work of the National Audit Office which watches over government spending. He covered its report on British Aerospace's purchase of the nationalized Austin-Rover motor company. The Government was so anxious to have a British buyer that it made valuable concessions to BAe. The Audit Office's critical report on these referred to an additional unpublished memorandum; and, because of Hencke's coverage, he was given a copy. This revealed £44million worth of sweeteners given to BAe and not disclosed to the European Commission, which keeps an eye on subsidies to industry.

Another Hencke inquiry concerned payments to MPs. Hencke believes that in the late 1980s some Conservatives got the impression they could safely profit from being in a long-governing party. He pursued one allegation about an MP's holidays; but the tour company concerned had gone bust and its papers had been shredded and so there was no documentary evidence.

As with the Poulson affair, it was an insider who gave access to the story. Mohammed Al-Fayed of Harrods lunched with Peter Preston when *The Guardian* was acquiring *The Observer*. Under its previous owner, Lonrho, then run by Tiny Rowland, *The Observer* had campaigned against Al-Fayed who had thwarted Rowland's ambition to run Harrods, At lunch

Al-Fayed disclosed he had paid MPs to ask questions, and he had also paid for a minister's stay at the Paris Ritz (the minister later reimbursed him).

The controversy over the subterfuge by which *The Guardian* obtained a copy of the Ritz bill illustrates one of the problems. If you are to publish an allegation, you need the documentary evidence.

Hencke has twice worked with an MP who received complaints of unfair practice. One concerned the manner in which brokers hired ships for the Gulf War. The other concerns aid to Turkey, and the National Audit Office has joined in investigating the Turkish aid programme.

When you are known for investigations, says Hencke, people start telling you things that are not publicly known. Pursuing these leads requires painstaking work, the aim being to find a source at the heart of the matter. Library work, with company accounts and other reports, can help complete a picture, but you need someone to tell you where to look.

Many government documents are available but you have to know which to ask for. It is also important to keep your name appearing in your newspaper so that you are known. The occasional by-line on a big exposé isn't enough.

Hencke's interest was first stirred when he worked at Wellingborough for the *Northamptonshire Evening Telegraph*. The council there discussed six options for an inner ring road and kept them secret. A councillor, however, gave him a copy. He realized then that in matters of public policy there is often a private agenda as well as the public one.

In theory there may be public consultation. In practice, someone could be calling the shots.

Peter Marsh of the *Financial Times* also found, when he covered the Treasury, that there were views other than the official view. He started talking to the people to whom the Treasury was talking. The result was a critical profile of Teflon Terry – Sir Terry Burns, the Permanent Secretary. Burns had escaped blame for Treasury mishaps but Marsh was able to show that what he had said had sometimes proved wrong.

The profile broke with the convention that you don't talk about the role of civil servants. It also cracked the practical difficulty of showing what Burns's role had been.

Marsh says it helped that he wasn't part of the Treasury community of journalists. It is hard to be critical of a host. He also points out that investigative reporting is not necessarily a matter of inquiring into mistakes and wrongdoing. It can also cast light on important matters that get overlooked. He spent a lot of time inquiring into how British factories have changed.

How does a small engineering works acquire the competitive edge to win a contract from Nissan when other factories could have done the job?

He talked not just to managers but to competitors and suppliers. He uncovered a web of industrial tourism: managers visiting other factories to see how things are done. This sort of inquiry is harder than it sounds: managers tend to be reluctant to discuss the factors in their commercial success in case they give clues to competitors.

Marsh points out that much journalism is one-sided, telling the readers what someone said about events or about themselves or about their organization or about someone else's organization. What people say is quite likely to be true but it may not be the whole truth. Other people will see things differently and know different facts. Investigative reporting is about collecting these different views and facts from people who don't leap into print with them.

One problem is how to get people to tell you what you want to know when they have no particular interest in telling you, especially if they don't want other people to know they told you. Marsh finds that the *Financial Time's* reputation for fair dealing helps. He is also persistent. Half-hour interviews, he says, are no good. It's towards the end of three hours, when you have got to know each other, that the interesting facts emerge. He spent over six hours with Professor Patrick Minford fathoming the ins-and-outs of Minford's influential economic views.

He went to a party conference simply to find out how the Conservatives raised money from companies. Once there, he gatecrashed a party and was introduced to a key fund-raiser by an MP who vouched for his reporting. This enabled him to interview the fund-raiser back in London and to understand the way money is raised through the Conservatives' industrial councils. He discovered that the chief attraction for directors joining these councils is to meet leading politicians and get on the inside of national affairs.

# CODE OF PRACTICE: PRESS COMPLAINTS COMMISSION

The Press Complaints Commission is charged with enforcing the following Code of Practice which was framed by the newspaper and periodical industry and ratified by the Press Complaints Commission.

All members of the press have a duty to maintain the highest professional and ethical standards. In doing so, they should have regard to the provisions of this Code of Practice and to safeguarding the public's right to know.

Editors are responsible for the actions of journalists employed by their publications. They should also satisfy themselves as far as possible that material accepted from non-staff members was obtained in accordance with this Code.

While recognizing that this involves a substantial element of self-restraint by editors and journalists, it is designed to be acceptable in the context of a system of self-regulation. The Code applies in the spirit as well as in the letter.

It is the responsibility of editors to cooperate as swiftly as possible in PCC enquiries.

Any publication which is criticized by the PCC under one of the following clauses is duty bound to print the adjudication which follows in full and with due prominence.

## 1 Accuracy

i)   Newspapers and periodicals should take care not to publish inaccurate, misleading or distorted material.
ii)  Whenever it is recognized that a significant inaccuracy, misleading statement or distorted report has been published, it should be corrected promptly and with due prominence.
iii) An apology should be published whenever appropriate.

iv) A newspaper or periodical should always report fairly and accurately the outcome of an action for defamation to which it has been a party.

## 2 Opportunity to reply

A fair opportunity for reply to inaccuracies should be given to individuals or organizations when reasonably called for.

## 3 Comment, conjecture and fact

Newspapers, while free to be partisan, should distinguish clearly between comment, conjecture and fact.

## 4 Privacy

Intrusions and enquiries into an individual's private life without his or her consent including the use of long-lens photography to take pictures of people on private property without their consent are not generally acceptable and publication can only be justified when in the public interest.

Note—Private property is defined as (i) any private residence, together with its garden and outbuildings, but excluding any adjacent fields or parkland and the surrounding parts of the property within the unaided view of passers-by, (ii) hotel bedrooms (but not other areas in a hotel) and (iii) those parts of a hospital or nursing home where patients are treated or accommodated.

## 5 Listening devices

Unless justified by public interest, journalists should not obtain or publish material obtained by using clandestine listening devices or by intercepting private telephone conversations.

## 6 Hospitals

i)   Journalists or photographers making enquiries at hospitals or similar institutions should identify themselves to a responsible executive and obtain permission before entering non-public areas.

ii)  The restrictions on intruding into privacy are particularly relevant to enquiries about individuals in hospitals or similar institutions.

## 7 Misrepresentation

i)   Journalists should not generally obtain or seek to obtain information or pictures through misrepresentation or subterfuge.

ii) Unless in the public interest, documents or photographs should be removed only with the express consent of the owner.

iii) Subterfuge can be justified only in the public interest and only when material cannot be obtained by any other means.

## 8 Harassment

i) Journalists should neither obtain nor seek to obtain information or pictures through intimidation or harassment.

ii) Unless their enquiries are in the public interest, journalists should not photograph individuals on private property (as defined in the note to Clause 4) without their consent; should not persist in telephoning or questioning individuals after having been asked to desist; should not remain on their property after having been asked to leave and should not follow them.

iii) It is the responsibility of editors to ensure that these requirements are carried out.

## 9 Payment for articles

Payment or offers of payment for stories, pictures or information, should not be made directly or through agents to witness or potential witnesses in current criminal proceedings or to people engaged in crime or to their associates—which includes family, friends, neighbours and colleagues—except where the material concerned ought to be published in the public interest and the payment is necessary for this to be done.

## 10 Intrusion into grief or shock

In cases involving personal grief or shock, enquiries should be carried out and approaches made with sympathy and discretion.

## 11 Innocent relatives and friends

Unless it is contrary to the public's right to know, the press should generally avoid identifying relatives or friends of persons convicted or accused of crime.

## 12 Interviewing or photographing children

i) Journalists should not normally interview or photograph children under the age of 16 on subjects involving the personal welfare of the child, in the absence of or without the consent of a parent or other adult who is responsible for the children.

ii)   Children should not be approached or photographed while at school without the permission of the school authorities.

## 13 Children in sex cases

1)   The press should not, even where the law does not prohibit it, identify children under the age of 16 who are involved in cases concerning sexual offences, whether as victims or as witnesses or defendants.
2)   In any press report of a case involving a sexual offence against a child—
   i)   The adult should be identified.
   ii)   The term 'incest' where applicable should not be used.
   iii)   The offence should be described as 'serious offences against young children' or similar appropriate wording.
   iv)   The child should not be identified.
   v)   Care should be taken that nothing in the report implies the relationship between the accused and the child.

## 14 Victims of crime

The press should not identify victims of sexual assault or publish material likely to contribute to such identifcation unless, by law, they are free to do so.

## 15 Discrimination

i)   The press should avoid prejudicial or pejorative reference to a person's race, colour, religion, sex or sexual orientation or to any physical or mental illness or handicap.
ii)   It should avoid publishing details of a person's race, colour, religion, sex or sexual orientation, unless these are directly relevant to the story.

## 16 Financial journalism

i)   Even where the law does not prohibit it, journalists should not use for their own profit, financial information they receive in advance of its general publication, nor should they pass such information to others.
ii)   They should not write about shares or securities in whose performance they know that they or their close families have a significant financial interest, without disclosing the interest to the editor or financial editor.

iii) They should not buy or sell, either directly or through nominees or agents, shares or securities about which they have written recently or about which they intend to write in the near future.

## 17 *Confidential sources*

Journalists have a moral obligation to protect confidential sources of information.

## 18 *The public interest*

Clauses 4, 5, 7, 8 and 9 create exceptions which may be covered by invoking the public interest. For the purposes of this code that is most easily defined as:

i)   Detecting or exposing crime or a serious misdemeanour.
ii)  Protecting public health and safety.
iii) Preventing the public from being misled by some statement or action of an individual or organisation.

In any case raising issues beyond these three definitions the Press Complaints Commission will require a full explanation by the editor of the publication involved, seeking to demonstrate how the public interest was served.

*Comments or suggestions regarding the content of the Code may be sent to the Secretary, Press Standards Board of Finance, Merchants House Buildings, 30 George Square, Glasgow G2 1EG, to be laid before the industry's Code Committee*

# INDEX